VANISHING ACT

VANISHING ACT

A Crashed Airliner, Faked Death, and Backroom Abortions

Jerry Jamison

ROWMAN & LITTLEFIELD
Lanham • Boulder • New York • London

Published by Rowman & Littlefield
An imprint of The Rowman & Littlefield Publishing Group, Inc.
4501 Forbes Boulevard, Suite 200, Lanham, Maryland 20706
www.rowman.com

86-90 Paul Street, London EC2A 4NE

Copyright © 2025 by Jerry Jamison

All rights reserved. No part of this book may be reproduced in any form or
by any electronic or mechanical means, including information storage and
retrieval systems, without written permission from the publisher, except by a
reviewer who may quote passages in a review.

British Library Cataloguing in Publication Information available

Library of Congress Cataloging-in-Publication Data

Names: Jamison, Jerry, author.
Title: Vanishing act: a crashed airliner, faked death, and backroom abortions
    / Jerry Jamison.
Description: Lanham: Rowman & Littlefield, 2025. | Includes bibliographical
    references and index.
Identifiers: LCCN 2024042309 (print) | LCCN 2024042310 (ebook) |
    ISBN 9798881802936 (cloth; alk. paper) | ISBN 9798881802943 (ebook)
Subjects: LCSH: Spears, Robert Vernon. | Swindlers and swindling—
    United States—Case studies. | Aircraft accidents—Case studies.
Classification: LCC HV6692.S64 J36 2025 (print) | LCC HV6692.S64 (ebook) |
    DDC 363.12/492—dc23/eng/20241206
LC record available at https://lccn.loc.gov/2024042309
LC ebook record available at https://lccn.loc.gov/2024042310

♾️™ The paper used in this publication meets the minimum requirements of
American National Standard for Information Sciences—Permanence of Paper
for Printed Library Materials, ANSI/NISO Z39.48-1992.

Dedicated to my loving parents, Ruth and Stan Jamison

My mother, who received one of America's first degrees in library science, served as a librarian for more than five decades. My father, who dropped out of elementary school during the Depression to help support his itinerant Kentucky family, was the most well-read and thoroughly studied man I ever knew. Though they are gone, through this story I hope to make them proud.

Contents

A Note from the Author		ix
1	One Spectacular Flying Leap	1
2	A God-Given Do-Over	9
3	Casseroles and Comfort	15
4	Sunshine Is Straight Ahead	23
5	That Hinky Feeling	31
6	Two Men on the Move	41
7	The Unholy Trinity	51
8	Under the Table and in the Shadows	61
9	Ticket to Paradise	69
10	A Fast-Talking, Slick Attorney	79
11	Hypnotism and Strange Sightings	89
12	Transformed into the Perfect Image	97
13	A Series of Seismic Shocks	103
14	Exploits, Perils, and Pitfalls	111
15	The Case of the Violet Paste	119
16	The Calm and the Storm	127

viii / Contents

17	Lighting the Fuse, Running Like Hell	135
18	Plastic Palm Trees and Peril	143
19	The Look of a Worthy Adversary	149
20	From Out of the Sea!	157
21	Zombies and Aliens	167
22	The Story of a Strange Love	177
23	Heroes in the Spotlight	183
24	A Burning, Searing Secret	193
25	A Side Trip to the House of Love	203
26	Twists, Turns, and Accusations	211
27	The Rock and the Role	221
28	A Book and Movie Deal	229
29	A Broadcast and a Bestseller	235
30	Laughing All the Way	243
31	In the Aftermath	249

Appendix A: Robert Spears' Alcatraz Case Summary	259
Appendix B: Civil Aeronautics Board Aircraft Accident Report: Case 1-0071	265
Bibliography	277
Index	297
About the Author	309

A Note from the Author

This book was a labor of both love and an incredibly meticulous research project. Any true story set deeply in the past comes with inherent challenges. This is definitely one of those. With a tale that begins to surface in 1913 and involves more than two dozen aliases for one man in nearly the same number of cities, there are a multitude of facts to uncover. As it turns out, much misinformation to sort through as well.

But this was simply too fascinating of a tale for me to pass up.

I first stumbled across the story while doing deep research in old newspapers for another project. I was almost instantly captivated by the bizarre nature of what I discovered: "Man Downs Airliner to Fake His Death." Could there be a more heinous crime?

From there, I took a deep dive and, along with the unparalleled work of my incomparable researcher, Julie Estrada, began to discover thousands of articles on the topic from hundreds of publications across the nation. In its day, it was a story that pushed nearly everything else off the front pages for months.

However—as is the nature of our fast-moving culture—the story quickly faded from the national consciousness and then completely disappeared within a year or two.

Like paleontologists, as we did our research, we felt like we were uncovering bits and pieces from a wide range of sources that all added up to what I believe you will find to be a quite compelling story of mystery, murder, betrayal, and intrigue. The

x / A Note from the Author

central character is as complex as they come, and to this day, undoubtedly, no one on earth knows the complete truth. What we do know, however, is fascinating in its own right.

I want to acknowledge an immense debt to the only two published works on the subject. The authors are due tremendous respect for their diligence and dedication to unearthing innumerable facts surrounding this virtually absurd and preposterous tale. The first of these is *Self-Styled* by Alan C. Logan. The second is a much earlier work, by Brad Williams—a public relations man for National Airlines—entitled, *Flight 967* (1963). Their fine work was invaluable in my own research and their contributions are much appreciated. There is more about them and their efforts in the bibliography section at the end of this book.

Although I was drawn like a magnet to the basic premise of the event—a downed airliner under suspicious circumstances—the backstory proved to me to be equally, if not more, interesting. Hidden in the background was the deep and disturbing reality of illegal backroom abortions and the men and women who made millions of dollars performing them, as well as protection, which was provided with a wink-and-a-nudge through law enforcement and the judicial system.

Abortion, which has been around in the shadows since the earliest recorded histories, has had its place in American culture despite the ongoing battle and political firestorm that has always surrounded it. Frightened, embarrassed, and shamed girls have always sought to prevent social humiliation and shunning through this manner, and their boyfriends, husbands, married lovers, and parents have often underwritten it.

The sad reality of the situation is that it was not uncommon for young girls—really women of all ages—to find themselves butchered and bleeding by the side of the road or, worse yet, on a marble slab in the coroner's office. From the 1930s on, activists told horrific stories of permanently maimed women who endured torture at the hands of unqualified practitioners who were so often billed as naturopaths, chiropractors, and osteopaths but only held licenses from "diploma farms."

And finally, this project would never have reached bookshelves without the exceptional work of my tireless assistant

A Note from the Author / xi

and head researcher, Julie Estrada. Her work on this project was invaluable, as it always is on every project. Thanks also go to my personal editor Kate Popa and the careful, expert editorial oversight of Becca Beurer of Rowman & Littlefield. Great appreciation goes to my loyal and long-suffering agent, Greg Johnson of WordServe Literary, who was by my side through both dark days and sunshine.

Now, prepare yourself for one of the most mind-bending, inexplicable, and unparalleled stories of the twentieth century that long ago disappeared from our current consciousness but remains, nevertheless, gripping and unpredictable at every stop along the way.

Jerry Jamison
Chula Vista, California
jerryjamison.com

Chapter 1

One Spectacular Flying Leap

November 7, 1941

The forest green and gray two-door Chevy coupe was spinning like a Texas twister in the red dirt-covered asphalt of downtown Weatherford, Oklahoma, causing gravel and dust to spew in every direction as onlookers dived for cover within the relative safety of storefronts and parked cars. Spinning like an out-of-control top, the thing was threatening to flip or tumble at any moment as mothers covered their children and shoppers tossed packages in every direction while they collapsed prostrate on the sidewalks.

To the four occupants in the automobile, however, everything seemed to be moving in slow motion. The pistol flying from the front seat—which now seemed suspended in flight—had just exploded a single bullet through the hand of one of the terrified passengers as acrid smoke filled the car's interior, and the deafening impact of the blast rendered the screams muffled.

Leo was desperately trying to gain control of his Buick. The other man and the woman trapped in the back seat tried frantically—but unsuccessfully—to exit the spinning vehicle in hopes of escaping this nightmare. Blood spattered their faces and clothing as Mollie—an older woman—yelped pitifully, her hands covering her face. She vomited seconds later.

2 / Chapter 1

Only one member of this sad group seemed to have his wits about him. That would be Robert Spears. The physician instantly reached back into his training and became preternaturally calm. Shifting into crisis mode, his mind was working like a finely tuned Swiss clock to develop a plan, to find a solution and get this chaos under control.

Unbelievably, the whole crazy thing had started three days earlier in the most peaceful place under the most tranquil conditions, with nothing but blue skies and sunshine ahead. So uneventful, so mundane was the meeting that it bordered on forgettable.

On November 7, in the tree-lined neighborhood of Lynnhurst—a bedroom community of Minneapolis—Leo Schertzer got behind the wheel of his two-door 1940 Chevrolet coupe while his 59-year-old mother Mollie settled in next to him for the 2,100-mile journey to Burbank, California. In the back seat was Leo's buddy and fellow 21-year-old Adam Novack and 47-year-old Dr. Robert Spears—his wedding planned for the same week.

College classmates Novack and Schertzer—who had been president of his Student Council and was a promising engineering student—were heading west to take positions at a military airplane defense factory. Mom was along for the ride and to help her son get established, while Spears was just a ride-along partner, sharing in gas money in exchange for the ride.

He had joined the group after answering the ad as a Mr. Herbert Erickson. However, when the car arrived in St. Paul to take on their passenger, they were met by Dr. Spears, who explained that Erickson had to take a last-minute trip to Washington and he would instead be traveling in the man's place.

Spears had no luggage—claiming it had been stolen only moments before—and carried only a small knapsack. Nevertheless, that sounded good to all, and they were happy to get an additional gas rationing card necessary during wartime. In minutes, they were on their way.

The first 500 miles of the journey were uneventful. The next 500 were not.

One Spectacular Flying Leap / 3

According to all involved, the group agreed to go south toward Kansas City along Route 66 so that Spears could visit his mother Matilda, who was in a nursing home in the area and reportedly dying, as well as see his sister Erna, who lived nearby. It would be a good break after driving through the night and a chance to get refreshed before the final leg of their trip toward a new and exciting journey into the burgeoning aeronautics industry.

While the others rested at the Econo Motor Court on West 9th Street, Bob met with his ailing mother for a 50-minute conversation. It was not a pleasant time. Words were spoken, things were said, and Bob left in a huff.

Still, whatever happened, the quartet was soon on the road with a now-moody Spears in the back seat, his arms folded across his chest and a scowl on his face. He was growing especially annoyed with Novack, who was loud, disrespectful, and crude from the older man's perspective.

Somewhere after crossing the Oklahoma border, Spears reached down into his knapsack and fished around for his traveling money, but he couldn't find it. Panicked, he pulled the bag up into his lap and madly dug around for the stack of cash—$485 then but equivalent to more than $10,000 today—and discovered it missing. Instantly he began shouting accusations, claiming that someone in the group must have stolen his cash when he was visiting his mother.

Stunned and dumbfounded by his charges, Novack began yelling back and denied that any of them had taken a cent from him. If anything, he had yet to cover his share of the gas money and more than once, they had picked up food and drinks on his behalf without reimbursement. Emotions were running high.

Seconds later, everything went quiet.

That was because Spears had pulled out a .38 caliber handgun and put it directly up to the side of Novack's head. Looking in the rearview mirror, Leo swerved the car while his mother screamed. The Chevy skidded to the side of the road and came to a stop in a cloud of dust.

"Gimme my goddam money, or I'll shoot you right here and now!"

4 / Chapter 1

The previously soft-spoke physician had transformed into a madman before their eyes. Mrs. Schertzer began to cry.

"Hand it over now, or I swear someone will get hurt."

None of this made any sense. There was no rational explanation for what was unfolding along this dusty Oklahoma stretch of Route 66. It was nothing short of a nightmare.

Ordering his traveling companions out of the car into a nearby field, Spears had them empty their pockets—despite loud protests of innocence—and demanded to know what they had done with his money. Adam produced $45. Leo came up with $14. Mollie Schertzer dumped the contents of her purse on the ground while sobbing hysterically.

Infuriated that they had not produced his missing money, the otherwise placid doctor began digging a hole—threatening to shoot them all and then bury them alive.

Next came something so inexplicable that the victims had a hard time later even describing it.

Ordering all three into the back seat of the automobile, Spears tied each of their hands, threw a wool blanket over their heads, and instructed them not to move an inch or "something bad was going to happen." Then, he poured an entire bottle of ether over them and demanded they breathe in the toxic fumes deeply.

In less than a minute, all three were quiet, motionless, and unconscious.

Starting the car, Spears turned on the radio and disappeared into the Oklahoma horizon to the big band tunes of "A String of Pearls" by Glenn Miller and His Orchestra. It would prove to be smooth sailing along country roads for the next 20 minutes until—quite unexpectedly—a foggy Novack sat straight up, yanked off the blanket, and began to lurch toward the driver.

Unfortunately, by that time, they were already rolling down Main Street in the heart of downtown Weatherford.

Leo Schertzer, who had also managed to free his hands as well, next leaped on the startled driver, pulled the ether-soaked blanket over the man's head, and held it tightly around his neck. With the three men struggling, the Buick began spinning sideways down busy Main Street, sideswiping a row of parked cars

One Spectacular Flying Leap / 5

and narrowly avoiding most, but not all, oncoming vehicles in the process.

Bouncing like a pinball, the occupants of the car were tossed around violently. In the terror of the moment, Spears began firing his gun wildly. Leo Schertzer took a bullet to the side of his head and lost consciousness. His mother, bashed by the butt of the gun, collapsed to the floorboard. The second bullet somehow pierced Spears' own hand before ricocheting off the back window. The third went straight through the center of Adam Novack's chest.

Despite his critical wound, Novack managed to wrest the gun from the driver, at which time the vehicle crashed headlong into the automobile of Tom Simpson, a local shop owner. With steam hissing from the radiator, gas spilling onto the asphalt, and a large Sunday evening crowd gathering, Spears crawled out of the driver's seat with Novack scrambling after him and waving the gun wildly.

Seeing it all from his front office window, Police Chief Bill Evans took chase down the street and demanded that the gun-bearing man drop his weapon and freeze in position. Dr. Spears, in the meantime, was teetering and staggering aimlessly down the middle of the street—still in a daze from the accident, the noxious ether, and the loss of the tip of one of his fingers—with blood dripping like breadcrumbs behind the middle-aged man.

Then, his chest soaked in blood—the bullet having passed less than an inch from his heart—Novack dropped the gun and fell to his knees in shock and exhaustion. As Chief Evans kicked away the firearm, Adam Novack unexpectedly jumped to his feet and began sprinting after Spears. In what the local newspaper later described as "one spectacular flying leap," the young pursuer caught up and drove his assailant "headfirst into the sidewalk and sat on him there."

But that's not where the story ends.

Weatherford's mayor, Leonard White—who happened to be in the lobby of a nearby theater—saw the commotion and hopped into his pickup truck, gunned the gas pedal, and headed toward the scene where the two men were now wrestling. Dragging the young and severely wounded Novack into the Eaton

6 / Chapter 1

Drugstore to receive medical attention, White then returned to his truck only to find Spears—now with the gun pointed directly at his forehead.

Ordering the mayor to drive out of town, the pair took off down Main Street—with the muzzle of the gun pressed to White's temple. However, at that point—fed up with the entire situation—he slammed on his brakes in fury and defiance. With a single wave of his hand, White knocked the gun away from his head, causing it to fire inside the cab, just missing White's head, as the car's interior filled with smoke.

Not just any smoke, though. Spears had been wielding a teargas gun. In seconds, the men were being asphyxiated by the burning, gagging fumes. Mayor White tumbled out of the truck, clawing at his throat while at the same time, local townsfolk—who had earlier joined in the chase—reached the vehicle.

At that point, Spears fired a second round of teargas in their direction, immobilizing the vigilantes who collapsed in a pile. Not to be out dueled, however, Evans clambered over on his hands and knees to reach the driver's side of the truck—his eyes red and raw—and yanked Spears out of the cab and sat on top of him, coughing and wheezing.

Robert Vernon Spears was arrested on the spot and shuffled off to the Arapaho Jail, charged with robbery involving a firearm. While sitting in his concrete and steel jail, with his hand bandaged and ego bruised, it was discovered that he had previously served time under two aliases.

Eventually, the miraculously healed California-bound party would continue. But the mystery of Dr. Robert Spears was just beginning to unfold for the clueless Oklahoma authorities.

It would turn out that this little scuffle in the sleepy, dust-bowl town of Weatherford, Oklahoma—a hamlet of just a couple thousand residents—was far from Spears' first run-in with the law. It would most definitely not be his last, nor his most outrageous—or even his most terrifying.

What Police Chief Evans, Mayor Leonard White, Custer County Sheriff Everett Stambaugh, County Attorney G. C. Loving, or Judge Donald Darrah could not have known at the time

One Spectacular Flying Leap / 7

was that Spears would ultimately have, in fact, 26 aliases in 20 different U.S. cities and Canada.

These included—but were not limited to—Clyde Stringer, EJ Manning, Robert C. Buchanan, GF Prescott, John Hill, Logan Hunter, CJ Fairchild, Robert Lane, Lee Byan, AW King, Dr. Clive Cushman, George Rhodes, Charles Howard, Clyde Porter, Fred. L. Bonney, Lewis Austin, Henry G. Tremmel, Oscar Delano, Lewis Harmon, Lionel Byam, Dr. Marion Campinella, Dr. Fred Farnsworth, George Searles, Frank Massey, Robert Howard, and the all-colorful and wonderfully named Kigab Gypterm—most identities replete with business cards, driver's licenses, personal letterhead, and photo identification.

However, it would be a full two decades and countless adventures later that the name of Robert Vernon Spears would surface in one of the most heinous crimes that could ever have been imagined and is virtually unparalleled in American criminal history.

And it would be that event which would come to define him.

Chapter 2

A God-Given Do-Over

November 16, 1959

A little over a week before Thanksgiving, William Allen Taylor—just "Al" to everyone who knew and loved him—was driving his pride and joy as the sun rose behind him. Breezing along State Route 90 and having just passed the turnoff to Panama City, he was preparing to exit Florida's panhandle heading west as the sunrise flashed brightly in his rearview mirror. His goal was to reach Dallas by sundown, though he was realizing that that might prove to be a bit of a challenge.

Taylor's "pride and joy" was, in fact, a 1957 Plymouth sedan with its smartly painted coral-and-cream exterior and matching vinyl interior, which screamed money and sophistication—everything Al believed himself to be. He was heading toward California but in no real rush. The holiday was still a full 10 days or so away. With money in his pocket and his Bulova watch tucked away in his pocket, he had nothing but time and unlimited freedom on his hands.

This was to be his fresh start. Leaving behind a muddled past, the man was anxious for this God-given do-over that had serendipitously presented itself, and he was damned if he wasn't going to take advantage of it. The sky ahead of him was still darkened, with a few stars that were managing to twinkle and capture his attention.

10 / Chapter 2

As he entered into the Gulfport area of Mississippi, Al flipped on the Philco radio on the dashboard and tuned it to *"WWL 870 on Your Dial"*—a New Orleans station featuring the new laid-back sound called Cool Jazz as dished up by the Miles Davis' Sextet.

Just a couple of minutes into a number called "Flamenco Sketches," the hip vibe was shattered by a breaking news story at around 9 am.

> We interrupt this programming to confirm that the Miami to New Orleans National Flight 967 crashed into the Gulf of Mexico at approximately two o'clock this morning, just a few miles from reaching land.
>
> Because of the darkness, rescue efforts were hampered, but nine bodies were spotted floating in the shark-infested waters, and it now appears that all 42 passengers were lost at sea.
>
> We will update this story as more information becomes available. May God rest their souls. We return you now to regular programming.

Shaking his head at the tragedy, Taylor was aware that this appeared to be just the latest in a rash of unexplained air disasters in the nation that had shaken the public and the industry. More unsettling was the fact that he had just earlier been meeting a friend at the Tampa airport—something that now just seemed a little too close to home.

"Hard to beat a fine driving machine," he said to himself as he cruised down the ever-brightening highway. With that, he affectionately patted the side of his perfectly polished car out the driver's window and retreated to the jazz tunes on the radio.

Deciding to press on as long as he could, six hours later, he was approaching Vinton, Louisiana—nearly out of gas and certainly out of energy. Emerging from the Plymouth, the six-foot-one, 220-lb. stocky man stretched and moaned as his body adjusted to being out of a car seat. After making a quick stop in the restroom, Taylor went into the small service station office while a boy filled his tank, checked the water and oil, and cleaned his windows.

A God-Given Do-Over / 11

An older man was behind the counter with his elbows settled on it and his eyes affixed to a flickering black and white television. Without turning, the clerk said, "Y'all hear 'bout this plane crash? Terrible. Terrible thing. Just went straight down, they's sayin'. Tail stickin' straight up in the air. Got no idea what happened . . . jus' dropped outta the sky is what they's sayin' now. Damned mystery. . . ."

Taylor had laid four dollars down for the gasoline and a pack of Luckys when he noticed a face on the television. "Hey, mister, turn the thing my way, will ya?" The man did as asked and adjusted the rabbit ears as he did. On the screen were the faces of several men, apparently some of the known victims of the crash.

"Holy Christ!" Taylor suddenly blurted out. "Oh my God . . . Robert Spears . . . I was the best man at his wedding. I just talked with him today. Oh my God, I can't believe it!" Taylor was jabbing a finger at an image on the screen. Under the photo, the name read Dr. Robert Vernon Spears. "He was heading to Dallas for a business meeting . . . I can't believe it."

"Dang, brother, I'm so sorry. Wow, don't know what to say. . . ." By the time the clerk had responded, Taylor was already out the door and heading to his car. Pulling out onto the main road, he turned the radio back on hoping to hear more news. *Crashed in the ocean. No survivors. Cause unknown. Forty-two assumed lost. Robert Spears included.* The thoughts jumbled around in his head and made his brain cramp.

Now unable to think of anything else, Taylor spotted the bright neon lights of the Del Rio Motel and Lodge through the fog up ahead and pulled into the nearly vacant lot. *Heated Pool. Television. Massage Beds. $5 per night.* It was perfect for his tired body and racing mind. The man needed a break. The past two weeks had been a real bear. Too stressful.

Walking up to the motel manager, he asked for a single room for the night. Without comment, the woman pushed a card across the worn, wooden counter and dropped a ballpoint pen on top of it. Dutifully filling in the information, he added in the license plate number of the Plymouth and then returned the form. Lowering her readers to review the card, she muttered,

12 / Chapter 2

"License, gotta see y'all's driver's license for ver'fication. State says, not me."

He complied, and the woman in the house dress glanced over it. *William Allen Taylor. Tampa, Florida.* "Good 'nuff," she replied as she pushed across a key attached to a plastic fob. "Room 107. Checkout is eleven. Use the ashtrays if you smoke. Throw the soiled towels in the bathtub when you leave." With that, she turned on her heels and returned to her chair in front of the television set in the adjoining room.

Taylor could hear the announcer saying, "Among the missing are two little girls, flying alone. Another was a man in his 80s who begged for a seat on the plane so he could see his ailing son in New Orleans, an Oklahoma college girl who just two days earlier had been a bridesmaid at her sister's wedding. . . ."

The little bell on the door jangled, and the lobby was empty.

Al's wife, Alice Taylor, had felt that over the past few weeks, her husband "just wasn't himself." Not that she could put a finger on it, or for that matter, what in the world he might have on his mind, but she just had what she called "a sixth sense."

Actually, Al was her ex-husband of four years, but they had remained reasonably close because of their son William Jr.—just "Junior" to everyone. He was always in touch, always around, always checking in. She was good with that, and by all accounts, so was he. He also dearly loved his son and was loved in return.

In the last few weeks, however, Alice noticed that Al was uneasy, unsettled. something just was not quite right. Not enough to really be concerned, but just off a bit.

At the moment, though, she was trying to reach him to see if he had heard the terrible news. Dr. Spears, after all, was Al's best friend for decades. Though she was not personally altogether fond of the man, Al and Bob were undoubtedly connected at the hip. The news of his tragic death would undoubtedly be devastating to her ex-husband, and she was trying to connect with him to see how he was handling the situation.

Making matters worse, he had flown to Atlanta that morning to check into a business opportunity, and she wasn't certain where he might be staying. As a successful salesman for the

A God-Given Do-Over / 13

Pioneer Tire Company, it was not unusual for him to be on the road—he had the southeast region to cover. However, because he was looking into a new job, he wasn't exactly anxious for his boss to know about the Atlanta trip.

Having told his supervisor that he wanted to take Monday off, Alice was unsure how to track him down. Making a few calls to motels where he had stayed in the past—a shot in the dark—she got no results. No problem, he had told Junior he would probably be home that evening. They could talk, and she could console him, then.

Having heated some soup, Alice and her son sat on the sofa in front of the TV and followed the news of the crash, which had pre-empted every channel—there would be no *Father Knows Best* or *Danny Thomas Show* tonight.

As with every national disaster, it was only a matter of time before the stories behind the faces of the lost came to light.

The newscaster began somberly, "It was a routine flight across water traveled by thousands of planes without a mishap. But Flight 967 ended in the deep waters of the Gulf of Mexico and brought horror to the 42 families of those on board. Each of those lives contained a spark of drama that assumes weighted importance in light of this tragedy...."

Chapter 3

Casseroles and Comfort

It is a sad reality in this modern age that until an unexplained but epic disaster occurs, most passengers on any flight are completely anonymous to the rest of the world. But as soon as a tragedy happens, every aspect of their lives is magnified and broadcast into the living rooms of total strangers. And those stories only exponentially amplify the heartache for everyone as the victims are no longer faceless.

As was the custom, journalists immediately began to dig into the backgrounds of each passenger—especially the fateful circumstances that brought them to this horrific moment. And, as was virtually guaranteed, the story of each lost life was gut-wrenching.

On board was Rev. C. L. McGavern, Dean of St. John's Cathedral in Jacksonville, and his wife. On their way to New Orleans to attend the funeral of a close friend, they had only moved to Florida from Macon, Georgia, months earlier. Left behind were their two devastated teenage children.

A grieving John Shutts was flying to California to try and reach his terminally ill sister while, at the same time, his parents were driving west from Ohio. When they arrived, they were devastated to find that their daughter had died just before they arrived and that their son had died in the plane crash—losing both of their children within 24 hours of each other at opposite ends of the nation. Their two other sons had been killed as Army fliers in World War II.

16 / Chapter 3

Dr. Joel M. Gibbons and his wife, of Van Nuys, were returning home from a long-awaited visit to Greece with their newly married daughter.

Eloise Pitts was a 25-year-old native of Tremont, Mississippi, who had recently been working as a dietitian in the Veterans Administration Hospital in Lake City, Florida. She was going to Long Beach to take a similar position in the VA Hospital there.

Pedro Marco, a prominent Cuban architect from Havana, was going to Los Angeles to visit his son, Pedro Jr., a sophomore architecture student at the University of Southern California.

There was the busy Dallas businessman who flew to Miami to drive home with his wife from a vacation only to miss connections and return alone on Flight 967. Unaware of her husband's tragic death, she drove along through the night with no idea what horror awaited her.

There was the veteran pilot, who had moved with his wife and children just two weeks ago into the large two-story house of his dreams that featured a swimming pool. He was still awaiting the delivery of their furniture. Four businessmen on three different sales trips ended in the Gulf of Mexico.

The 51-year-old man who elected to make a sales trip to Florida to escape a harsh Detroit winter but decided at the very last minute to fly to Dallas and back. The bread truck delivery man, who decided to make a quick trip on a last-minute impulse. The 33-year-old merchant marine, who was trying to catch up with a ship he had missed.

The 20-year-old Oklahoma college girl, who had been an excited bridesmaid at her sister's wedding just two days earlier. The Coral Gables electrician, who decided on an impulse to visit his grandchildren in California. Several who were making inconsequential trips that turned into the most consequential moment of their lives.

A young flight engineer, a boyhood airplane enthusiast and nephew of a chief pilot for the airline, was aboard. As was a pretty 23-year-old blond stewardess with hazel eyes, Patricia Ann Hires, who had tried clerking in a bank but gave it up for the glamor of being an airline attendant. "I'll never marry if it

Casseroles and Comfort / 17

means giving up flying," she had proudly told her mother just before leaving.

There was also Ellis "Itchy" Mandel, a longtime associate of the notorious Los Angeles mobster Mickey Cohen, who was traveling with two companions. Then, curiously enough, there was another man who was discovered to have two wives when they both showed up to meet with investigators simultaneously.

Forty-two lives, each with a story.

Although the experts were careful not to tip their hands—and denied the possibility of sabotage from the very beginning—the first theory to be developed was based on the presence of Itchy Mandel on the flight. A mob hit was not out of the question, though it was a bit inconsistent with the Mafia's known adherence to certain unwritten ethics. Even for gangsters, taking down a plane full of innocent civilians was considered immoral.

Still, it was the best lead they had initially, and so the first FBI statement that was released said: "We are attempting to determine if the presence of Ellis 'Itchy' Mandel on National Airlines Flight 967 had something to do with the crash. There is no basis for substantiation at this point, but Mandel is not an ordinary person aboard an ordinary flight. We have a number of conjectures and one of them is that there could have been foul play because of Mandel's presence."

In fact, Itchy Mandel—along with his brother George and a companion—had left Chicago a short time earlier and flown to Miami for what was called a contentious meeting. He was en route to Las Vegas to meet with other "associates" after just the brief stopover in Tampa.

Police departments in all major cities were asked to check with their informants to see if Itchy might have fallen into disfavor with any of his associates, especially Mickey Cohen—the high-profile Los Angeles mobster.

During this time, at police headquarters in Los Angeles, Lt. Herman "Bud" Zander overheard Mandel's name mentioned during the investigation. "What's up with him?" he asked curiously. "Just routine," he was told. "Itchy was on the plane that went down over the Gulf last night, and there's a check to see if anyone was mad at him."

18 / Chapter 3

With plenty of other work to do, Zander just shrugged his shoulders and continued on to his desk. He had heard of the plane crash but hadn't read anything beyond the headlines. It would come back to him with added impact later in the morning, however, because of a casual call he received from a well-known female Los Angeles crime reporter.

"Hey, Bud, there was a Dr. Spears from Dallas on the plane that went down just outside of New Orleans," the woman said. "Isn't he the same man you picked up on an abortion charge out in San Pedro?"

Zander paused for a few seconds and then admitted, "I don't really know for sure" and then promptly forgot about it. Less than 15 minutes later, the reporter called back. "Yep, that's your boy," she said cheerily. "That's one court appearance you can cross off your calendar now . . . he's at the bottom of the ocean."

A few moments after the woman hung up, Zander stared at the calendar on his desk. The trial for Spears was set for December—just a few weeks away. Now curious, he pulled out the Spears case file and perused the contents for a few moments before heading over to the office of his captain.

"This character who has a court date with us is listed as a passenger on the plane that went down in the Gulf," Zander said, placing the open file on the desk. "Do you think he could have somehow slipped his name on the manifest?" His boss shrugged with disinterest. "No idea. Don't think you can do that kind of thing, though."

Indeed, the passenger in question, Dr. Robert Spears, was a renowned physician who lived in an exclusive neighborhood of Dallas with his wife and children. A board member of the American Naturopathic Association—a well-regarded organization in the 1950s—he was an in-demand speaker and writer and traveled in the elite circles of Dallas society.

It would be safe to say that with a sophisticated young wife of 10 years, two young children, a thriving practice, and a majestic home, Dr. Spears was living out his dream. Hosting Gardening Club soirees, dinner events, and cocktail parties with regularity at their Gaston Avenue home, the Spears were both

Casseroles and Comfort / 19

popular and influential—even bending the ear of Texas Governor Allan Shivers on occasion.

However, all that made this moment even more tragic as Bob—husband, father, admired doctor, and society gadabout— was apparently now lost forever more than seven hundred feet underwater. Making matters worse, at the time, Frances and the kids had moved to their posh California vacation home near Palos Verdes and could not immediately be located.

Eventually notified of the tragic news—the family was staying in their Dallas home briefly to check on a deadbeat renter— Frances was shocked, confused and grief-stricken. The newly widowed mother of two was frantically trying to put together the pieces of the puzzle. Later, recording the events as they unfolded for her, Mrs. Spears dictated the following to Special Agents Doyle Williams and Charles Brown, Jr.:

On Saturday night, November 14, 1959, I received a call from my husband in Tampa, Florida. He stated that he would be coming home on National Airlines Flight 967 which would make him arrive in Dallas at approximately 4 am on Monday, November 16. He said he would try to sneak in order not to awaken me.

Later on, at approximately 7 am on November 16, I received a long-distance phone call from Mr. McKay of National Airlines in Tampa who advised me that the plane Dr. Spears was on was overdue in New Orleans, Louisiana, but that the plane had five hours of gas beyond that.

The next call from the airlines was approximately 9 am the same day and they told me that they had sighted some wreckage, but they had not gotten to it yet and did not know what they would find. He told me not to make any travel arrangements to the area until they contacted me back and let me know what the conditions were when they got to the plane.

Apparently the first news of Bob being on the plane broke on the radio sometime in the vicinity of 11 am our time the same morning because the house was suddenly swarmed with friends coming in. The next call from the airlines was about one in the afternoon that day and they said they had found the wreckage and had gotten to it, but there were no survivors.

20 / Chapter 3

My family came down and were here on Tuesday morning, the 20th of November. I had been at the house completely by myself until then. I started to grow concerned about what this meant regarding Bob's arrest in California and called Mr. Joseph Forno in Los Angeles, who was Bob's attorney there, and told him of Bob's death. I explained that Dr. Spears had been on the plane that went down and that he was dead.

Frances Spears then related something very odd that the FBI agents immediately noted and flagged for further investigation. She said: "I then asked Mr. Forno if everything was *all squared away out there,*' and he told me that everything had all been taken care of as planned except that Bob had not yet paid him his fee. I was concerned that my parents would find out about his arrest and the circumstances."

The next pieces of the puzzle for Frances would fall into place when she received a call from Alice Taylor, the wife of her husband's dearest friend, Al. Expressing her deepest condolences, Alice mentioned that there was word going around that three gangsters—associates of famed mobster Mickey Cohen—were on the passenger list. "It might have been a gang hit, Frances," Alice confided. "It's all just so terrible . . . my heart is breaking for you, dear."

With that, friends and neighbors led by Ella Mae and John Martin quickly rushed to bring hot casseroles and covered dishes while offering comfort at a gathering of friends in the Spears' home. There they were joined by dozens of friends including Eva Houseman, owner of the Wild Cherry Cafe in town, who later explained:

"Frances was distraught and upset and cried throughout the entire time. Mrs. Spears stated she would have a formal funeral service performed about thirty days later when she was planning to leave Dallas to go back to California."

Few of the people who came to pay their respects noticed the three airmail letters postmarked two days prior to the plane crash that were now resting on the bureau. Those letters from her husband had come on the same day as two packages mailed to her by Mrs. R. M. McElreath of Los Angeles.

Although she waited until the "wee hours of the next morning" to open everything, she would discover that the packages inexplicably contained her husband's insurance policies, his will, and related legal papers—something she would never be able to explain nor the timing of the deliveries.

What she would treasure however, were those three letters with some of the last words he wrote to her, ending with: "I have been gone only a few hours, but I'm so lonesome I don't know what to do. I guess this business of having two wonderful kids and a wonderful wife has become chronic—it's a habit I can't, and one I don't want to break."

But on this evening, the friends and neighbors on Gaston Avenue were all mourning how Frances Spears' perfectly idyllic and privileged life—the very picture of the ideal 1950s family—had suddenly crashed and burned as surely as that plane.

Chapter 4

Sunshine Is Straight Ahead

November 17, 1959

By daylight, after the accident, the scene of the crash was swarming with a flotilla of boats—some curiosity seekers—who primarily had been called in to assist with a search and rescue mission that almost immediately was changed to the tragically titled *recovery mission* with all its horrific implications.

Only nine bodies would be found floating in the area—one of them half-devoured by sharks. The remaining 33 would never be located. A 10th individual would be identified much later by what was called "a very small portion of a finger bearing a ring."

Somewhat surprising to the team from the Civil Aeronautics Board, which was called in quickly to conduct an investigation, was that the remnants of the plane were all relatively small pieces—the largest no bigger than a small card table. Considering that the plane was a full-sized DC-7, this was telling.

Originally thought to have lost engine power during a thick fog bank and virtually gliding into the ocean, the investigators were now looking in a different—more concerning—direction.

The first reports had indicated that the plane was sitting on an underwater shelf with its tail in the air featuring its distinctive markings. If this was the case, the aircraft, flying at 15,000 feet and only 30 miles from shore, could have undoubtedly

24 / Chapter 4

easily coasted for some distance with no power and landed roughly—but safely—on land.

However, the water scene told a different story.

The plane had virtually disintegrated—the small pieces covering a two-mile area indicated that such significant damage could not have been caused by water impact. The fact that life jackets were floating on the surface without ever having been inflated or any evidence that seat belts were in use now was giving credence to the fact that the plane was downed by an explosion of which the passengers and crew had no foresight.

Stewardess Donna Osburn's injuries, in fact, were consistent with those of a person who was walking at the time—implying that she was performing her normal duties when the plane came apart.

Maybe that was why there was no SOS signal broadcast by the experienced pilot. And why radar trackers had followed its flight path before watching it disappear at 1:51 am in a blip from the screen. And why the crew had communicated with air traffic controllers in New Orleans that there was nothing but clear skies ahead just 25 minutes before they went silent.

Eighteen-year-old Coast Guardsman Richard Prince, in fact, indicated that he saw a large, bright red flash, from his position in a watchtower, that was "as big as the sun which lasted for several seconds" in the early morning sky at roughly the same time and location that the plane disappeared from radar. "The light then dropped with a white tail straight into the ocean and was gone."

Perhaps it was a mob hit after all?

Worse yet, in an era before "Black Box" recorders were required by the FAA, the plane, in fact, after impact, had descended more than 700 feet into an undersea ravine at the bottom of the Gulf—an unreachable depth in 1959—where it would remain with its doomed passengers for eternity. Today, it is still entombed by tons of silt and sediment.

Investigators, Navy divers, and Coast Guard vessels would continue to scour the site for weeks in hopes of finding any clues as to the cause of the downed plane. Ultimately, the Civil Aeronautics Board's eight-page report—dispassionately entitled

Sunshine Is Straight Ahead / 25

Case 0-0071—simply listed the cause as: *Unknown*. The detailed report, signed and dated by the five-person panel, was issued some two-and-a-half years after the event and was incredibly detailed, including the specifics of an extensive search for survivors. A portion of their summary reads as such:

> National Airlines Flight 967, a DC-7B, numbered N 4891C, crashed in the Gulf of Mexico while en route from Tampa, Florida to New Orleans, Louisiana, on November 16, 1959, at about 0055 Central Standard Time. All 42 occupants—36 passengers and 6 crew members—were killed. There was no radio message of impending trouble.
>
> A radar-observed descent was close to a position about 108 miles east-southeast of New Orleans, about 30 miles east of Pilottown, near the mouth of the Mississippi River, and very nearly on the planned course.
>
> Intensive sea and air searches resulted in finding nine floating bodies and one partial human remnant, as well as a significant amount of floating debris the following morning. None of this disclosed conclusive evidence as to the genesis of the accident. The main wreckage has not been located despite several well-executed searches.
>
> Because of the lack of physical evidence, the probable cause of this accident is unknown.

Not that the official findings mattered much to local fishermen, residents of the area, and regional law enforcement. They all knew what they had seen, and the evidence was in plain sight for all to judge, as was clearly stated by a Louisiana bayou shrimper who simply said, "The damn plane just blowed up inna million pieces."

For some time, pieces of mail—the plane was filled with airmail letters for the U.S. Postal Service headed for Dallas—would wash up on the shores of the small islands at the mouth of the Mississippi in New Orleans along with bits of clothing, personal items, and fragments of the lives lost.

Al Taylor—after a long stretch of emotions and inner turmoil—was relieved to finally see the towering 15-foot steel

26 / Chapter 4

replica of an oil derrick welcoming visitors to oil country. He was getting weary of the drive but still had a stretch to go. It was no longer the road trip he had anticipated.

News of the crash was also preempting nearly all of the local area stations—taking away his anticipated jazz tunes—with the continuing concern over what had caused the crash. At the moment, an unexpectedly dense fog bank seemed to be the culprit, but local observers and eyewitnesses were immediately questioning that theory. Everyone seemed to have an opinion, and the radio station managers were more than eager to put anyone willing to voice an opinion on the air.

But Al was focused on something entirely different. In his rearview mirror was the familiar but dreaded sight of flashing red lights. Pulling his battleship of an automobile to the shoulder, he coasted to a stop and involuntarily dropped his head to the steering wheel. This was the last thing he needed.

His mind racing, his pulse pounding, Taylor stepped out of the car with a broad smile and a big ol' country "Howdy" for the approaching state trooper. The officer didn't say a word other than to ask for the proverbial license and registration. Quickly responding, Big Al handed over the pieces to the cop, who studied them carefully in the uneven glow of his flashlight.

"William Allen Taylor? You from out Tampa way? Whatcha'all doin' out here in these parts?"

Al explained that he was heading west "for some business opportunities," explaining that he was in sales. "Sorry, sir, if I was goin' too fast, but my mind is just all caught up in this airline crash news. You see, my best friend was on board, and, gee, it's just so damn hard to accept that he's gone. Was a real good guy . . . a doctor, you know, with a wife and kids."

The officer nodded disinterestedly and added, "Left rear tail light out. Get'ter fixed when you get into town." With that, the trooper returned to his car, and Taylor pulled uneasily out into the open road. He still had another 250 miles and probably five hours to go before he reached his next stop.

Nightfall had descended during the roadside interlude, so Al, finally locating a music station, revved his Plymouth up to 60 and began to sing along to "Yakety Yak" by the Coasters. The

Sunshine Is Straight Ahead / 27

sky was awash in stars and traffic was relatively light, so, under a waning moon, excitement was beginning to rise in his heart as he sailed along Highway 20 past Marshall, Longview, and Kilgore in the east Texas portion of the state.

It was probably close to midnight when Taylor entered the Lake Highlands neighborhood of northeast Dallas, and about 10 minutes later, he pulled up to the tree-shrouded home at 6116 Gaston Avenue. It was a two-story, stately brick home on a large lot that spoke of affluence and social status at the time. Surprisingly, the lights were still on in several of the rooms and from where Al parked across the street, he could clearly see people moving around inside.

The scene was homey and friendly and seemed to be a house filled with love. He could see two women standing in front of the living room picture window talking. One had her hand on the shoulder of the other. That woman was holding a small baby and making that rocking motion that young mothers naturally know how to perform. Always moving, never settling.

From his driver's side seat, he could also see other silhouettes in other rooms. Two men drinking from beer bottles. Another woman, apparently sitting in a chair and smoking. Getting out of his car, surreptitiously, Taylor made his way to the base of a large oak tree in the neighbor's yard where he would be hidden from the house's occupants.

As he did, a couple emerged from the front door, pausing briefly on the front step to hug the woman holding the baby. She was dabbing at her eyes with a handkerchief. "Thank y'all for coming over . . . so sorry to . . . sorry to keep y'all up so late," she added.

"Don't you even say that, honey," the other woman implored. "We'll be here ever' day if y'all want us to, or we'll make ourselves scarce if that suits you better. But remember me and the ladies from church will be bringing a hot meal every night, so don't you pay no nevermind to cooking during this terrible time. You hear me, now?"

The woman in the door frame nodded, the tears starting again, and waved goodbye to her friends. Walking down the sidewalk carrying an empty Pyrex dish, the man—presumably

28 / **Chapter 4**

the husband—said, "Man, that's a hell of a tragedy. I don't know how she'll make it through. . . ." His comments went unanswered. Nothing needed to be said. Nothing could be said.

After they passed, Taylor emerged from behind the tree to get a closer look at the living room and the woman with the bouncing baby through the window. She was standing there alone now, just peering out into the inky blackness of the night with tears streaming down her cheeks. His eyes moved slowly to a placard next to the front door.

There in black script letters were the words *The Spears Family.*

With that, the man strolled back to his coral-colored Plymouth and slid inside, careful to keep the overhead dome light from coming on. Sitting there for a minute or two, he exhaled a sigh and then started up the engine on the automobile.

Before heading out of town, however, he reached into his back pocket to pull out a worn leather wallet. Crammed full of cash, notes, and business cards to the point of bursting, he extracted the license that read William Allen Taylor, tore it into pieces, and tossed them out the window into the cool night air where they fluttered and eventually landed in an empty field.

From his pocket, the man next pulled out a second license and slid it into the empty slot where the previous one had been. Taking a glance before tossing the wallet into the glove compartment, he looked hard at the name. *Robert Vernon Spears.*

It felt good to be himself again, even if it was at the cost of Al Taylor—his best friend in the whole world.

Smiling to himself for a brief second, Bob began to concentrate on the dark, wooded stretch of highway that was up ahead. Somehow, the drive already felt lighter, better, more promising.

Before turning the radio back on, however, Spears found himself repeating the lines of his favorite Robert Frost poem, as he remembered it. When he reached the final lines, an enigmatic grin involuntarily crawled across his face.

The woods are lovely, dark and deep,
But I have miles to go before I sleep.

Indeed, miles to go—for the umpteenth time in his life—before setting up yet another identity. Another life. Perhaps

Sunshine Is Straight Ahead / 29

another family. His heart couldn't help but break for his dear wife Frances, and he would forever miss his little eight-month-old Robin and her older brother Kenneth, who was about to turn two. However, they would recover and hopefully enjoy full and meaningful lives.

He loved them all, and if there were any way—any way at all—he would make it back to them. Then, if the stars aligned, maybe they could all be together again. That was the dream, anyway.

They, of course, would have the benefit of the million-dollar (in today's value) life insurance policy he had taken out on himself just a few short months ago. Back when he and his best friend Al Taylor—*may he rest in peace*—were developing their. . . . Well, this was not the time to think about that. *Poor, poor Alice*, he managed to remember for a second. Poor Alice Taylor and young Junior.

They didn't deserve the pain, but unfortunately it was just part of the plan.

But now was not the time for being melancholy. There was work to be done. No, now it was time to start over. Find a place to hide out for a while and devise a new strategy. A new name, certainly, but also a new life. He had some business ideas, and there were some promising opportunities. All he needed to do was to reach the home of his good friend Dr. William Turska, and all would be good. Turska would also have a plan. He always did.

And as he pondered his future, the Plymouth's headlights flashed on a hand-painted sign featuring a large saguaro cactus and the words *Arizona Sunshine Is Straight Ahead!*

That sounded good to Bob Spears.

Chapter 5

That Hinky Feeling

It was November 18, 1959—two days after Flight 967 ended up on the bottom of the Gulf of Mexico—and Robert Spears had been driving virtually night and day to make his way across the country and put distance between him and that tragic disaster.

Far, far away on the other side of the country, however, Alice Taylor was pacing around her kitchen with the telephone in hand—the long, coiled cord stretching from the living room. She was growing increasingly desperate to reach Al and see how he was doing emotionally in the aftermath of the death of his closest and dearest friend. Alice knew her ex-husband would be distraught.

With his recent uptick in drinking, she was concerned he might do something foolish or harm himself accidentally. She knew that there was no one more important in her husband's life than Bob Spears—not even herself or their 17-year-old son—and she knew she needed to get a hold of Al quickly.

However, Alice was not making any progress, and it was rapidly becoming concerning. No one had seen or heard from Al in three days. It was not like him. If anything, he checked in with Junior every day, whether he was home or on the road. She was beginning to get a "hinky" feeling without being able to identify what that was.

In her mind, Alice reviewed what she knew: Al was flying to Atlanta on Sunday. There, he would spend one night and then be home in time for dinner on Monday evening, or so he had

32 / Chapter 5

told Junior. It was now Tuesday, and his boss at Pioneer Tire had called inquiring where he was. He, too, had been trying to reach him regarding a missed sales appointment.

Al had casually dropped by the house on Saturday to see his son, but now Alice remembered that "he seemed off a little. A bit distracted or nervous. Preoccupied might be the best word." With Junior out of the house, the two talked briefly, but Al left in a hurry—again distracted.

That Sunday evening, he called two more times for Junior, who was still not home. "He said it was important but wouldn't tell me what it was about," she later remembered. When Wednesday rolled around with no word from Al, his boss at Pioneer, Robert Christie, called the Tampa Police Department and officially filed a missing person report, saying, "Al is very prompt, very attentive to detail . . . this is not at all like him."

While the FBI was looking into the possibility that organized crime was involved in the airline crash—the clues now pointing more toward a bomb aboard—Alice Taylor was on a concentrated search of her own. From the moment she was interrupted during her weekly bridge party that Dr. Robert Spears was on the ill-fated flight, she had a knot in her stomach that just would not go away.

It was no secret that she was not a fan of the doctor—who she saw as arrogant, pretentious, and shady at best. However, she would not allow her personal feelings to stand in the way of supporting her ex-husband at the time of grief.

Alice, now in her late fifties, had enjoyed a socialite past, having come from one of Florida's more influential and wealthy families. Formally trained in voice in piano at the Conservatory of Music in Ohio, she had "a certain air about her at all times."

She was also universally described as a "stubborn and hard-headed woman," though not unpleasant, and she regularly admitted to still feeling fondly toward Al—having been married for 18 years—after they separated five years earlier. Attractive and sophisticated, she seemed unwilling to let go of her coarser, easy-going salesman of a husband who was well beneath her socially.

That Hinky Feeling / 33

Unable to make any progress in her search, Alice drove over to Al's small, two-room efficiency apartment in the sketchy Hyde Park section of South Tampa. Using her key and stepping inside, she was instantly struck by how sterile and sparse it was. She knew her ex made good money—very good, in fact—but there was nothing in his home that reflected that. It was a spartan existence at best.

More concerning was the fact that there was nothing that revealed Al was planning on being away for any length of time. Everything was where it should be—his shaving kit, toothbrush, even luggage. It appeared to her, as she would later comment, "as if he had just stepped out to pick up a newspaper." Especially concerning was her discovery of his denture cream. "He could not possibly eat without it," she would add. "His teeth won't stay in."

Alice also made a mental note that his tan overcoat was missing.

Rifling through his drawers and papers, hoping to find some clue as to what he was up to, she was surprised to come across a large bundle of string-tied letters. Unashamed, she pulled them out and, sitting down on the sofa, read through each one. They reflected a long and enduring series of correspondence between Al and Bob Spears.

At times, they had almost written daily to each other—sometimes writing on the back of each other's sheets. Sometimes writing between each other's lines. Other times, using all the margins. To her, they felt uncomfortably like love letters, perhaps trophies of some sort.

Alice was simply unable to shake the gnawing feeling that the crash of Flight 967—which had left from the same Tampa airport where Al was heading on that day—and the disappearance of her husband were somehow connected. Add to that the element of the always-mysterious Robert Spears, and it was all just too coincidental. Not that she could get anyone to listen to her.

In a final effort, she went to the post office, where she knew Al received his mail. After some arm-twisting, she was able to obtain the contents of his box. Nothing unusual there—sales fliers, bills, advertisements, Rotary notices—until she came across

34 / Chapter 5

a legal-size envelope with a red, embossed seal in the corner marking it as important. It was addressed to Junior but mailed to his own address. *Curious.*

Opening it somewhat shyly, she discovered that it was a receipt and policy information for airline insurance that was purchased in her husband's name, with the beneficiary designated as William Allen Taylor, Jr., their son.

But there was something else that jumped out at her.

The insurance policy, according to the paperwork, had been purchased at the Tampa International Airport at exactly 12:16 am—just nine minutes before Flight 967 was scheduled to depart. Her heart dropped. And then it dropped even further when she saw that her husband had listed the airline as National and his destination—not as Atlanta as he had told her—but rather as Dallas, Texas, the destination of the doomed plane.

Racing back to her car, within minutes, Alice was on her way to the Tampa Airport—little more than a stopover airfield at the time with an unimpressive two-story flight tower—and parked in one of the spaces.

Entering the glass double doors to the terminal, Alice hastily asked around to find out where the airline insurance vending machine was located. Finally spotting the Mutual of Omaha unit, she stood for a moment, reading the words plastered on its face:

Get $62,500 of Coverage
for only 10 Quarters!
Free Postage Stamp With Each Policy!

She had only begun to let it sink in that her missing husband had been standing in that exact spot just days earlier when a harsh realization struck her—the machine was located steps from the gate through which the doomed Flight 967 passengers had passed, unaware of their fate.

"Nine minutes," she said to herself. "Nine minutes from the time he purchased the policy and the airplane was set to take off. Al was on that plane. . . ."

That Hinky Feeling / 35

Alice would later confess that she nearly vomited at the thought of what she was now coming to believe—it was her husband on that flight. Her husband . . . using Dr. Spears' ticket! Spears' name on the manifest, her husband sitting in the seat. *Al Taylor was dead, not missing.*

Her mind now a blur—spinning uncontrollably with terrible, dark thoughts—Alice hopped in her car and sped directly to the Tampa Police Headquarters. Greeting her, Police Sergeant John Daniels listened patiently as the harried, frantic woman tried to explain her situation. Then, he stopped her in her tracks with a simple question, "If your ex-husband were on that flight, then his car would still be in the airport parking lot or at home, wouldn't it, Mrs. Taylor?"

At that moment, Alice remembered that when she had parked her car earlier in the small airport lot, she would have most certainly seen his unmistakable salmon and cream Plymouth—it was so distinctive and memorable. Would have seen it, that is, if it was there. *But it wasn't.*

As her mind raced, Sgt. Daniels was carefully explaining what she already knew to be fact: that either Al had driven to the airport—in which case his car would still be in the parking lot—or he had taken a taxi to the airport. In that case, his car would have been left at his home or, perhaps, at his workplace. "The Bureau," he continued, "had already checked every possible place, as a routine matter, where he could have parked his car, and they had been unable to locate it.

"I think at this point, Mrs. Taylor, it's reasonable to assume that your ex-husband and his car will be found together. There is a search for that car as we speak, and as soon as. . . ."

Alice interrupted, "What about checking the local. . . ." This time, it was the officer's turn to interrupt. "Ma'am, we have checked all of the hospitals and clinics between here and Atlanta, and there has been no accident involving anyone answering to Al Taylor's description."

"Of course not!" Alice barked back sharply. "Of course not, because the plane with my husband on it went down in the Gulf of Mexico, not between here and Atlanta!"

36 / Chapter 5

"Well, Mrs. Taylor, I assure you we will keep looking. I'm sure something will turn up. You'll see . . . he was probably just out for a Sunday drive and airing things out in his head."

Then, sensing the woman's patience was growing thin, the police sergeant went on to explain. "But, ma'am, every passenger on board that flight has now been accounted for by some relative . . . each and every one," he said kindly.

"Even Dr. Robert Spears?" Alice asked.

"Even Dr. Robert Spears," Sgt. Daniels replied.

What the sergeant didn't say was that he was pretty certain that this was just another case of domestic conflict. Whenever an ex-husband or an ex-wife disappeared, in his experience, it resulted from one of the parties wanting to be done with the other. Daniels had handled hundreds of similar cases as head of Tampa's Missing Persons Bureau, and the missing spouse almost always eventually surfaced.

Feeling sorry for the distraught woman, however, he suggested, "Why don't you see a lawyer? He can probably help you more than I can."

Alice, frustrated and now angry, thought it was a good idea and immediately headed across town to the offices of Hill, Hill and Dickenson, Tampa's oldest and most influential law firm. Bursting through the doors and demanding to see Robert Mann, the office was suddenly abuzz.

Trying to calm down the woman, Mann took her into his office and pulled up a chair across from the frazzled woman, motioning for her to slow down. With a stenographer a few feet away, Alice began to share her suspicions and the evidence she felt backed them up.

"My ex-husband, William Allen Taylor, was on National Flight 967. I am convinced of it. I am not a crank. I am not just anyone, and I need you to look into this case and find the truth so that the world will know. I believe Dr. Robert Spears—a man with a criminal record—somehow switched places with Al, and he is now dead as a result." Her words were sharp and abrupt, but they also had the ring of truth—at least as she saw it. Instantly, Mann was intrigued.

After she had unloaded emotionally on the attorney, Mann agreed to take on the case and suggested she go home and get some rest while he began the exhaustive process of following each lead and requesting every report. From that moment, he and his expert team would gather every scrap of available information to construct a comprehensive accounting. From that day on, he began a crusade on behalf of Mrs. Taylor that would last for years.

Robert Mann's investigation began at the beginning—the early days of the romance and marriage of Alice Mae Steele and William Allen Taylor and their fateful intersection with Dr. Robert Spears. There would be some twists and turns, some mystery, some dark corners. Still, he appreciated the challenge.

Alice arrived in Tampa in 1930 from her hometown in Ohio after marrying William Henrie, a wealthy builder who was capitalizing on Florida's reclaimed land as a result of the Great Depression. With bank-owned properties easily coming by for pennies on the dollar, Henrie successfully secured large parcels of land and then was perfectly poised to begin construction on new homes as the nation recovered under President Franklin Roosevelt.

Rich and well-positioned socially, Alice Henrie, however, became disillusioned with her workaholic and loveless husband and filed for divorce in 1938. Their union had produced one son, Blaine, who had been showered with everything he could have ever wanted from birth. Unfortunately, all who knew him said his personality reflected that sense of entitlement and privilege. He was a boorish young man at best—and a narcissist at worst.

Alice was now in search of a new husband in her early forties—guided by her parents, who were anxious to remove the family's social disgrace of divorce. It wasn't long before she ran into a charming and successful salesman by the name of William "Al" Taylor. He had recently relocated from Washington, DC, where he had held a position in the government.

Drawn by his self-effacing and sensitive nature—the opposite of her ex—she accepted an invitation for a date, and soon the pair were officially a couple. Telling him that she was only 36,

38 / Chapter 5

she especially appreciated that her new beau had no issue with her being a divorcee with an impertinent and feisty 11-year-old in tow.

The two were married in Ft. Meyers in a lavish ceremony on April 23, 1942—only months after America had entered the war. In less than a year, Alice was pregnant with their son, William, Jr. The new family of four was reasonably well-established financially. Alice soon made it her mission to draw her husband out of his shy shell by having him join church committees, several fraternal orders—including the Masons—and forced him to host regular cocktail parties in their home where Alice could flit around as queen bee.

William also came from social royalty of sorts. His grandfather, Charles Newton Taylor, was a renowned Memphis attorney and a state senator, and the Taylor name meant something in the status-driven South. After moving to Tampa, Charles was named a federal circuit judge while serving in the socially prominent position of editor of the *Tampa Tribune*.

Al himself had been described as "an all-around good fellow, who is intelligent, quick-witted, good with numbers and money, and has a real head for business." Popular on campus, a top student, and a star football player at Central High School, he was considered as the one student "most likely to succeed."

With both families having roots in power and money—as well as her new husband's sweet nature—Al was exactly what Alice had always been looking for.

Robert Mann, however, would discover some darker chapters in Al's life.

Although William Allen Taylor was born into an influential and well-heeled family, he never seemed to fit. Bouncing from job to job on the mean streets of Memphis, Al took on clerking positions and various jobs in the coal-mining industry but never amounted to much until he found his true calling—sales. After being hired by the nation's largest office supply company, a new concept at the time, he began to specialize in mechanized accounting systems and quickly moved up the ladder.

Just as quickly, he determined that he could make more money going directly to his customers and cutting out his parent

That Hinky Feeling / 39

company—a decision that promptly got him fired. Undeterred, and with all the company secrets in hand, he went out and quickly signed up one of the nation's largest accounts—a firm that would eventually become Terminix.

Hired to set up the company's centralized bookkeeping systems, Taylor was given full access to their banking and records and did a masterful job at the task for which he was handsomely paid.

Before long, William—as he was known then—had a wife, Ruth, and a son, Jack, and a brand new house at 1708 Union Avenue with a shiny car parked in the driveway. Life was good for the Taylors.

Unfortunately, young Taylor soon became restless and devised a second way to make money from his client. This one somewhat skirted the law. Taking home a section of business checks along with samples of the firm's officer's signatures, he learned to forge them with impressive skill and began writing checks to himself under various aliases, the first of which—at $30,000 in today's money—was just a test. It grew from there in a matter of days.

Knowing, of course, that it was only a matter of time until his embezzlement scheme would be uncovered, Taylor did the only reasonable thing and skipped town. Heading 300 miles due north to St. Louis, he quickly found a boarding house and settled into his new home—never again to see his wife Ruth and five-year-old son Jack.

Alice had never known that her husband had been married previously. She never knew he had a son. Never knew he had owned a house in Memphis. Never knew anything about a "former life."

Never knew that that former life included much more than Alice could have known or Robert Mann had expected. It was, in fact, a whopper.

Chapter 6

Two Men on the Move

If William Taylor had first discovered himself in Memphis, he was destined to truly flourish in St. Louis. There, with a new identity—he was now simply "Al"—and a bundle of stolen checks in hand, he immediately opened two accounts at different banks in town and began depositing funds into them with rapid efficiency—$200,000 in today's money, in fact, in just a matter of days. Withdrawing the money as quickly as seemed reasonable, he next made some inexplicable decisions that would come to haunt him.

Instead of laying low, Taylor instantly went on a weeklong spending spree that would have rivaled the Rockefellers. Moving into the exclusive Coronado Hotel, the 27-year-old flashed cash and had jitterbugging flappers on both arms as he lavishly purchased gifts for the girls and bought rounds for anyone who would cheer him on.

Now, with tailored suits and polished Italian shoes, Taylor was the man-about-town—a living embodiment of Jay Gatsby in real time.

It wasn't long before he was on the lot of the local Packard dealership, where he wrote a check for a glossy new Roadster convertible and was pulling out on Washington Avenue to cruise across the Eads Bridge and into the ritzy St. Charles District with a backseat full of girls waving scarves in the breeze.

42 / Chapter 6

Two days later, he was gracing the society pages of the city's newspapers as "one of the most eligible and available bachelors with a flair for fashion and a sense of unmistakable style."

What he had yet to learn was that conspicuous consumption also attracted the authorities, who were increasingly growing interested in this young man with no discernable source of income yet plenty of cash on hand. Parading around the downtown area in outlandish golf attire, he was resplendently photographed for a feature article in *The St. Louis Star*.

Not long after, his high-profile living prompted the headline "Flashy Clothes Lead to Arrest on Check Charge" with the description: "His white flannel trousers, sport shoes and red necktie attracted the attention of two detectives at Ninth and Olive streets. Taylor admitted his forgeries and said he had purchased a brand new Packard with other worthless checks."

Upon his arrest—he apparently had been followed by detectives for some time—he calmly confessed to everything and simply explained, "I wanted to live rich and have a good time ... so I did." Years later, Taylor shared that this incident "taught me an important and valuable lesson—if you want to live rich on the dime of others, try not to draw attention."

With Ruth and her child having returned heartbroken and in shame to her parents' home in Mississippi, her husband was now facing a judge alone and receiving a three-year sentence for second-degree forgery. Headed to the penitentiary was Al, who would disappear from public view for some time.

As if the dark hands of fate were at work behind the scenes, a 32-year-old inmate by the name of Robert Vernon Spears had just been admitted into Missouri State Prison just mere weeks before another inmate—Albert Oliver Thompson—was assigned a cell there. Spears, who had just finished a six-month stint in famed Leavenworth Federal Penitentiary for mail fraud, was now inmate 33194 at Missouri State.

The two men almost immediately gravitated toward each other—each possessing something the other man found attractive. Thompson—known as "Ollie" in the pen—shy and non-aggressive by nature, was drawn to Spears' suave, high-powered leadership and bravado. Spears, for his part, was attracted to Thompson's intelligence and refinement.

Thompson, who had never been incarcerated before and was little more than a white-collar criminal of the lowest level, had been instantly overwhelmed by the harsh and unforgiving prison life he was now experiencing. Thus, he found refuge in Spears, and ultimately, they would form a bond that would sustain both men for the rest of their lives.

Years later, when Missouri Governor Henry Caulfield eventually paroled Ollie Thompson, he was a man without a country. Thus, it was Robert Spears, six years his elder, who provided both a home and a sense of family as a big brother after being released himself a few months prior.

For the better part of the next decade, Spears and Thompson worked in tandem to perfect and enrich themselves through confidence schemes up and down the Midwest and Eastern Seaboard. Sometimes they were hugely successful—securing tens of thousands of dollars in elaborate cons—and other times, they were not.

They came to be what was known in the era as "Flim Flam" men—gentlemen bandits of sorts who never hurt anyone who didn't deserve it, in their opinion, and then who spread their booty with joy and generosity. Friends and partners, it was by all accounts a fun and profitable time for the pair, and they began to identify and appreciate each other's strengths.

In an odd blend of personality and trickery, Thompson's innate sense of innocence and trustworthiness—"he had such honest eyes," said one victim—nicely counterbalanced Bob's natural energy and aggressiveness. One found they could easily draw in "the mark," while the other seamlessly closed the deal.

In one instance, Spears elected to become Mr. Henry G. Tremmel, the actual name of an affluent Cleveland manufacturer. Taking residence at the exclusive Hollenden Hotel, Spears began writing "rubber cheques" while the pair lived a life of luxury and excess—flashing and spending a bankroll a day. Purchasing hand-tailored suits with regularity, one early December, the two hucksters each ordered new wool outfits—$2,800 in today's value—from the W.B. Davis Men's Store and instructed them to be delivered to their offices in the Standard Bank Building.

44 / Chapter 6

Thompson then, posing as Tremmel's personal assistant, received the packages just outside of the office doors as his boss—arriving moments later—signed for the delivery. Ten steps and one minute later, the pair—parcels in hand—walked into the arms of the police. In less than a month, they were cellmates once again—this time in the Ohio State Penitentiary, where they enjoyed a brief stay before being released.

Once again free and on the street, Thompson and Spears— now changing aliases as easily and quickly as changing their socks—managed to work dozens of cons among the trusting and naive citizens of the Bible Belt. Although it would be impossible to enumerate and detail the many crimes the fraudsters committed during the decade, suffice it to say, they were cleverly conceived, expertly executed, and highly profitable.

Chief among their scams was the "Conference Grift," which employed a technique that, curiously, has made a resurgence in our recent era. The scheme involved securing the identity of a conventioneer—an easier task a century ago—and calling his wife or boss or best friend with a cry of distress.

In a time long before credit cards and cell phones, Thompson would meet someone at the hotel bar, gain his name and home phone number, and then Spears would place a call to his wife saying, "Your husband was (jailed/mugged/hospitalized), and he needs you to wire ($250/$500/$1,000) immediately to this person to provide him help."

That person, of course, was Spears under an alias and, after producing identification at the local Western Union office, would walk away with the cash. Although the amounts might seem small, the gentleman bandits—often perceived as cultural heroes in the era of Bonnie and Clyde—could easily and regularly clear hundreds of thousands of dollars in today's value in just one week.

If anything, writers of the time had become enamored with the idea of the dashing and dapper outlaw—many of whom seemed to have a sense of humor while thumbing their noses at fat cats and authorities. Taunting police at every turn, they were becoming the stuff of legend.

Robert Spears and his band of fraudsters even bemused the judges, who seemed to run circles around law enforcement and make them look foolish. In many ways, as long as no one was injured, the "confidence man" was seen as one of the charmingly good bad guys.

Though their plan would work surprisingly well for the better part of nine years, during his lifetime, Spears occasionally would run into an unexpected roadblock—as it once did with a leery and clever wife. When Mrs. Jarvis, back home in Albuquerque, received the distress call—as so many others had—regarding her husband's plight at a State Farm Insurance convention in Topeka, Kansas, she quickly wired the money. Still, she added the following note: "My husband is completely bald."

When Bob Spears showed up sporting a full head of hair, the clerk detained him while presumably gathering the funds, only to notify the authorities. In minutes, they arrived and took Robert Vernon Spears into custody. Upon his arrest, Spears congratulated the artfulness of the woman and offered her a virtual tip of the hat.

"Too Much Hair Traps Man in Wire Frauds: Impersonation of Bald New Mexican Leads to Arrest of Robert V. Spears," the tongue-in-cheek headline in the *St. Louis Star* blared the following day from its front page.

More serious was the con that the traveling team of Thompson and Spears attempted to lay down years later in Baltimore, Maryland. This time, they had singled out Mr. C. C. Willis, a sales executive for a tire company in California, who Ollie Thompson spotted at the registration counter of the Southern Hotel. Eavesdropping on a conversation the man was having with the desk clerk as he checked in, Ollie quickly relayed key information to his co-conspirator, who immediately contacted his employer's office by telegram requesting additional funds as a result of "a clerical error."

In less than an hour, Spears—acting as Willis—received nearly $10,000 cash in today's value, and after hitting up a few more hotels in Baltimore, the pair were soon on the road for Florida. This time—anticipating a more complex Miami score— the team brought in some accomplices to help pull off the scam.

46 / Chapter 6

These primarily consisted of women who regularly worked in conference rooms with less than honorable intentions.

They quickly enlisted the aid of five individuals to defraud a wealthy executive from the Westlake Construction Company who was pretentiously bragging about the commissions he received and was picking up drinks for girls at the prestigious Breakers Hotel in Palm Beach—at the time called "the nation's most magnificent and successful example of a palatial winter resort."

As per their established protocol, Thompson had gathered pertinent information on a Mr. George Reed and relayed it to Spears who then contacted Reed's home office requesting a wire of $5,000 in today's value. As always, without question, the transfer was made, but this time, as Thompson himself elected to pick up the funds at Western Union, the police were waiting with handcuffs ready—betrayed by one of their accomplices to escape legal problems of their own.

With Thompson in jail, Robert Spears now needed a new partner, and that person turned out to be Joey May, a New Yorker with a record for petty crimes. After testing the waters with Joey and finding success, Spears began to ready himself for the annual migration of wealthy individuals from the northeast and the winter sales conventions that were inevitably scheduled for Miami.

Identifying Charles Fredrick Cunningham of South Bend, Indiana, as a prime target, the pair took up residence at the ritzy, celebrity-favorite Hollywood Beach Hotel and Golf Resort. All was going well—intel gathered, phone numbers procured— with Joey May posing as Robert Howard, a business associate. Contacting Cunningham's office to request that emergency funds be wired to Florida, Howard casually made his way over to the telegraph office.

Unfortunately, Charles Cunningham turned out to be one of Indiana's most high-profile and respected citizens. As president of Merchant National Bank, his office was instantly puzzled by this unusual activity and contacted him directly at the hotel to confirm the request.

Two Men on the Move / 47

A stunned Cunningham then slyly instructed his office manager to go ahead and wire the money, recognizing it as a scam. At the same time, he notified the authorities to be at the Western Union office in Miami when "Mr. Howard" arrived.

According to newspaper reports from the time, "The so-called Mr. Howard strolled in wearing a cream linen jacket, azure dress shirt open at the neck, and expensive round-frame sunglasses, looking every bit the South Florida tourist." In seconds, badges were in his face as detectives arrested the perpetrator. Unfortunately for him, Mr. Howard—Joey May—started singing like a canary and gave up not only this scam but all of their previous schemes.

In little time, Robert Spears was heading to the Florida State Penitentiary for a one-year term. Shortly after arriving, however, Baltimore authorities came calling about a string of similar cons in their state. CC Willis quickly fingered Spears as Thompson's accomplice in his case, and the prisoner was extradited to Maryland to face charges there.

After going through the now familiar court process, both Thompson and Spears were reunited in the Maryland State Penitentiary with matching five-year sentences. This time it would be different, however. Thompson was 40 years old and rapidly growing weary of the erratic life of a rogue on the run. Lucrative though it was, the life of a gentleman's bandit was turning out to be tedious, with little to show for all of their efforts at the end of the day.

Throughout their run of fraud and foolish spending, the pair had shared five prison stints together in several states—most of the time readily admitting their crimes and accepting the subsequent punishment without complaint. But for Thompson, the thrill of it all was diminishing.

So, Ollie Thompson made the difficult but correct decision to walk away from their partnership and try and "go straight" after a decade of wild living on the edge of the law. It was a crushing decision for Spears, who had grown fond of his partner in crime and was confident that there would be even larger scores awaiting them in the future. But Spears respected his friend's decision and said a sad goodbye as they parted outside the prison gates.

48 / Chapter 6

Albert "Ollie" Thompson, of course, was none other than William Allen Taylor all along—an alias he had conjured up in his early days in St. Louis. Still, regardless of the names they used, the two men had forged a genuine friendship during those halcyon days that proved to be a bond that was stronger than any other throughout their lifetimes.

Returning home to his mother Genevieve's hometown of Tampa in 1940, Al Taylor moved into a boarding house and began to look for honest work. This eventually led the ex-con to an entry-level sales position for Pioneer Tire and Appliance, and soon, his life began to approach some normalcy.

At this time, he met and began to date Mrs. Alice Mae Steele Henrie and got to know—and adore—her young son Blaine, who, in some ways, reminded him of his own abandoned son, Jack. A little more than a year later, the two had a child of their own, Junior, and moved into a nice new home in a good neighborhood in Tampa.

Mrs. Taylor, of course—knowing nothing of her husband's checkered past—wholly accepted that he had been working for the federal government for the past 10 years without question when, in fact, he had been in federal prison.

Ironically, Robert Spears—who was to have participated in his good buddy's wedding—sadly could not attend. That was because he was presently a resident of the Oklahoma State Penitentiary where he was serving a four-year sentence for check forgery.

In another world, this should have permanently ended the Spears-Taylor criminal partnership but it did not. Instead, the two men drove their relationship underground while still occasionally joining forces to work scams, pull off petty frauds, and work the convention circuit from the shadows.

Despite the geographical distance between them, when Robert Spears met and married Frances and became a family man, the two couples would meet and come together for vacations and holidays even if the wives never really became friendly.

A writer would later say, "Taylor was in touch regularly with Spears through phone calls and letters. It seemed to sustain him. When they met up from time to time, Al felt alive—it was so good to be *himself* again. He felt his stress and tensions drain away when he was with Spears."

Alice, in turn, watched this relationship with some consternation and trepidation. "I would see them yukking it up about their past adventures, never really realizing that they were actually talking about crimes they had committed together. I always had an uneasy feeling when they were together. I could see that Al worshiped Bob, and I had a sense he would do anything for his friend. They were always there for each other, no matter what."

Frances Spears, for her part, just was happy that her new husband had a good friend. Though she didn't appreciate Alice's condescending tone toward her, it wasn't anything she couldn't deal with. Besides, Bob—with his past far behind him and completely unknown to his wife—had recently launched into an entirely new but equally profitable career.

He was now the renowned Dr. Robert V. Spears—president of the Texas Association of Naturopathic Physicians and the leading spokesperson for this exciting and burgeoning new medical field.

The man was indeed going places.

Chapter 7

The Unholy Trinity

After years of being on the wrong side of the law, Robert Spears decided to flip the script and become—in the eyes of society at least—one of the most respected men in the nation by becoming a physician. This stunning, head-shaking reversal would only add to the lore of the man who had reason to be called "one of the most fascinating men of his, or any, era."

Not all of it for good, unfortunately.

In this most recent iteration, Robert Spears took on the mantle of being a naturopathic practitioner—though he readily and wrongly attached the professional designation of MD after his name and on his letterhead. It was a tweak of the truth, to be sure, but in reality, it represented a much more nefarious and insidious lie—one that would fool people into trusting him for the rest of his life. But then, such was the goal of a serial scammer.

After serving an extended sentence in prison, Spears was trying to determine where his next score might be. At first, he scuffled around the oil fields of the southwest in hopes of "landing a whale" that he could take advantage of in some way. Despite the free-flowing money that was ubiquitous during the Texas oil boom, there seemed to be no promising leads nor anyone to partner up with as he had in the past.

What he did notice, though, was an unusual number of clinics popping up in every community—large and small, urban and rural—that were curiously called Naturopathy Medical

52 / Chapter 7

Centers. Unfamiliar with what the term referred to, with a little research he came to understand that these were doctors who specialized in practices just outside the realm of the American Medical Association.

Their approach was to utilize natural means—herbs, vegetable powders, ancient remedies, nutrition, exercise, and positive thinking—to heal almost anything. Believing that the medical industry had partnered with the pharmaceutical industry to form a monolithic for-profit monopoly, it no longer served in the best interests of patients.

And they were not alone in their thinking.

In the first half of the twentieth century, there were nearly as many practicing naturopaths as physicians, and the jury was still out as to which discipline might subdue the other. Even as medical practices became more regulated and were proven effective and medical technology produced incredible results, the public was still not wholly sold on inoculations and pills made in secret laboratories.

Instead, home remedies, superstitions and mother's herbal potions and treatments still held sway in most American households, as well as "doctors" who utilized such approaches.

Capitalizing on these homegrown philosophies toward medical treatments—popularized by a funder with the interesting name of Benedict Lust—several individuals rose to the forefront. They began to make a fortune on questionable medical advice.

One of those, Harry M. Hoxsey, was an extraordinarily successful naturopathic doctor operating out of Dallas. In fact, by the 1950s, he was listed as one of the wealthiest men in America through his clinic, which claimed to be able to treat cancer through natural, non-invasive means.

Hoxsey's cancer creams would eventually be proven to have no medicinal value and, after several court cases, were even deemed hazardous to the point that he was named by both the American Medical Association and the U.S. Food and Drug Administration as "America's number one cancer quack and charlatan."

The Unholy Trinity / 53

It proved to be only a minor setback for Hoxsey, though, as he had turned his clinic profits into oil leases in south Texas and was now rich and powerful beyond belief. Furthermore, in the 1940s, he had carefully nurtured the enthusiastic support of politicians who respected his money and influence, fundamentalist Christians who believed prayer and mother's poultices were best, and ultra-conservative citizens who were convinced that vaccines and fluoridation were Commie-plots.

Even more important to Hoxsey and the naturopathic movement was that the world's richest man, H. L. Hunt, was a fervent advocate of health elixirs and alternative medical treatments.

Hunt—worth $700 million in 1950—was a character in his own right. A staunch Baptist conservative, he was a bigamist who managed to father 15 children with several mistresses. One of those, Lamar—who assumed family control after his older brother and heir apparent was lobotomized—launched the American Football League and created the Super Bowl while his family still owns the Kansas City Chiefs to this day.

The legend of H. L. Hunt also couldn't be accurately covered without mentioning his connection to the assassination of John F. Kennedy.

Madeleine Duncan Brown, an advertising executive, maintained that she was present at a party at the Dallas home of oil tycoon Clint Murchison, Sr. (whose son owned the Dallas Cowboys) on the evening prior to the assassination that was attended by Lyndon Johnson as well as other famous, wealthy, and powerful individuals including Hunt, Murchison, J. Edgar Hoover, and Richard Nixon.

According to Brown, Johnson had a meeting with several of the men, after which he told her, "After tomorrow, those goddamn Kennedys will never embarrass me again. That's no threat. That's a promise." Brown's story received national attention and has become part of the JFK conspiracy theories that abound to this day.

One of the founders of the current conservative evangelical movement, H. L. Hunt, was an avowed lifelong racist and unrelenting political power broker who vocally advocated for "the deportation of all Negroes to Africa."

54 / Chapter 7

But as Hunt relates to this story, he was also a major force in promoting quackish medical treatments and in spite of his billions, never stopped promoting his own bogus health product, *Gastro-Majic*. Going as far as to plaster his limousine with bumper stickers for the product, he also required his thousands of employees to do the same.

So, with naturopathy skyrocketing like that in Dallas, Spears would soon be lured there as the place he intended to make his fortune.

However, the naturopathic tide would begin to turn during the great polio epidemic in mid-century America when the Salk vaccine proved capable of wiping out the disease—despite virulent calls from the alternative medical community and anti-Communist legions to reject the drug. By the late 1950s, the practice of naturopathy was in disrepute and on the wane.

In the post-war era, however, the alternative "doctors" were still held in the highest regard. To Robert Spears, that was like a beckoning call. After doing his research, he found out that Texas—with its Wild West culture of lawlessness—had allowed naturopaths to thrive while other states were in the process of shutting them down as "Quack Farms."

In late 1949, Texas established the State Board of Naturopathic Examiners to keep the practice on the straight and narrow, requiring a certified college degree from a qualifying institution and passing a state-certified medical exam to be licensed. They also—inadvertently or not—provided a very large loophole: for a $50 fee, applicants presenting a license from any other state would automatically be certified in Texas.

Thus, all Spears required was a license from some state and—impatient to claim his piece of the pie—was unwilling to do the study or the apprenticeship to get a degree in the field. He badly needed a shortcut, and he found that in the person of Dr. Robert H. Reddick—a bonafide and highly regarded psychiatrist who had been assigned to the famously groundbreaking Manhattan Project, which produced the world's first nuclear weapon and effectively ended the World War.

Reddick, coming out of that momentous and exhausting clandestine effort, had taken a position at Apple Creek State

Mental Hospital in Ohio and quickly became appalled by the barbaric treatment of the patients there—from electroshock therapy to testing unproven therapies and drug regimens. When his concerns were not addressed, he turned to the press and created an instant scandal for which he was fired and banned.

As a whistleblower before the term was coined, he brought a critical spotlight on mental health practices in America and began to work toward important change. At the same time, his disillusionment with the medical world drove him toward alternative modes of healing. He—completely inexplicably and out of character—began issuing phony Maryland medical licenses to anyone who fell in line with his recent thinking.

Spears' diploma cost him $5,000 in today's value while auto mechanic Joseph Biscardi later complained that he had plunked down the equivalent of $50,000 for his.

As soon as Robert V. Spears had a "certified" license to go with his already forged academic degree—going from a cattle slaughterhouse worker to a respected physician overnight by virtue of a counterfeit sheepskin—he opened his first naturopathic clinic, with the blessing of the Texas state examiners, in a rented office in the upscale Dallas suburb of Lakewood. At the same time, his stationery and business cards arrived featuring the professional, but wholly untrue, designation of MD after his name.

That was at the beginning of 1950. Over the next five years, Spears' practice expanded dramatically, as did his reputation in Dallas and his standing in the international community of naturopathic clinicians. Specializing in female issues—an evolving medical specialty—he dealt with everything from gynecological and digestive matters to general health concerns and weight loss treatments.

Aside from a certain "backroom" surgical procedure that was proving to be quite profitable, he also had realized a degree of success in the lucrative area of helping wealthy and vain women get slim, or at least slimmer in theory.

He was doing this through several programs he had developed that took off like a rocket in Dallas' exclusive and prestigious suburbs. These centered around his "Milk Routes"

56 / Chapter 7

by which he meant several well-populated groups of society mavens—usually 20 to a group—who paid him $10 each per month. For this they were able to attend a weekly group meeting in one of the ladies' homes where Dr. Spears provided group consultation, an invitation to purchase his bogus "Radionics Machine" or a "Neuro-Calometer" and deliver sixty "B-Slim Reducing Pills."

He once bragged to a friend that he had one group for each day of the week and estimated his income to be $4,000 a month from this source alone—more than $50,000 in today's value.

By 1954, he had also been named as president of the Texas Naturopathic Association—greatly increasing his reputation and clientele. His Radionics Machine—a contraption he had purchased from some failing business years earlier—became the rage for a while and attracted the original "desperate housewives of Dallas" with expendable money and an intense fear of losing their husbands and social status.

Radionics—based on pseudoscience—claimed that diseases could be diagnosed and treated by applying electromagnetic radiation (EMR), such as radio waves, to the body from an electrically powered device.

This so-called treatment was immediately dismissed as "hokum" by mainstream medical practitioners because it literally contradicted the principles of physics and biology. That of course did not dissuade Dr. Spears' patients from begging and paying for a turn on the machine.

The same was true of the "Electro-Psychrometer" which promised to provide insights into the mental state of an individual and thus provide—in much the same way as a licensed therapist might—some coping mechanisms for the triggers that cause weight gain.

In Waco, Texas, Frances—somewhat surprisingly—had taken a class on the use of an Electro-Psychrometer—which was invented by a man by the name of Joseph Matheson and which purported to be able to record the reactions of people when they were presented with certain words or questions. It was a sort of emotional aptitude test based on the perspiration a person

The Unholy Trinity / 57

exudes during responses and was designed to provide psychological analysis based on those physiological changes.

Frances was soon beginning to fancy herself as a "psychiatrist"—without any training or education whatsoever aside from spiritualists and snake oil salesmen—and over the years would actually attract a steady stream of "patients." The FBI file on her would turn out to be filled with many pages of their testimonies—they interviewed every known patient of Mrs. Spears for the record. Her $5 treatments ($50 today) seldom extended beyond what was described in this excerpt from her FBI file:

> In the Summer of 1956, I was directed to Frances Spears when I had a nervous breakdown. She would take me to an upstairs room where she would have me lie on a daybed and give me a handle type object on a cord to hold in my hand. The cord was attached to some type of machine but I don't think it was plugged into an electrical outlet.
>
> She would tell me to imagine that I was in a mental institution and how terrible that would be and tried to make me concentrate on the absolute worst situations I could imagine. At the same time I had headphones on listening to a record with extremely high-pitched notes and she said this would fix any sinus trouble I might have. After that, I determined that Mrs. Spears was not competent to help me and I did not return.

Also, at the same time, Dr. Spears was developing an "electronic machine which was for the purpose of testing a single drop of blood and then from that test particular diseases can be ascertained." Unfortunately the word for "disease" had mistakenly been replaced by the word "decease," an especially troubling typo. One potential buyer—who was totally sold on the value of the piece of equipment—explained that the testing went even further, however: "The electrical impulses made by the machine could cure polio."

During this period, the newly minted Dr. Spears was living in the Marsalis Apartments in the Oak Cliff neighborhood of Dallas and he began to fall for one of his neighbors down the hall. His eyes were apparently turned by a 26-year-old secretary working at RCA—more than 35 years his junior at 64—named

58 / Chapter 7

Frances Massey. She was generously described as homely, long- and sad-faced, tall and without any discernible figure.

His appeal, according to her friends, was that he was wealthy and socially respected—she had grown up in poverty as one of 13 children—and could lift her out of her circumstances. It seemed to work for both of them and, after dating for three or four years, they were married on December 22, 1954, by Justice of the Peace William Richburg. Eventually the newlyweds moved into an elegant and finely appointed home from which they welcomed their first child, Kenneth, at Baylor Hospital.

The house would also serve as a base for the new couple to entertain Dallas' elite, wealthy, and powerful. Before long, he was also well-connected politically to the administration of Governor Allan Shivers—ultimately tainted by an administration of massive corruption.

Earlier in 1950, at the National Convention of Naturopathic Physicians in St. Louis, Spears made several connections that would be at the core of both his practice and his fraudulent activity for the rest of his days. It was at that event where he would meet Donald Loomis and William Turska. Each man, as had Al Taylor before them, proved to play a pivotal role in his life.

Donald Loomis was a star among stars—more accurately, the health and fitness guru of MGM Studios in Culver City, keeping their marquee idols in top shape, tanned, and beautiful for the fans. Every ingenue was assigned to him at one time or another to slim their bodies and build up their busts, while the leading men were expected to add muscle, lose flab, and become darlings of the tennis set.

All of this was part of a new Hollywood trend sweeping the nation in the late 30s and 40s that came to be known as the "Physical Culture." And the unchallenged leader of this parade was an individual whose name was Donald "The Flesh Sculptor" Loomis. Usually photographed sporting body-hugging shorts while flexing the massive muscles of his bronzed, well-oiled body, Loomis was, in his heyday, as popular as any star of the silver screen and a regular on covers of both movie fan magazines and fitness journals.

The Unholy Trinity / 59

As the mid-50s rolled around, however, Hollywood gave way to unabashed glitz and excess, and vices began to overwhelm the desire for healthy living and good nutrition. The smoking, drinking, and carousing Rat Pack mentality had taken root, and it would be decades before the trend would reverse.

With his income and interest from the stars beginning to fade, MGM let him go, and Loomis was suddenly scrambling to find a new source of revenue. The answer was, at first, the pseudo-medical field of chiropractic and then, rapidly on its heels, Loomis became intrigued with naturopathy.

By 1950, Dr. William Turska had already established himself as one of the leading voices in this exciting new field, which was now receiving a significant volume of positive coverage. Cutting a dashing figure with both his fashionable outfits and his choice of sleek and sexy European sports cars, he was the face of naturopathy. Well-connected, affable, and extroverted, he was always on the prowl for "the next big thing."

And he, like Loomis and Spears, found exactly the right chemistry in the other two—each providing the missing link in their own lives and delivering the potential for more money, more fame, and more risk.

As the new decade of the 50s began—flush with the unbridled optimism of a booming post-war economy and a willingness among the public to explore new ideas—each of the players in this 50s drama found themselves inexorably attracted to each other.

Loomis had the looks, the charisma, and the Hollywood pedigree that the other men virtually worshiped—as well as an enviable black book full of high-profile clients. Spears was the ultimate smooth operator who knew how to work any system to his advantage—pulling the right levers to generate the funding he required.

William Turska had the chutzpah, the moxie, and the aggressiveness required to either go big or go home. He was a prime mover and shaker who was virtually fearless in every regard as he zoomed around town in his European sports cars with girls on his arm. Eventually he would wed six of them.

60 / Chapter 7

However, all three men also had dark pasts which they were loath to have revealed. Still, this was perhaps the strongest bond that drew them to each other and then would hold them together during the storms to come.

William Turska had a lengthy rap sheet and a history of questionable activities. Oregon-based, he had been busted there a year earlier for having a marijuana farm on his property, which landed him a five-year suspended sentence and probation. That unwanted attention resulted in the state board of medical examiners taking a closer look at the doctor and ultimately stripping him of his license.

Prevented from earning a living the traditional way, Turska turned to a series of shady ventures and "medical devices," which were promised to "produce incredible outcomes." Undisciplined with a serious drinking problem, Turska—younger than the other two—was always on the verge of reeling out of control or of scoring a million-dollar payday.

Of course, Bob Spears' lengthy criminal past with innumerable aliases was well-documented. But his new image as a respected doctor provided a perfect disguise for his ongoing illicit activities, which always involved fraud of some sort and usually included forgery and passing bad checks.

But it was Don Loomis who had been—and still was—the mastermind of something so great and so nefarious that his two new friends and cohorts literally idolized him. That was because Loomis—health guru, muscle man, and friend to the stars—was making the equivalent of millions of dollars through a backroom trade that existed only in the twilight of American society.

Donald Loomis was one of the nation's leading abortionists.

Chapter 8

Under the Table and in the Shadows

Abortion, of course, was illegal in America and in the "pre-pill era," unwanted pregnancies were rife. It is estimated that during this time, *several* million women tragically found themselves "with child" and terrified by that reality. For an unmarried woman, it was a social disgrace and an economic hardship made all the worse by the fact that it had often occurred during a secret affair.

What wasn't a secret was that more than one million of these women and young girls—many crushed by unfulfilled wartime romantic promises—decided that an illegal abortion, frightening though it was, in fact, was their only solution.

The American abortion mills of the 30s, 40s, and 50s—as well as long before that—were massively successful and highly profitable businesses that operated in the shadows but generally with the full knowledge and even protection of law enforcement, judges, and politicians.

It was deemed a "necessary evil" and clandestinely propped up by highly respected and influential power-brokers who were convinced it needed to exist—famed attorney Harry Umman once said, "Society condones abortion and then condemns those caught practicing it."

But the abortion industry had no intention of being controlled or caught.

Running slick and sophisticated operations—far from the back alley butchers who would forgo anesthesia and sterile

61

62 / Chapter 8

practices to abort a baby, often at the cost of the mother's health or life—one group held the monopoly on the industry. James Weiss and his sister Vivian Hubbard, along with three other family members, had a virtual lock on the business and, working in tandem with sideways-looking authorities, they would charge as much as $5,000 in today's money per procedure and were raking in an average of $5 million each year.

Running their practice out of a mansion in Los Angeles, there was no shortage of business. With their pristine operating rooms and medically trained practitioners, they regularly received hidden referrals from police departments, the courts, legitimate physicians, and even clergy. It was a well-managed and well-respected—though completely unacknowledged—profession in mid-century America that served, in the eyes of many, a needy population during a difficult time.

Donald Loomis, however, had an edge on his competition.

As the official abortionist for MGM Studios—later confirmed through previously hidden memos—and the Hollywood movie community in general, "Dr." Donald Loomis was the "fixer" when it came to unwanted pregnancies.

Appendicitis was the code word for "pregnant" at the time, which, of course, required an "appendectomy." Even a casual reading of the fan magazines of the day—of which there were dozens—reveals that a large number of actresses required appendectomies, so much so that it was labeled "a Hollywood epidemic" in the press.

Loomis, with a built-in clientele and the imprimatur of his employer, quickly built up a lucrative business—even providing a "mobile service to the stars." Arriving at the Beverly Hills mansions in his white paneled van, the health guru would show up for a purported workout, perform his duties, and be on his way, receiving compensation from both the studios and the patient willing to pay well for his services and discretion.

Thus, Loomis—preferred abortionist to the rich and famous—not only found himself wealthy but in demand. Clark Gable, it was once said, nearly kept Loomis busy on his own.

However, the man wanted more. Deciding that he could expand and franchise his operation with offices on Crenshaw

Boulevard and in Van Nuys, he began advertising to the general public through the legitimate newspapers of the era that he offered "Free Rectal Exams"—code for abortions. Business from the general public boomed and, more importantly, he had the tacit approval and protection of the LAPD.

After meeting Loomis through the naturopathy conference, Turska and Spears were taken into his confidence. The three decided that they could do better working in concert in different markets than as competing entities and thus formed a bit of a loose and unholy alliance.

From 1950 through 1956—when the trio reconvened at the national conference in Colorado Springs—things were going well. Still, the heat was beginning to come down on the industry, and there was a mutual sense that their business efforts should redirect toward the more acceptable fields of alternative treatments, medications, and devices.

It appeared that naturopathy, with its largely unregulated practices and procedures, seemed like a much safer bet. Spears soon began to apply all of his energy in this direction.

Rising up the ranks quickly, first in Texas, then nationally and eventually internationally, at the Colorado event with more than a thousand attendees present, 62-year-old Dr. Robert Spears was introduced as the new president of the organization with a vision of busting the monopoly of the American Medical Association by imploring the group to "rally around the flag of professional freedom."

Spears was undoubtedly riding high at this point. At the time, Loomis was busying himself with an odd assortment of money-making ventures that landed him a multi-million dollar home in the exclusive enclave of Palos Verdes Estates. Turska, now with a fresh start in Phoenix, had turned to exploring "Female Issues" and was finding equal financial success—though he managed to find a way to blow every penny.

Bob Spears, however, was content to settle in among the suburban elite of cash-rich Dallas with a wife, a child, and a beautiful new home—along with a respected position in a segment of the medical community.

64 / Chapter 8

In fact, life was very good until a twist of fate would change his—and thousands of others—fortunes.

With the hubris and ego of the Texas naturopathologists, the group was readying to do battle with the AMA, believing they could bust their powerful lobby and find equal footing through Congress and local politicians. Taking an aggressive stance, the association—led by Dr. Robert Spears—almost taunted their adversaries to fight with confidence that this was their moment in history.

It would prove not to be.

With a series of horrific incidents throughout the nation where naturopathic advice went wrong—resulting in tragic deaths and permanent disability among patients—the Texas State Medical Board began to pressure legislators to take action and weed out the bad actors and illegal operators.

Spears, now the fearless leader of the association, was unmoved by the allegations, knowing full well that they had been bribing state officials and politicians for years—named on the books as "educational expenses"—to gain protection. This system had always worked efficiently, and there was no reason to believe they couldn't quell this most recent uprising.

However, Robert Spears had not anticipated that this time the challenge would come from within his own ranks. One esteemed and legitimate member in particular, Dr. Howard Harmon, launched a crusade to clean up his industry and enlisted the aid of an expert private investigator with the promise of unqualified support from one of the few remaining honest legislators in the state.

Instead of going after Spears, Harmon out-maneuvered his adversary by focusing on the most egregious bribe-taker of all—Rep. James Cox—who had, ironically, just introduced a bill to basically shutter all "nature doctors" in the state. Harmon set a trap for the politician from tiny Conroe, Texas, through a sting operation in a room at the Stephen F. Austin Hotel.

Dr. Spears countered by negotiating with Senator Doyle Willis of Fort Worth—for a price tag of $60,000 in today's money—to support his side on the legislative issue. Unfortunately, that all fell apart when Rep. Cox was caught on tape demanding his

Under the Table and in the Shadows / 65

own $60,000 (today's value) tab to withdraw his bill and switch his support to naturopathy practitioners. Caught red-handed, the full House of Representatives was in the spotlight. Before long, the entire administration of Gov. Robert Allan Shivers—corrupt to the very core—began to collapse.

As key players on all sides began to tumble, one of the first to go was Robert Spears, the face of the bribery scandal on the naturopathic side. His license to practice was immediately revoked, but not before more than a half-million dollars in today's value somehow inexplicably disappeared from the association's coffers. A secretary later testified that she was aware of an additional $220,000 that disappeared from a petty cash fund—called the Program for Progress—which "was the result of an inordinate number of outgoing checks for cash."

Also, with his exit, however, went Spears' newly minted reputation, his standing in the community, his ongoing source of income, and his ability to show his face anywhere in town. Humiliated and desperate, Spears, this time, turned to an old acquaintance to help him create the next chapter in his story of fraud and deceit—with hopes that an unparalleled grift would restore his prestige and wealth.

He knew beyond any doubt that the big money was to be found in the abortion trade but this time he would turn to neither Loomis nor Turska—whom he had begun to lose confidence in—but rather to a man by the name of Charles Faiman.

Faiman was an infamous abortionist at the level of the greats in the industry who had no problem flaunting his wealth and status. Flashing Hollywood quality fashion, with rings on both hands, he had married a girl more than half his age who shared his lakefront mansion and a lineup of luxury vehicles.

With botched abortions headlining newspapers on a daily basis and several practitioners already behind bars, the industry was under a frontal attack. Faiman responded by choosing to—literally—no longer get his hands dirty through surgical procedures but rather by introducing his proprietary product "guaranteed to resolve the matter." It was called by the uncomfortable-sounding name of Metro-Vac, consisting of a vaginal creme that came in a toothpaste container.

66 / Chapter 8

The purple, sweet-smelling paste could be squeezed into the cervix, after which a miscarriage would occur usually in less than a day. Faiman had somehow managed to get the abortifacient approved by the equivalent of the Texas FDA, though it was banned elsewhere. That didn't stop Faiman from creating a vast national and global sales network, which generated ungodly amounts of money while distancing the doctor from the unpleasantness of the issue.

The creator of the creme, of course, was protective of his secret formula, so Spears—seeing immense value in following the same path—enlisted the aid of the colorfully-named Napoleon Bonaparte Barbee, a pharmacist with a checkered past of his own.

Together, they were the inventors and manufacturers of Euro-Clear Creme—"safe and effective up to the first four months of pregnancy"—and the money, as it did for Charles Faiman, began to roll in. Spears, however, couldn't bring himself to give up the vastly more lucrative surgical procedures and, through his "Mobile Motel Service," was performing abortions on a daily basis.

That was until the Dallas Vice Squad raided Cabin 346 of the Alamo Plaza Motel on March 3, 1958, and caught Spears performing a procedure for a couple who had just paid him $200 (around $2,000 today). According to a confidential FBI report filed by Special Agent Doyle Williams, the tip came from none other than druggist Barbee himself.

When Officers Erich Kaminisky and C. A. Moore broke down the door, on the bed was a 32-year-old secretary of a major oil company with her older married lover at her side, a powerful executive in Dallas. Arrested, charged with a felony, and released on a $4,500 bond, it looked to be the end of Robert Spears' freedom.

But that would not be the case. With a few well-placed phone calls, his powerful and expensive lawyer, Charles Tessmer, miraculously managed to negotiate the charge down to a hand slap and a $50 fine. Spears had dodged yet another bullet, and this time, he decided to clear out of town.

Under the Table and in the Shadows / 67

That decision was based in part because it was the first time Frances had learned that her husband was involved in the practice of performing abortions. Later, during an FBI interrogation, she related her experience:

> I first heard of my husband being in trouble with the law when someone called me on the telephone to draw my attention to a story in the *Dallas News* about a naturopath who had been picked up for performing an abortion. When I read the story, I saw that it fitted my husband's description.
>
> Later that afternoon I read in the *Dallas Times Herald* the same story in which my husband was identified by name. When I confronted Bob, he said something to the effect of, "Yes, baby, that's me."
>
> After that arrest I nagged him and pushed him pretty hard telling him I wanted him to quit his abortion activities and get into something moral and ethical.

In fact, that event meant it was time to move to "someplace where Robert said it would give him a chance to turn over a new leaf." That would not turn out to be the case, but it gave Frances the assurance she needed, despite the fact that she was loath to leave her beautiful home and friends. Dr. Wenton Welch, a friend, told the FBI that Spears left Dallas because "things were getting too hot for him in the abortion field" and he wanted to find new turf where he could ply his trade.

Eyeing California as their future home, in the summer of 1959 Frances and Robert bought a new place in the upscale Rolling Hills estate community near San Pedro at 1802 South Rena Drive. The four-bedroom, 2,800 sq. ft. home was purchased for $27,500 with monthly payments of $141. As a side note, the same home was most recently appraised at $1.9 million.

There the Spears moved closer to Don and Elsie Loomis, where Don seemed to have figured out how to perfect the surgical abortion business and was now eager to join forces with Spears, who was promising to bring him in on the lucrative Euro-Clear pharmaceutical abortion distribution business.

68 / Chapter 8

Though there was every reason to believe that this new partnership would soar from the outset, there was a wholly unexpected twist ahead that would push over the first domino that would ultimately result in some mind-bending decisions that could have been impossible for anyone to predict.

Initially, however, this new venture was producing revenue in unimaginable amounts. In today's value, the men were generating an income of more than $22,000 *monthly*, with that average steadily rising for most of the year. The sky, as they say, was the limit, but there were dark clouds on the horizon.

Sailing along without a care in the world, Robert Spears was thus surprised to get a phone call in late July 1959 from the UCLA Medical Center, which explained that they had a very ill 22-year-old schoolteacher in their clinic who claimed he had performed an abortion on her in a Santa Monica motel room. Additionally, she had used a paste she said he prescribed that had destroyed the soft tissues of her inner organs.

Before he could finish denying the charges, the Los Angeles police were at his doorstep, where they both arrested him and confiscated surgical tools, Euro-Clear manufacturing equipment, and a bushel of blank medical diplomas and licenses.

Unshaken, Spears quickly dropped the name of Donald Loomis—assured by him that they had paid richly for police protection—and was shocked to discover that he, too, had been brought into custody.

The magic, apparently, had finally run out.

At their preliminary hearing, the two men immediately turned on each other. Don Loomis was beyond furious that the unsophisticated Spears had destroyed his well-run machine, which had operated smoothly and seamlessly for years, with his carelessness. The judge set a trial date four months from then, and so, with a December case now looming, the pressure was beginning to get to both men.

This time—for Robert Spears at least—there was a good chance significant prison time was ahead. For a man heading toward age 70, it meant some extreme actions needed to be taken.

And that was exactly what he decided to do.

Chapter 9

Ticket to Paradise

Bob Spears—having completely abandoned his earlier Al Taylor impersonation—blew past the New Mexico-Arizona state line, fully aware that he had dodged his upcoming trial date through this deception. Scheduled for the following month, now the trial would never happen—for him at least—because Robert Vernon Spears had been officially proclaimed deceased. Thus, all the charges against him just melted away.

He knew, of course, that his wife would soon get well over $100,000 in a life insurance payout—more than one million dollars in today's value. There were other policies as well which would tack on the modern equivalent of an additional quarter-million. Spears was assured that he had set up his two children for life.

However, he knew all too well that he would have to create a new identity and start life over again, something he had already done many times in the past. But at the moment—as he cruised along the brand new "Interstate 10"—he was also certain he knew just the man who could make it all happen: *Dr. William Turska.*

"What's done is done," he thought to himself, trying desperately to push away from his mind the horrific consequences of what he had done just days earlier. "There's no changing anything now."

70 / Chapter 9

No bringing back his best friend, Al Taylor. No chance to explain anything to Frances. No opportunity to return to his suburban life in tree-lined Dallas.

Now, it was about survival, and in the moment, that meant connecting with Turska and hiding out until he could come up with a new plan—any plan, actually.

After several days on the road—and an exhausting stretch through the barren wastelands of West Texas, New Mexico, and Eastern Arizona—Robert Spears pulled the coral-colored '57 Plymouth into one of the parking slots at the Deluxe Motel just outside Benson, Arizona, on Thursday evening, November 19. He killed the ignition with a massive sigh.

The Deluxe, despite its promising name, was a dilapidated series of stucco cabins which attracted only the lower end of travelers. Before heading to the manager's office, Spears, however, circled to the side of the building where a pay phone booth was situated. Dropping in a dime, he dialed the number written on the inside of a matchbook cover that he had saved for some time. He knew it would come in handy eventually.

Scrawled in ink was the phrase: *Ring #6-7097*. Under this was the name, *Mary Ford*. "Ring #6," was circled. "7097" was likewise circled with the word "Code" written above it. In addition, the words "3pm Safeway" appeared on one of the maps later found in his possession.

Mary Ford, a friend and neighbor of Bill Turska—who did not possess a telephone—spoke for about 10 minutes with Robert adding change as the operator directed. Spears explained that he was on his way to Los Angeles and wanted to stop and say howdy to his friend. The two later met in the Safeway parking lot where Mary indicated that she and Turska were no longer really friends but she had no doubt Bill Turska would welcome him to stay at his place up in New River—about 50 miles north up along Route 51.

Bob would leave the next morning, Friday, November 20, for the dot on the map called New River and, in little time, was leaving the rural highway and traveling five miles along a narrow, rocky road before pulling into the dirt and dust driveway of the low-lying, boxlike, clapboard and stucco home. It looked

Ticket to Paradise / 71

like an abandoned outpost surrounded by a never-ending desert to Spears. However, that made it a welcome sight to the fugitive, and the two men embraced genuinely.

After explaining that he had to leave right away for a business connection—and to pick up some documents and items from his Rolling Hills home—Spears was off on the road in little time but not before returning to pick up an unknown and mysterious passenger back at the Deluxe Motel, according to Turska.

After nearly an eight-hour drive, Spears and his unidentified companion pulled onto the street in Rolling Hills, where his home was located and almost immediately got a bad vibe. Convinced that the house on South Rena Drive was under surveillance, he made a quick U-turn and headed back the way he came—never even stopping at his home.

Later, Robert Spears confessed to FBI agents that this was the first time that he'd thought that he'd better ditch the distinctive vehicle with Florida plates that was now regularly being identified in the news. "This was when I decided that I really needed to get rid of the Plymouth and my first thought was to dispose of the car by running it off into a lake or a river."

"Secondly, I thought it would be better to drive it into a canyon or rockslide area and cover it by means of an explosion. My third thought on the matter was to attempt to get rid of it through Turska in some way in Phoenix."

Four hours later, he and his mysterious companion were in Yuma, exhausted, hungry, and annoyed. Checking into yet another roadside motel, Spears called Turska one more time, who—based on whatever he was told—immediately hopped in his Mercedes sports convertible and zoomed off into the dark desert night toward Yuma.

As he drove, William Turska reviewed the events of his recent past and tried to decide what his next step might be. Like Spears, he was considering going on the run—Yuma was, after all, less than 10 miles from the Mexican border. And, like his Spears' buddy Don Loomis, he was facing certain jail time. His mind racing—working on overdrive—he pulled into the last space in the parking lot of the El Primero Motel.

72 / Chapter 9

From a second-floor room window, Turska saw a hand waving him up. Entering the room, he saw that Spears was now alone—no longer with any mystery companion, nor would there ever be any mention or later identification of him.

Spears had not been idle, however, during the time that it took Bill Turska to motor over to Yuma. Calling every junk yard in the southwest, Robert was feverishly searching for one that had a '57 Plymouth with a similar two-tone paint job that matched Al Taylor's quite distinctive automobile that no doubt was now being sought throughout the nation.

On the phone Bill Turska had suggested that Bob find a vehicle similar to Al's, buy it, switch the plates, and then abandon it for the authorities to find. When they did locate a perfect match—though partially burned—in a nearby Phoenix wrecking yard of all places, Turska was angered to discover that the proprietor wanted $150 for the body of the vehicle. Walking away from it, Turska turned to Plan B.

When no one was looking, he stole the license plate from the burned out '57 Plymouth junker—prying it off with a screwdriver—and then attempted to switch the Florida plates, which could so easily entrap Spears, with Arizona ones. After trying several times to affix the new plates with airplane glue and failing, the pair gave up and took off for Nevada to try the same thing in a different state.

Reaching Ely, Nevada—a tiny, rural hamlet—Turska and Spears gave up and eventually the only solution seemed to be to just park the thing in a long-term garage and be done with it. Which they did.

Having dealt with that concern, the pair took off once again for California in Turska's Mercedes, hoping to recover Spears' valuable items from his home. The plan was to have Turska masquerade as a visitor and secretly grab the desired items— primarily expensive and difficult-to-obtain abortion tools. This time, it worked, and so, to celebrate their success, the two men stopped at the Las Vegas Strip to live it up until all hours.

Eventually making it back to Turska's desert hideaway, the pair settled into a bachelor life—William's wife Annette having abandoned him prior to this bizarre ordeal—that seemed to suit them both. Spears enjoyed cooking and often made grand dinners while his housemate enjoyed eating them. Spears was not a fan of alcohol but Turska liked to drink despite being an outspoken evangelist for a healthy and nutrition-based lifestyle.

Time passed as the decade of the 1950s came to an end and the two felt like it was a sign from the stars that they had both been given a fresh start and a chance for a new beginning. There was something about the ring of "1960" that just exuded optimism and opportunity, and the pair began to discuss the potential for expanding the New River outpost into an "Abortion Spa" of sorts where patients could come and stay, get their procedure, and then relax and get restored in a healthy and stimulating environment.

The idea had great possibilities except for two important factors. Less than two years earlier, William Turska had been popped by the Phoenix police for performing an abortion from the back room of his Seventh Street doctor's clinic in downtown Phoenix after a 28-year-old woman turned him in and directed the cops to his door.

To make matters worse, while that case hung in the balance, Turska was arrested for driving under the influence and being in possession of banned medications. On top of that, the authorities quickly discovered that he was operating the supposedly legitimate clinic without a medical license. There were dark clouds on William Turska's horizons, to be sure.

However, in Bob's case, the situation was quite different. Though he didn't express any particular concern about downing an entire airliner with 42 souls and at the cost of his best friend's life, he had begun to feel a pull on his heartstrings for his wife and babies. For all his flaws and despicable actions, Spears truly was in love with Frances and dearly longed for her and the kids. He knew it would be impossible for him to resurrect his old and nearly perfect life in Dallas . . . but he wanted a taste of it.

"I want to let Frances know that I'm okay. Just get a message to her or a phone call to say that I'm alive while I'm figuring out a way to get us back together." Bob tested the waters to see what his friend might think of the idea.

74 / Chapter 9

"You're nuts. Completely bananas," William delivered his answer tersely and quickly.

"Hear me out, Bill. If we could drive out that way and I stay in a motel on the outskirts of town, then you could contact her—slip her a message in case she is being watched—and then maybe we could get together for a couple of hours . . . maybe bring the kids. It would work, I'm tellin' ya."

In less than an hour, the two were sailing along the highway on a crisp southwest January morning in Turska's Cadillac with the radio blaring and the excitement of a road trip adventure ahead.

Ten hours later, the two had checked into a room at the Lakewood Hotel on January 7, 1960—Spears registering under the name of George Rhodes. Bill Turska then placed a non-descript call to Frances, simply saying he was an old friend of her husband and wanted to stop by to pay his respects.

Back in his room at the Lakewood Hotel, however, Spears was pacing nervously.

How would Frances respond to the news that he was alive? Would she be furious? Would she turn him in to the authorities? Was this the end of the run for him? They were all very real, very legitimate questions and as he sat on the generic motel bedspread with head in hands, beads of sweat were forming. At any minute, his life might take a sharp left turn.

Just a few blocks away, Bill Turska knocked on the door at 6116 Gaston Avenue and when it was opened, handed the startled woman a large bag of oranges as a gift. Soon they were sitting in the living room of the Spears' home where Turska explained in hushed tones—assuming the FBI bugged the house—that she needed to meet with a "Mr. Rhodes" at a nearby hotel in regards to something related to her late husband.

Suspicious but curious, Frances cautiously agreed to the meeting and slipped out under cover of night at around 9 pm for what appeared to be—to those surveilling her house—a casual drive through the neighborhood.

In five minutes, she was in the hotel lobby where Bill silently led her to the staircase, which delivered her to Room 26. Then, pushing open the door, she saw him—her dead husband.

Robert Spears was alive.
She would later describe the situation to the FBI.

At first, I thought it wasn't for real, you know. I asked Mr. Turska outright, "Is this some kind of trick?" I had to know. He again replied that it was not and that someone was waiting at the Lakewood Hotel and gave me a note. It was from my husband in his own handwriting. I read it and then tore it into a thousand pieces and flushed it down the commode.

After that, I quickly left the house in my own car and drove to the Lakewood Hotel. I was hesitant to leave the children with my maid, Mrs. Kay McNeill [who is referred to by Frances in the FBI reports as "the colored girl"], and told her that since Dr. Turska had not had a bite to eat, we were going to Lakewood to get him something.

He accompanied me there from my house. I started to park the car in the rear of the hotel, or down the street, but then decided that I would not try to hide from anyone who might see me enter the hotel. So I just parked the car, a 1959 Pontiac Sky Chief, directly in front of the hotel.

When I entered the hotel room my husband was there. It was quite an emotional meeting—for I thought, of course, my husband was dead . . . but then, there he stood right in front of me. I don't remember our first words. It was extremely emotional. I had a hard time breathing.

Their meeting would only last around 40 minutes, and neither of them would ever fully say what was discussed though Frances did later mention to FBI agents that the first words she said to him when she saw him were: "What the hell are you trying to pull?"
She also added an interesting twist.

I told him that a few days after the crash that I had received a phone call from Allen Taylor, Jr. who told me that he knew his father was on that plane and he had found an insurance policy in their post office box. He claimed that he and his mother had spoken to a Mr. McKay of National Airlines and he had told them that they found your dentures in the debris from the trash.

In the end, I told him that I had tried on numerous occasions to get him to follow my line of thinking on things and that this

76 / Chapter 9

was one time that I could not allow him to do something that not only would harm him, but me, the babies, and all those who believed in us. I tried to use the children as a lever against him to get him to do what was right.

But he said too much time had elapsed and that no one would believe him anyway, and he did not see how he could go back now. He said he knew it was a mistake coming to see me, but he had to know how things were going. As I stood in the doorway, Bob told Dr. Turska to see that I got home safely. I assured him that I could do that on my own and then walked away.

Nervous that she might have been followed, Frances was uncomfortable staying any longer or saying any more and left quickly, returning to her car confused, filled with anxiety and stress, and clueless about what her future would hold. "I was trying to figure out the things necessary to reestablish myself as a widow," she would later confess. "I was unable to sleep for months after that meeting."

What she was able to do, however, was to continue seeing or talking to her husband over the next several days. After their first meeting, however, Dr. Spears moved over to Cabin 35 at the Grande Lodge Motel in Oak Cliff—further from their house so as to not raise unwarranted suspicion and to avoid accidentally running into an acquaintance in his own neighborhood.

There—still using the alias of Dr. George Rhodes of Tucson—Spears made a series of almost inexplicable decisions. Deciding—for some unknown reason—to play the role of an invalid, he required that the hotel staff serve him meals in bed and run his errands. Yet, on one occasion, he blatantly picked up a taxi from the hotel lobby to visit a restaurant—Little Bit of Sweden—that had been a favorite of his and where waitress Elsie Abadie cheerfully greeted him as an old friend.

At one point later on, Frances Spears would admit to avoiding his calls after a while. "When I got home from running errands one day, my other colored girl—Vernice Darby, who has done day work for me for a number of years and knows both Bob and I quite well—told me she had answered two or three telephone calls from a man and, after considerable hesitation, asked me if I knew of anyone whose voice sounded like Dr.

Spears. In trying to cover up, I mentioned the names of several other people, but she didn't buy it.

"After that I told him not to communicate with me at the house. He tried to get me to come up with a way he could keep in touch with me and the babies and I tried to appeal to him that there was no way he could contact me without placing me in a mental turmoil not knowing where he was or whether he had anything to eat or a roof over his head or what his conditions were."

There were also other visits and forays into town as well, as Spears' conduct during this period ranged from extreme recklessness to extreme timidity. It seems obvious during this period, however, that Spears decided he would have to remain in hiding for a considerable length of time at the retreat in Arizona. Seeing headlines about the plane crash everywhere he turned, it was clear that Dallas could no longer be his home.

If Frances found herself losing sleep, Spears and Turska certainly weren't.

Their minds churning, a plan was developed to retrieve all of the medical equipment that was stored in the garage and a shed at the Gaston Avenue property and drive it back in a large, wood-paneled trailer that Spears owned. After re-registering the vehicle with the Texas DMV in his name, Turska, along with Spears, made four trips to the garage and packed the trailer to the limit—more than enough to start up a full-scale abortion clinic back in New River.

Frances would later admit to the FBI that "I packed many items collected from inside the house which included a homeopathic Kardex File, an assortment of his medications, medical instruments, and two half-gallon jars of pharmaceuticals that had been used for abortions. Then I gave him a clipping from the Jacksonville newspaper saying that Al Taylor had also disappeared on the night of the crash."

Mrs. Spears also remembered this: "When Dr. Turska was loading the trailer, I observed a cardboard box in the trunk of his Cadillac with the word 'EXPLOSIVES' stenciled on the side of it. When I asked him about them, he said that they used them on the ranch for prospecting. I dropped it after that."

78 / Chapter 9

Thus, a little less than a week after his arrival in Dallas, Bob Spears said a sad farewell to his wife. In a touching moment, Frances gave him a packet that, along with $2,000 in cash, included photos of their children. The pictures had been taken at their son's second birthday party on December 22, 1959. Written on the back of each was their names, the date and the occasion. She did not expect him to ever see the children again.

Minutes later, Spears and Turska—pulling the overloaded trailer behind them—began a leisurely evening drive back toward New River, Arizona. After traveling for just three hours, the pair checked into the Juanita Motel in Abilene on Monday, January 11, 1960. The next morning, according to FBI records, "Spears attempted to purchase a 1957 Plymouth sedan from a man who had advertised one with the same coloring which was very similar to the one owned by Al Taylor and later possessed by Spears."

It was on this return trip, however, that Spears was taken by a strange but generous impulse. It was close to dusk, and they were driving along one of the interminable highways in the New Mexico flatlands when Spears reached over with his hand and gripped Turska's shoulder.

"It is good for a man to have a close friend," he said affectionately. "Someone he can trust." His fingers tightened on Turska's shoulder. "You have done so much for me. I'd like to do something for you."

"Forget it."

"No, seriously," Spears continued. "Have you ever been to Hawaii?"

Turska shook his head. "No . . . that's pretty rich for my blood."

"Well, my friend, you're going there on a vacation as my guest!" Spears suddenly shouted out exuberantly. "I'll buy the plane tickets for you and take care of everything. I just need you to carry a package over there for me and give it to a friend. You'll have the time of your life in paradise, believe me!"

Thinking over those words and remembering the recent headlines, Turska shook his head. "I think I'll take a raincheck on that, Bob," he replied.

Chapter 10

A Fast-Talking, Slick Attorney

Satisfied that they were now traveling incognito with Texas plates, Turska's Mercedes sports car chugged away, straining under the load of the trailer packed to the limit. By January 14 at the New River compound—his wife and children now left far behind both emotionally and geographically—Spears was in the process of setting up an abortion clinic once more with a vision of going bigger, better, and bolder than ever before.

Unbeknown to him, however, the FBI was also hard at work on the Flight 967 investigation and had just leaked a stunning admission:

> Robert Vernon Spears may have had someone travel for him to collect a large insurance policy for the benefit of his young wife. The aircraft may have been sabotaged, and there is the probability that Mr. Spears is still alive.
>
> A confidential informant has indicated that Spears was planning to shake down Donald Loomis—his partner in a Los Angeles-based abortion ring—to keep him silent about the extent of their massive operation and then disappear to Mexico. He may also have explosives in his possession.

Angry and vindictive over apparently being betrayed by Spears, Loomis fired back in the *Los Angeles Times,* stating that he indeed knew Spears was still alive because the man was trying to extort him to keep quiet on their upcoming court case.

80 / Chapter 10

"Spears kept asking me for anything from $15,000 to $25,000 and warned me half a dozen times that if he didn't get the money to 'get lost,' he would testify against me in every way he could and try to make me look bad," Loomis barked to the press. "And to top it off, the last threat I received from Spears was just shortly before Flight 967."

It was a damning statement indeed and threw open the premise that Bob Spears was still alive—something which, to this point, hadn't been openly considered. It was a shocking turn. More concerning to Spears, however, was the fact that newspapers throughout America and around the world decided to make this front-page news with headlines blaring in large type: "Passenger Swap Eyed in Plane Crash" and "'Dead Man' May Be Alive."

At the same time that the Civil Aeronautics Board and the FBI—with a personal directive from J. Edgar Hoover—were digging deep into the mysterious circumstances of the Flight 967 disaster, enterprising journalists were making some interesting connections. Primary among these was the legal situation that Robert Spears found himself in with co-conspirator and Hollywood legend Donald Loomis.

With a serious court case looming—one with the possibility of a lengthy prison sentence—it seemed more and more curious that Robert Spears was officially listed among the dead in the Flight 967 crash. Also, with the presumed cause considered to be an on-board bomb and the disappearance of Spears' best friend, Al Taylor, there were increasingly more questions and reporters were pressing hard.

The Loomis-Spears case in Los Angeles was bigger than either man had ever faced before. Though the exercise guru was pretty confident that he could bribe and buy his way out of it, Bob Spears was a loose cannon. It was, after all, his damn fault that Loomis was even in this mess and now—with Spears trying to extort him—the waters were muddier than ever.

It had all started when Robert Spears, as part of their partnership in Los Angeles, had performed an abortion on a shapely, tanned UCLA student in her early 20s with long, brown hair that fell past her shoulders who was a full four months pregnant.

A Fast-Talking, Slick Attorney / 81

Something had gone terribly wrong, and the young lady was now in an emergency room in critical condition.

Spears and Loomis had created a nice network for themselves in the Southern California market and were raking in money at unprecedented speeds. According to the FBI, people—local cops, priests, pastors, social workers, prosecutors, and attorneys—would slip the distressed girl a note with a name and a pickup point which was usually just a street intersection. Dr. Spears would then go to that address and pick up three or four girls at a time.

From there they would head to one of their pre-selected motels in the Los Angeles area where the medical equipment was located. Frances Spears would later explain more about the operation to FBI agents.

"Dr. Spears performed all of his abortions in California in various motels, most of them cheap and along the beaches. I had no idea how many abortions he performed and I had no idea how much he charged for an abortion. I didn't like this business of his and these were subjects we never discussed. I was once told, however, that the fees varied from $200–$500 per abortion [$2,000–$5,000 in today's value]—just depending on what the traffic would bear."

After paying the equivalent of $5,000 and meeting an unknown "gray-haired man with a paunch at a beachside motel," apparently the "doctor" had inserted "such a copious amount of a caustic chemical inside her—one with a lye base—that it was now literally burning out her womb."

The attending physicians at the Westwood Village hospital notified the authorities when their patient quickly gave up the name of her abortion practitioner and provided a wealth of information on his practice. Lt. Herman Zander, head of the Abortion Squad for the LAPD, in turn, went to Robert Spears' suburban residence on South Rena Drive in the San Pedro area and waited at the house for his return with Frances acting as the perfect hostess.

Soon enough, Spears arrived and was surprised to find "company" waiting for him. Immediately informed that he needed to go with the officers to the police station, he requested

82 / Chapter 10

permission to say goodbye to his wife. Going over to reassure her that everything would be alright—this was just a misunderstanding after all—he hugged Frances tightly while surreptitiously slipping a key into her meager cleavage.

"When I saw him drop something into her bra, I demanded to have it, and she fished it out without protest. It was the key to a beach motel room, and so I decided to swing by there to see what Spears wanted to keep to himself," Zander later explained. "I put the Doc in the back seat of my cruiser, and then on the way, he said, 'Being a cop must be a pretty poor-paying proposition.' He was trying to bribe me, and I just answered, 'You're already in enough trouble, Doc.' That's when he really started to sweat."

Spears also did something else. He began talking. Well, more accurately, singing like a canary.

At the motel, along with abortion-related equipment, Zander seized a letter Spears had been writing to the IRS detailing Donald Loomis' complex abortion operation, including the names of more than 20 local doctors who were regularly referring multiple pregnant girls to Loomis for a percentage of his fee.

Zander asked Spears if he was turning in his competition to get him out of the way. "No," Spears responded, "he's my partner." This head-scratching admission—clearly, he was implicating himself as well—was soon cleared up when Spears explained his reasoning.

"You see, the Internal Revenue Service has a program that will pay a 10% informant's fee and knowing how much Loomis' operation brings in—I just made pennies compared to him—well, I decided I'd end up with a mighty tidy sum by turning him in." It was still a head-scratcher, but at least the motive was cleared up.

Around the same time, Don Loomis had also been arrested at his luxurious Palos Verdes estate and booked into jail with bail set at an unusually high equivalent of $100,000. Loomis was shocked. He had managed to be in the abortion business for decades at this point and never gave any concern that he might be arrested for what he felt was "just performing an important public service."

A Fast-Talking, Slick Attorney / 83

Protected by both police and judges—for which he had paid significantly over the years—Loomis was doing his business in the open.

However, this was an unexpected turn, and he had no idea at the time that it was his own partner who had fingered him and was even planning to betray his good friend to the FBI and IRS for a finder's fee.

Spears quickly enlisted the aid of attorney Joe Forno, who once boasted that he had gotten more defendants exonerated than anyone in history. He instantly informed him that he wouldn't take the case for anything less than the modern equivalent of $50,000.

Robert Spears, the experienced con man that he was, suggested the lawyer charge Loomis $100,000 which would also cover his fee. "He's a rich man. He can pay for it," Spears told Forno. "That's when I knew he might be a difficult client," the attorney later commented.

Joe Forno, however, boasted his own dark and questionable history and he was known to both local authorities and the rich hoodlum underworld of Los Angeles during the gritty era described famously in detective novels by Raymond Chandler, Mickey Spillane, and Dashiell Hammett. But Forno was no fictional character, and he had forged a lucrative practice in making and receiving payoffs and being on the take in any number of illegal, back-alley enterprises.

Attorney Forno, in fact, was at the center of the entire payoff scheme and served as a mediary between the crooks and the cops. It was a simple arrangement that was overseen and managed by Forno. The cops would notify Forno that they had the goods on someone and demand a fee for not busting the guy. The attorney would take his cut, and the arrest would never happen.

In the abortion trade, it was even simpler. The cops and Forno both got a set percentage of every fee paid by the desperate girl in exchange for not raiding the event. But something had gone wrong in the UCLA case and Loomis was at a total loss.

All along, Joe Forno had been telling both Loomis and Spears not to worry about the case as the payoff arrangement would

84 / Chapter 10

ultimately take care of everything and no one would serve any time. Frances Spears—now aware her husband was back in "the business" in California—was incensed at this turn of events and told her husband that he "was a fool because the officers would demand more and more of a cut as time went on and he would pretty much just end up working for the Los Angeles Police Department."

In fact, the biggest mystery was who were the corrupt cops in the LAPD who were at one end of the scheme? It was apparently common knowledge, but everyone clearly refused to name names. It was Juana Martinez, secretary to Attorney Forno for six years, who was the first to shed light on the racket for the FBI.

She explained during an interview with special agents that Spears was confident that her boss was taking care of the abortion case—even though he and Loomis had been arrested—and that the case would never be prosecuted. The cost to put in the fix, outside of Forno's stiff legal fees, was $10,000 which was what the dirty cops demanded to sweep the case under the rug.

According to Martinez, however, Spears was unable to get in touch with Loomis to discuss the matter, because of what Spears called his "crackpot attorney, Bill Kraker, and the fact that Loomis has no mind of his own." As a result, the matter rested comfortably on the legal back burner awaiting a payoff. Eventually charges were filed—a shock to Spears—and Forno explained that the cops had been after Loomis for years and this time they weren't letting him off.

As a result, what was expected to be a minor bump in the road soon became quite serious. Some judges and prosecutors in the Los Angeles system were dirty but not all and they could not afford for their case to fall into the wrong hands.

Fortunately, Joe Forno had a solution. He had negotiated a new payoff deal with the cops, but this time the fees had gone up: it would take $35,000 to fix the charges—$25,000 for Loomis and $10,000 for Spears (well over 10 times that in current value). Martinez said this so disturbed Bob "that he thought he would go straight to the source himself—the cops—and negotiate a better deal. Unfortunately, they—and I won't identify who 'they' are—indicated that it would take the full 10 grand for his end of

A Fast-Talking, Slick Attorney / 85

the case to make things go away. After that he decided to put his Texas home up for sale to cover the $10,000 price tag."

With this, Spears was ironically released on $10,000 bail. That was August of 1959. Just weeks later on September 2, he purchased $100,000 in life insurance from the American Fidelity and Casualty Company by writing a check for $60.

Shortly after that, he applied for a $20,000 mortgage insurance policy with Surplus Underwriters which would pay off his home loan in the event of his death.

Shortly after that he took out a $10,000 double-indemnity death and dismemberment policy through the Mutual Benefit Health and Accident Association.

And then, not long after all of that, National Airlines Flight 967 ended up at the bottom of the Gulf of Mexico presumably with the insured aboard and the abortion charge became a moot issue.

However, with the troubling concern over the still-looming court case in Los Angeles and the added heat it was bringing to the search for a possibly alive Spears—his wife Frances was still steadily denying to the FBI that he had ever contacted her, and she assumed he was dead. But it was soon to be an entirely different tragedy that began to populate the front pages of national newspapers with the name of Robert Vernon Spears conspicuously at the center.

From somewhere in his secret desert compound, it would be hard to know if Spears was grinning or trembling.

January 16, 1960: The headline on the front page of the *Los Angeles Mirror* screamed the breaking story with three-inch, all capital letters, in bold: "2ND AIR BOMBING: L.A. DOCTOR LINKED!" Newspapers around the nation quickly picked up the story, which began to spread like wildfire.

It was already big news that Robert Spears, one of the passengers on the doomed Flight 967, might actually still be alive—worse yet that he might have been responsible for its explosion—but now came the stunning news that he might be connected to yet another horrific air disaster.

86 / Chapter 10

On January 6, National Airlines Flight 2511 was downed during a routine flight from New York to Miami, crashing along Highway 17 in the rural eastern area of North Carolina.

After investigators quickly identified the cause as "a dynamite explosion emanating from row seven," they noticed that every one of the 29 passengers—except the individual who was in the window seat in that row, had been identified. The missing passenger would eventually be located 18 miles away with his legs blown off by a handmade bomb with detonation wires embedded in his torso.

They identified the remains of the man—Julian Andrew Frank, a prominent New York attorney married to a stunning fashion model with two young children, a most unlikely suspect in an airline bombing.

Until they looked further.

At the time, the 32-year-old Frank was described by *Life* as "a fast-talking, slick attorney from Westport, Connecticut, whose high-flying financial capers had proved too much for him." The article went on to provide additional details, including the fact that only weeks before, he had taken out insurance policies on himself in excess of $10 million in today's value.

His wife Janet had really no idea about her husband's professional life or activities—she was primarily a socialite—and was shocked to hear that the FBI was suggesting that the crash was caused by him in order to mask his own suicide as an accident so that his massive insurance policy could be collected.

While aeronautical engineers began the laborious task of reassembling the plane in a massive hangar with the goal of determining if the explosion was the result of a bomb, federal and state authorities were trying to piece together "the crazy quilt pattern of Frank's activities."

Apparently, until just a few years previously, Julian Frank had been known as a wealthy lawyer who continually boasted about his grand business deals. At the time of the crash, however, he had been making frequent and mysterious trips around the country and abroad with rumors swirling of financial pressures. On these, he would regularly disappear for weeks at a time.

Shortly before the plane crash, though, the authorities had begun to close in on him, and he was in the process of being

A Fast-Talking, Slick Attorney / 87

disbarred for unethical legal activities. Julian Frank had, it appeared, been pocketing money estimated at hundreds of thousands of dollars given to him to pay fees on million-dollar deals.

With her husband already identified in the wreckage of the plane, unlike the wives of Al Taylor and Robert Spears, there was no doubt in Mrs. Frank's mind that Julian was dead. And, although it was not official, reporters were already inferring that Julian Frank was the likely cause of the explosion.

The aspersions and anxiety of that reality—as captured by a *Life* magazine photographer at a particularly excruciating moment of grief with her children and mother—was clearly crushing for Janet, a stunning and sophisticated New York fashion model. Pregnant with their third child, a few weeks after her husband's death, Janet collapsed on a south-bound train.

At the nearest depot, she was transported by ambulance to a nearby hospital in Charleston, where she suffered a miscarriage. Holding a makeshift press conference, her attorney told the hounding press "that this personal tragedy was brought on by grief over her husband's death and the worry caused by irresponsible conjecture and speculation in connection with the airline crash."

In the end, investigators would eventually conclude that Julian Frank had indeed committed suicide at the expense of 34 other innocent individuals. His wife Janet would never receive a penny of the insurance money—apparently, his primary purpose for dooming National Airlines Flight 2511.

But the breaking news that came 10 days after the crash was about a most unusual connection.

Donald Loomis—who had his million-dollar abortion practice ruined by Spears' sloppiness—was now eager to get revenge. He proudly squawked to reporters that his former partner was an expert in explosives from his military training.

"He told me that he had figured out a way to disappear forever and would never spend a day in jail for these abortion charges. In fact, he once offered to blow up a hospital where I had been employed—and still had some issues with—if I paid him $500. He said he was good with explosives, and no one would ever know."

As shocking as that was in its own right, what Don Loomis said next made headlines on January 16.

Chapter 11

Hypnotism and Strange Sightings

Sitting down with reporters and FBI agents, Donald Loomis swore that there was a solid link between Spears and the dead attorney Julian Frank. Maintaining that his former partner had gone to New York to seek counsel on their Los Angeles abortion case, he said, "Mr. Frank knew how to get things done and could find a way out of any jail time. Spears told me they discussed some creative solutions to their problems and how to take care of their wives. He gave me all the particulars."

Apparently, one of those "particulars" included the fact that in September of 1959—less than two months before he would board a doomed airliner—Al Taylor took a thousand-mile road trip to New York City from Tampa with his annoying stepson Blaine. The stated purpose was for Blaine to try and get a foothold in the gallery world of the Big Apple, but Loomis had some insights on that which he was willing to share.

The two-week journey would indeed give Blaine a taste of Manhattan's art world, but Loomis inferred that the trip was about much more than that. "It was just an excuse, really. Al wanted to meet up with Bob to talk over some business opportunity that was supposed to make the two of them a lot of money."

Alice Taylor would later mention that her husband never made any mention of him meeting up with Spears in New York—nor did Blaine ever see them together. Though, by his own admission, he was relatively self-consumed during that period.

90 / Chapter 11

But clearly, Al Taylor had his reasons for the trip. Loomis explained to authorities that Taylor and Spears had been planning this rendezvous for some time as the perfect cover for them to develop a new scheme. Apparently, Taylor was becoming disgruntled with his life in Tampa and tiring of being around his nagging ex-wife. With his son having joined the Marines, there was little left for him in Florida.

> Dr. Spears said that Al related to him that he was fed up with his old life—his ex-wife's money demands, expensive tastes, and those infernal society bridge parties. His job at Pioneer had become monotonous and unfulfilling. He lived in a dumpy apartment and had few friends. It was a depressing lot in life.
>
> For some reason, the two also wanted to meet with Julian Frank, the attorney, though I'm not sure why. I know why Dr. Spears did, at least I think I do, but the whole thing is a bit of a mystery.

If it was a coincidence, it was a strange one. Spears and Taylor were in New York together—all arriving secretly—and meeting with Julian Frank. In a relatively short time, two National Airlines planes would be downed—exploded by someone on board—and two of the three men in that meeting would be dead as a result. The third man—who was the only connection between Frank and Taylor—would be on the run and in hiding in the Arizona desert.

This revelation rocked investigators and brought the Robert Spears/Flight 967 connection back onto the front pages. Could Julian Frank have followed in his client's footsteps and decided to either fake his own death or commit suicide just to escape certain prison terms while rewarding their wives? It was an intriguing possibility in an already bizarre case.

Then, just to make the entire affair even more fascinating—if that was even possible—the Civil Aeronautics Board uncovered an accomplice who admitted to participating in the insurance ruse. He described a "connection" that was made in the Tampa airport on November 16, 1959—*the exact date of the ill-fated Flight*

Hypnotism and Strange Sightings / 91

967. It was a development that appeared to be beyond mere coincidence. The CAB report read:

> On November 16, 1959, Frank sent a close associate to Florida on an airplane on what was referred to as a "dry run."
>
> First, asking him to get passport photographs and a copy of his birth certificate, Frank also gave the associate a number of calling cards and a credit card and an airline ticket in Frank's name, along with a locked suitcase.
>
> Frank would then take the associate's car and drive to Tampa to pick him up. The following morning, however, Frank called his hotel in Florida and said, "This was just a dry run. Come on home now."

Aside from the eerily obvious parallels to the suspected Robert Spears scenario, the accomplice's testimony reminded the Flight 967 investigators of reports of a mysterious man in a tan overcoat and suit who several people saw in the airport as appearing nervous and uncomfortable while obviously looking for someone. Could it have been Frank's associate? Or could it have been Al Taylor, with Spears' airline ticket in hand? Both were distinct possibilities at the moment.

As a result, nothing would ever be considered ordinary about the Robert Spears situation. Nor, for that matter, about the unresolved and quite troubling disappearance of Al Taylor. Then—as if the Frank matter didn't add enough mystery to the story—the entire suicide-by-proxy theory was thrown for a loop when a man who was a close friend of Taylor's swore he had spotted his good buddy on the streets of Nashville.

Just one day after the crash of National Airlines Flight 2511—the one in which Julian Frank was on—a coworker of Al Taylor at Pioneer Tire claimed that he saw "without any doubt in my mind" that he had spotted Al on Christmas Eve among the holiday crowds in Nashville.

The FBI immediately labeled this a "credible report"—several others had also mentioned they had seen him—as Taylor had been born in Tennessee and had spent most of his life there. It was not unreasonable to assume he had gone there on a

92 / Chapter 11

holiday visit to see family and assure them that he was fine after all the conjecture.

Informing local authorities that he was "one-hundred percent certain that I sighted the man," he explained what he saw. "It was in a busy shopping district off Route 41, and as soon as I saw him, I called out, 'Hey Al!' I knew for a fact it was Al Taylor. The man immediately turned and glanced in response to me, and I waved. Then he hastily looked both ways and quickly and deliberately slipped away into the crowd. I have no doubt it was the man I had been working with side by side. I know it was Al Taylor, no doubt about it."

The news also caused Alice Taylor's heart to leap with the hope that her husband might still be alive. She renewed her enthusiasm for and commitment to defending his reputation in the press and pointing all the blame at Robert Spears. At the same time, Frances was managing her own public relations campaign to protect her husband's reputation.

The newspapers—which had discovered that the story increased sales with every headline of the saga—feasted on the war of words between the two women and readily gave them the platform they each desired.

The Civil Aeronautics Board investigators were gathering new and additional information regarding the odd circumstances surrounding the crash of Flight 967 almost daily. Much of this was out of the view of the public, but reporters—desperate for any news connected to the case—were working diligently to pick up bits of information or at least clues from anyone in the know.

To fill the void, several individuals stepped into the gap to be the eyes and ears of the two women—one or both who might be widows at this point—and to deal with both the ongoing legal issues as well as manage the rumors constantly swirling around them.

On behalf of Alice Taylor, attorney Robert Mann led her efforts to redeem the name of her missing husband—which was being dragged through the mud by the press—and hopefully still locate him alive somewhere. He, in turn, had employed an

Hypnotism and Strange Sightings / 93

experienced investigator who began digging deeply into Al's past, hoping it might give a hint toward where he might be or how he got mixed up in the Flight 967 story, if that was truly the case.

Alice was absolutely convinced that Bob Spears had somehow talked her husband into swapping places with him on the Dallas-bound flight. On that day, several travelers in the Tampa airport concourse mentioned seeing a man in a brown coat acting nervously and fidgeting with a wrapped package in his hand. Alice reported that her husband's sole brown coat was missing from his closet. She was certain that her husband was a victim of Spears' treachery and that the perpetrator of this madness was still alive and in hiding.

Operating on that assumption—but ready to follow the facts wherever they might lead—Robert Mann and his investigator began the difficult task of tracking down William Allen Taylor and his true story.

Unfortunately, Alice couldn't be of much help. She didn't know much about her future husband before they met. Taylor had explained that he had been a government employee in Washington, DC, before moving back home. His mother, Genevieve, confirmed this, and Alice had no reason to doubt her. Early on, he eagerly became involved in community events and joined several social clubs. But with time, he seemed to grow increasingly morose and began to withdraw, never making any close friends.

No friends except for one: Robert Spears.

Even Alice recognized that only Spears seemed to be able to lift her husband's spirits. It seemed to her, however, to be a one-sided relationship. Al had casually mentioned his name while they were dating and invited him to their wedding, but of course, Spears never showed up or even bothered to drop by during the initial years of their marriage.

However, she soon began to notice that Al was regularly receiving phone calls from Bob—often several times a day—and letters came at almost the same rate. "I could see that he became quite excited, even animated, with every contact. After a few years, Spears did start to visit. I can't recall exactly when, but

94 / Chapter 11

he would stay in a local hotel. They would meet together, sometimes for days at a time. Al became strange and silent."

Throughout the decade, Spears evolved into becoming the most important person in Al Taylor's life. Alice felt that her husband had come to worship the man and, most bizarrely, looked forward to receiving gifts from him regularly. Almost beyond belief, these consisted of boxes of his own used clothes, even though they were far too big to be of any use.

But Taylor had each of the pieces tailored to fit him. "I couldn't understand it," Alice complained. "Al could easily afford his own suits, but he said he didn't want to hurt Spears' feelings, and that's why he wore them. But I think there was more to it. It was almost as if they were a magical thing. It seemed to make him feel more powerful. Al would use up all of our family vacation time just visiting with him—sometimes for weeks."

Alice later recalled that once, in the mid-1950s, Al traveled to Dallas for what was to be a short stayover.

She later recalled:

> It was strange because I got a telegram from Mr. Spears, who said my husband had been in a terrible automobile accident and had a broken neck.
>
> I frantically called all the local hospitals, the Texas Rangers, all the police stations, but there was no record of anyone who fit Al's description in a car crash. Three days later, he just turned up back in Tampa in perfect health with no explanation of the supposed accident or injury. I never asked, and to this day, I still have no idea what they were up to.
>
> Another thing . . . that man made good money and a lot of money too, but I don't know what happened to it. He worked day and night—you've never seen anyone so applied to his work.

Immediately, people began to speculate that the missing funds constituted his "go-money" and were part of a larger plot to disappear. But, according to one of his coworkers, Taylor was deep in debt, once complaining, "I came to Tampa owing $5,000, and years later, after all of this work, I still owe $5,000."

Hypnotism and Strange Sightings / 95

The money was a mystery, just one of many in Taylor's secretive life.

As Mann's investigators seemed to be having a difficult time coming up with anything substantial, Alice contacted the *Dallas Morning News*—Frances' hometown newspaper—and delivered a bombshell that would generate a front page headline: "Hypnotized Man, Not Doctor, Killed on Plane, Ex-Wife Says." Indeed, Alice was now promoting the theory that Robert Spears had hypnotized her husband—he was reportedly an expert in the dark art—and sent him to his death to fake his own.

Now working through the press and becoming more outspoken—more animated as an evangelistic protector of her husband's name—Alice was always good for a quote, a comment, an opinion, or a reaction for hungry reporters.

"It was Al Taylor on that flight," she proclaimed. "And it was Robert Spears who put him there. Al was merely a puppet with Spears pulling the strings. The two of them spent several days together in Tampa before that night, and I think he was hypnotized then. When he got on that plane, he didn't know what he was doing. Bob just handed him a package and said he would meet him in Dallas and then just took off with my husband's car."

Alice then took her campaign a bit further and directed her next shot at Frances Spears—her bitter adversary in this battle through the press—by saying, "I called Frances long distance when I heard the news about her husband being on the plane as I felt sorry for her. But I guess I should have been feeling sorry for myself instead. When I told her that it would have been wonderful if they had simply decided to drive to Dallas in Al's car instead of Dr. Spears flying, she simply responded with an unusual statement, telling me never to doubt the integrity of her husband. I found that quite odd."

Now, becoming increasingly infuriated by the fact that authorities seemed unable or unwilling to come to the conclusions that she had—primarily that Robert Spears sent her husband to his death and was still alive and in hiding—she doubled down on her efforts to smear the doctor and paint her man as a

96 / Chapter 11

loving father, faithful husband during their time together, and an affable, generous, civic-minded member of the community.

Her loud and haughty proclamations in the press continued unabated daily until a neighbor stuck a newspaper under her nose—with a picture of her husband featured prominently on the front. It detailed his long criminal history as well as a string of aliases including Albert "Ollie" Thompson, Spears' longtime co-conspirator. Along with that, the article provided details on his first marriage with Ruth and his son Jack—something of which Alice was completely unaware. *It was an immeasurable shock.*

Alice was suddenly silent and began to slink away from the press. And that was all the opening that Frances Spears needed to launch a public relations campaign of her own. The war of the widows was now heating up and would soon burst into flames fanned by national headlines that read: "Wives of Missing Men Differ on Plane Substitute."

As Alice had found her advocate in Robert Mann, Frances enlisted the aid of high-profile Dallas TV personality and KRLD radio favorite Eddie Barker. It would be this rather unassuming man who would ratchet up the entire controversy to new and unexpected levels.

Chapter 12

Transformed into the Perfect Image

Dallas newsroom editor Eddie Barker—short, sporting a crew cut, and round-faced with dark, heavy-framed glasses—would eventually become famous as the first reporter to break the news of President John F. Kennedy's death. Still, at the moment, he was the leading figure and spokesperson for Frances Spears as she mourned the loss of her husband while remaining in the harsh glare of the public spotlight.

Of course, Frances knew something that no one else did: that her husband was actually alive and in hiding. But that did not prevent her from covering up that fact from the authorities nor preclude her from playing the role of the heartbroken, grieving widow with two orphan babies. At this point, she was undoubtedly complicit in a serious crime and needed some assistance navigating this entire unfathomable saga.

And it was Eddie Barker who would come to play that role in her life, though it was questionable whether or not he had her best intentions in mind.

At this point in his career Barker was still trying to make a name for himself and the Spears-Taylor case—with a pair of feuding wives and more than enough soap-opera mysteries—was just the thing that could put him on the national stage. He didn't plan on missing out on this opportunity.

Up to this point, Alice Taylor had been providing the narrative for the entire case from Tampa, and the nation had grown sympathetic to her pain—a missing husband, a puppet master

98 / Chapter 12

fiend of a friend, and the implication of a greedy, evil insurance plot. Frances Spears, on the other hand, had remained largely reclusive throughout the ordeal and had shied away from telling her side of the story.

However, that was all about to change.

Frances' attorney, Charles Tessmer, was the first to suggest that it would be in her best interest to speak to the press, which had grown to be critical and accusatory of her because of her silence. Wanting to change that lopsided narrative, Tessmer contacted Barker and set up an exclusive interview.

Barker, a friendly and engaging sort, immediately set up an interview on local radio station KRLD, and Dallas housewives everywhere tuned in and were glued to the soft-spoken, clearly distressed young wife—the official widow in the case.

"I don't really like any publicity," Frances began from her home with the sound of her children behind her. "And I don't know anything. If my husband was on that plane, I can accept it, although my life will be hard. If he were not, I don't know anything I could do about it." Her voice broke as she said the words. The sloshing of a bath can be heard in the background as her children play in the water.

"I know one thing: we had planned on celebrating my son's birthday and we had even bigger plans for Christmas. I know that he loved these babies and that if he were alive, I'm sure I would have heard from him. I believe him to be lost in the crash. Nothing that I have heard gives me any other impression. I have had a communication from the airlines that confirmed he was aboard the plane, and that's all I really know.

"I wanted to go to Biloxi to satisfy myself from an emotional standpoint and see what was recovered," she added hesitantly as her baby daughter cried in the background. "But I felt it would be much too depressing, and in the end, I chose not to go. But I can tell you, sir, that if he were alive, he'd be here with me and the babies right now."

The interview came off as empathetic, and the tide of national opinion began to slowly turn in her direction and—more importantly to Eddie Barker—Frances Spears now had placed her complete trust in him. From this point forward, she

Transformed into the Perfect Image / 99

would speak to no other reporter. In time, Barker's exclusive relationship with Frances began to anger other reporters who were shut out of the story. Soon, Barker was at the center of his own controversy—even garnering criticism nationally.

However, not to be outdone or excluded from the hottest topic in the land, other reporters began to redouble their efforts to dig up more dirt on Robert Vernon Spears. They would ultimately deliver a blockbuster of their own.

Dorothy Hayes had just settled in at the kitchen table of her modest home with a cup of coffee and was adding in some cream and sugar as she unfolded her copy of the *Oakland Tribune*. It was early on a Saturday morning in January, a good day to catch up on errands and chores, but she was still half asleep and rather casually glanced at the headline: "Insurance Plot Hinted in Gulf Air Crash."

Initially pushing it aside, she pulled out the section that included the horoscopes, curious to see what the stars held for her on this day. At the same time, she was drawn back to the headline blaring from the front page and began to read, starting with the column heading that stated: "Exchange of Identity Suspected."

Dorothy hadn't gotten two sentences into the article before she gasped, her hands involuntarily covering her mouth. Perhaps she had read it wrong, so the 60-year-old single woman picked up her reading glasses and took a second look.

> The FBI revealed today that a passenger who bought a ticket on the National Airlines plane that crashed into the Gulf of Mexico last November may have arranged for another man to travel for him in order to collect on a large insurance policy. The man who bought the ticket was identified as Dr. Robert Spears of Dallas, Texas.

Robert Spears. The name leaped off the page as Dorothy tried to steady herself in the light of this stunning revelation.

Could this really be her ex-husband?

100 / Chapter 12

Dorothy Eastwood Hayes was once a stunningly beautiful socialite in the upscale community of Oakland, California, where she lived with her sister, Kitty Lou, and her parents, Joel and Kathleen Hayes. Descended from a renowned eighteenth-century English family of distinguished artists—headed by portraitist Sir Joshua Reynolds—she enjoyed a protected and entitled life.

On this day, however, she served as the head archivist and librarian for Bank of America, working from their downtown San Francisco offices. By all accounts, it was a quiet and serene life and one, thankfully, now far from the turmoil that Robert Spears had brought into her life some 40 years earlier.

Still in some dusty box on her shelf was his photo that reflected a dashing and impressive military aviator in the Great War—resplendent in uniform and beyond handsome. That was when he was serving proudly in the U.S. Army's 314th Aero Squadron which was attached to the Royal Flying Corp based in Stonehenge, England.

According to Robert, he was a hero, a First Lieutenant, and a popular squadron leader. That was 1920, and Dorothy would eventually discover that that was just the first of his many lies.

But on this day, 40 years later, no one on earth knew about her connection to the suspect in an airline bombing, and no one in her world ever would. They all assumed she was just an old maid, a spinster. No one except for her sister Kitty, an invalid being cared for by her loving sister in the home they shared.

Robert Spears had indeed served in the 314th Aero Squadron.

For years, he would regale friends and neighbors with his tales as a flying ace over France, locked into bi-plane dogfights with the German Luftstreitkräfte. Eventually, severely injured and retired with The Badge of Military Merit—the precursor to the Purple Heart—he was considered one of the heroes of the skies in the fierce battle for Europe.

But, of course, none of that was true.

Spears' military records would reveal that he never was involved in any airborne battles and only served for one year. The sole injury he received was a chest infection, for which he was sent to the military hospital in Oxford, England, where,

Transformed into the Perfect Image / 101

according to one report, "for the next three months, he was transferred between the lounge sections of various hospitals in Oxford, Steventon, Liverpool and London where he became a favorite with all the nurses."

Ironically, this would become the basis for his future claims that he received training and studied medicine—more accurately, studied nurses—at Oxford.

After being discharged with the rank of Sergeant at Camp Fremont in the Bay Area of California, Spears initially found a room with a family who owned a tailor shop on Telegraph Avenue in Oakland and was immediately taken by the Swedish family's two gorgeous daughters. From one of their rooms, the women had a business of training the social elite in matters of etiquette, elocution, and carriage. Their clients inevitably ended up appearing prominently in the society pages of the local newspapers.

Learning from the shadows was also young Robert Spears—tall at six-foot-two and handsome enough to be a fashion model. Soon, he acquired the charismatic skills needed to charm both men and women. With his brilliant blue eyes, impressive height and build, well-groomed presence, and shiny, new tailored suits from the family's shop, Robert Spears had completely transformed himself from a military grunt into the perfect image of a corporate executive.

That proved important when he took on a sales position for a business machine company and quickly became their top performer—earning the equivalent of thousands of dollars in commissions every month. Now able to rent and furnish his own apartment and stock his closets with new suits, Spears evolved into a gallant man-about-town. Obsessed with the new "physical culture" movement in California—exercise, nutrition, positive thinking, and natural medicines—he began to seriously consider homeopathy as a future career.

It was this forward-thinking, good-looking, and almost aristocratic young man who Dorothy Eastwood Hayes—a popular and stunning 23-year-old socialite—met one day and was immediately convinced that he was the right man for her.

102 / Chapter 12

Once the two began to court, he explained to her parents that he was from a highly educated, prestigious, and well-regarded family in Ohio—the son of Dr. and Mrs. George Spears of Toledo. He had graduated with honors from the University of Ohio as an electrical engineer but—he humbly shared—had made his fortune early on as an investor in the oil fields of Oklahoma.

Dorothy was impressed. Her parents were impressed. Sister Kitty Lou was impressed.

And Robert, of course, was lying through his teeth.

Chapter 13

A Series of Seismic Shocks

On June 25, Dorothy Hayes and Robert Spears were married in a glorious ceremony. The newlyweds were the subject of a featured article in the *Oakland Tribune* that described the bride's dress, flowers, and bridesmaids and reiterated everything that Robert had told his future inlaws about his family history, thus formally establishing his recently created past. That same afternoon the couple boarded a ship for Seattle, where Robert had just been promoted to serve as a northwest regional sales manager.

However, Seattle did not turn out to be the emerald city for the young lovers as Robert—inexplicably to his new bride—almost instantly upon arrival came to be bored with his job. There was no challenge to it, and though the money was significant, he began to develop a fear that he was looking his long-term future in the face, and it was dull and unimaginative. It almost made him miss the risk and tension of being in the war.

He quickly found that by developing and prospering from a robust bootlegger smuggling operation. With the nation struggling through Prohibition in the 1920s—Spears began to once again feel the excitement of danger by purchasing whisky made in Canada and outrunning the authorities to smuggle it across the border into Seattle where it was then distributed throughout the West Coast by boat and wagon.

But as it would turn out with so many of Robert Spears' ventures, the bootlegging eventually went bust as Eliot Ness and his

104 / Chapter 13

famous rough-and-tumble officers known as The Untouchables began to bring down operations like his. Escaping major jail time, he nevertheless was picked up a time or two and eventually the newlyweds were reduced to relying on a stipend from Dorothy's parents.

In little time, the couple began to tumble into financial distress as Robert fell into a bleak depression without the excitement of the chase. What he didn't stop doing, however, was spending, and soon, he was the proud owner of a brand new Duesenberg accompanied by a bundle of debt.

Disillusioned and frightened by the course of her husband's life, Dot nevertheless stood by his side, encouraging him to find a satisfying and fulfilling job. The young Spears family continued on this path for some months until, one morning, Dorothy opened the front door to see two suited men standing on her porch with muted expressions and asking to speak with Robert.

Without saying a word, a minute later, he walked out the door without explanation, got into their car, and drove away. Dorothy was left dumbfounded until, just 20 minutes later, she answered the phone and heard her husband's voice.

"Robert informed me that he was at the jail in Seattle, and I couldn't believe my ears! I was so astounded! Then he told me to come down and see him, but I didn't even know where the jail was. After rushing around to find the address, I finally managed to get over there to see him. He told me to wire my family, requesting $750 [$12,500 today] at once. Not knowing what else to do, I did that."

Panicked and confused, Dorothy rushed over to the Western Union office immediately and sent a desperate telegram: "Mother, Bob in great trouble. Send $750 right away tonight. Borrow on my piano and from Uncle Vernon, Auntie Lillie, anybody for God's sake! Dot."

Dorothy, who had trained throughout her life to be a concert-level pianist, counted her grand piano as her only item of worth, and she now was pawning it for no reason that she understood. It was a heartbreaking decision. The next day, Mrs. Hayes rounded up the bail money from several sources—placing the family in deep debt. Soon, Spears was released from jail.

A Series of Seismic Shocks / 105

Eight days later, through the help of a good but pricey attorney, the charges were dismissed.

Dorothy would never come to know what had happened other than he had been arrested for theft. Still, whatever it was, Robert decided that he wanted to pack up and move out of Seattle as fast as he could. And so they did, and Dorothy was soon setting up a house in Portland.

In Oregon, however, her husband never seemed to have a job but always had spending money. As it turned out, there was a good reason why: Robert had redeemed the bail money when the Seattle charges were dropped and then proceeded to spend all of it, leaving his in-laws in debt and his wife without her beloved piano. In the meantime, Dorothy had moved them into a rooming house and was struggling to manage the household on a pittance of a weekly allowance her father mailed her.

When Dorothy found out about the squandered bail money, it was crushing.

The humiliation and betrayal were great, but equally concerning was the fact that her husband had forced her parents and family members into financial distress. While she was still reeling from that blow, her mother Kathleen called with more bad news: her wedding rings were missing, and they had discovered that Robert had stolen and pawned them.

One year after she had worn a white lace wedding dress and carried a bouquet of orchids and lilies down the center aisle of St. Paul's Episcopal Church, Dorothy had left Robert and returned to her parents' comforting arms in Oakland. Forced now to take an entry-level position at a furniture store—an embarrassing turn for a one-time debutante—with the goal of repaying her parents for her husband's financial misdeeds.

A penitent Robert followed after a while and—willing to go the extra mile for their beloved daughter—Dorothy's parents set him up with a sales job at an appliance store owned by one of their close friends. A born salesman, he quickly excelled and was bringing in good money—bringing it in but not bringing it home. Dorothy never knew what happened to his paychecks, and apparently, Spears felt that it was his prerogative to spend

106 / Chapter 13

his income on anything that suited him. No one pressed him on the matter.

It was also during this time that Dorothy, embarrassingly, confided in her mother that her husband had an insatiable appetite for sex—requiring it every evening and often several times a day. She was exhausted by his animal desires, ashamed of what he was requiring of her, and in great physical pain.

That was the straw that broke the camel's back, and Mrs. Hayes ordered her son-in-law out of the house that day. Without saying a word, without defending himself, without expressing any concern for his wife, Robert Spears simply picked up his coat and hat and headed for the door.

"Without one word and unable to look us in the eyes, he took the Duesenberg that we had bought for him, and he just drove away," Kathleen Hayes would later testify to a judge during her daughter's divorce proceedings.

Robert Spears responded to the insult and humiliation by calling up a local quarry and regularly placing orders for one-ton loads of coarse gravel. He then would have them dumped at intervals on the Hayes' front lawn—only the beginning of a series of childish and spiteful pranks to which he would subject the already wounded family.

It would be the last time Dorothy would ever see Robert Spears. She would never again have the confidence nor the courage to marry again.

The pain of Dorothy's life with Robert would sting even more a month later when she was granted a divorce. Less than two years after her marriage, she would once again grace the pages of the *Oakland Tribune,* but this time in shame.

It was once written of the one-time society darling: "The almond-eyed beauty is one of the most talented children in the Piedmont area. She is very pretty and a charming entertainer, artistic, having inherited her love of the finer arts from a gifted family." Now she was being memorialized in humiliation under the headline: "Husband Keeps Bail Money, Drops Wife."

It would be just the beginning of a steep and tragic descent for the entire family as beloved sister Kitty Lou soon contracted polio and would be bedridden for the rest of her life. Followed

A Series of Seismic Shocks / 107

by the death of Dorothy's mother and her father falling seriously ill, the Hayeses disappeared from Oakland's society circles and tumbled into poverty. The ripples of tragedy initiated by Robert Spears would continue for some time as Dorothy tried to hold the remaining household together on her meager pay as a bank stenographer.

However, 40 years later, sitting at her kitchen table on a crisp Saturday morning in January—newspaper in hand—all those bitter memories that had been long buried suddenly came rushing back to the 60-year-old, slightly built woman with graying hair. Subconsciously nodding as she read, she was convinced that it was him—Robert Vernon Spears—her husband of a little more than 20 months who did several lifetimes worth of damage.

But if Dorothy assumed she was the first woman in Robert's life to have felt his treachery and betrayal, she now knew she certainly wasn't the last. She would soon be delivered another seismic shock when she learned that she was, in fact, actually Mrs. Spears Number Two.

The questionable honor of being number one belonged to Miss Ora Clayton. Should Dorothy feel the devastation of a marriage that lasted less than two years, she was about to learn of a first wife who enjoyed a marriage with Robert Spears that lasted less than two days.

Years earlier, after Spears was discharged from the military in San Francisco, he made a quick trip home to Oklahoma to visit his mother. Within a week, he was married to Ora—a 41-year-old wallflower—whom the 25-year-old groom had told that he was in his forties. The combination of his charisma and charm—along with an absolute desperation to be married on her part—swept the lonely woman off her feet in a matter of hours.

The newlyweds spent their honeymoon night at a boarding house room above a corner store in Muskogee. However, in the morning, Ora Spears awoke to find her new husband had disappeared along with her expensive watch and all of her money. Oklahoma headlines blared: "Bride of Two Days Says Her Husband Jilted Her. Watch Missing." A second newspaper led with "Husband and Watch Both Disappear Says Wife."

108 / Chapter 13

The new Mrs. Spears, according to the articles, was mostly confused about what her name should be. "I don't any longer know what my correct name is. I am convinced he has another and more genuine name, with which I am not familiar." She would never get the answer to that concern—though she would be proven to be accurate in her assessment—when she read four weeks later the headline: "Two-Day Hubby Arrested for Deserting Wife" and learned "that he will be soon charged for wife abandonment and maybe for some other things!"

Deputy Sheriff Jack Hedrick commented at the time, "This man Spears is one of the smoothest crooks we've ever had here in Muskogee. We already got him on a grand larceny charge, which he committed just days ago." After a short stint in jail, Spears was on the road again, but this time to California, where he would soon be courting a naive and innocent Dorothy Hayes—destined to become the second Mrs. Spears, but not the last.

Ironically, poor Ora was correct about her husband's—and now her—last name. Not that it would provide any consolation, but Robert Spears would turn out to be just one of nearly two dozen known aliases that the man would employ during his lifetime.

In fact, Robert Spears never even knew his real name from birth. His mother, who went by a long series of surnames, ended up with any man who would take her in. By the time Robert—Clyde Stringer at the time—was barely a teen, he was already on his own riding the rails, stealing at will, and writing bad checks, which landed him an extended stay in a juvenile reformatory as a 16-year-old.

The officer who picked him up noted that he became suspicious "when a young man was spotted with a hefty bankroll, flashy clothes, staying in nice rooms, and working cash frauds."

It would prove to be a weakness that would follow him throughout his life and cost him dearly.

By the time he was 18, Robert Spears had become a dedicated criminal. If anything, during his teenage incarceration he had managed to perfect the art of forgery.

A Series of Seismic Shocks / 109

His first opportunity to test his new skills on the outside was when, through the help of an old friend Emmet Hale, he got a job with the railroad and promptly stole a check from his buddy's father. The *Mayes County Democrat* in Pryor, Oklahoma, picked up the story from there.

> Bogus Check Cashed—Katy Depot Robbed
> A young lad of 17, supposed to have been Clyde Stringer, put one over on DC Blakely, Katy Depot nightman, between midnight and one on Thursday morning. About that time a young man presented a check drawn on the First National Bank for $9.00 in favor of Clifford Fusselman and purporting to have been signed by Thomas Hale.
> After cashing it, the nightman learned that the check was bogus. About this time, Mr. Blakely went to the post office to file a report but while he was away, he discovered that someone had extracted $15 from his money drawer.
> Next, the Pryor Dry Goods Company and the Pryor Bakery each discovered that one of their cashiers had also cashed more bogus $9.00 checks. Two railroad detectives were investigating the robbery and fraud, and it is supposed they are hot on his trail. The railroad expects that the young fellow will soon be doing hard labor.

The railroad detectives—major law enforcement officers of the day—were not about to be outfoxed by a scrawny teenager and, indeed, were soon on a multiple-state chase that would leave them angry and frustrated as their perpetrator seemed to elude them at every turn. Special Agent Pete Porham would later comment, "I chased that boy from Kansas City to Oklahoma City and across several states from east to west, but I finally nabbed him."

> The Sheriff was notified by railroad detectives yesterday that they had finally landed an elusive young fellow in Kingman, Kansas, supposed to be Clyde Stringer, who is wanted for check forgery and robbing the Katy Depot. Deputy Tom Thompson is accompanying young Stringer back to face charges after railroad detectives run him down.

110 / Chapter 13

Tried and convicted, Springer would celebrate his 19th and 20th birthdays in the state reformatory. But after going into the reformatory as Clyde Springer, he emerged as Charles Howard with every intent of picking up where he had left off—more dedicated than ever to perfect his craft as a master criminal.

In his early 20s, Howard—along with several other aliases—made his way through the Midwest states, committing petty crimes and passing forged checks with ease. Already quite experienced, he was no match for naturally trusting small towns and rural hamlets, which he saw as populated by rubes just waiting for someone to take their money. Often, he would get a job and immediately begin stealing merchandise and supplies from his employer before moving on after a day or so.

Now, as Clyde Porter, he was honing his skills at the expense of shopkeepers and businessmen and living the good life in the process. In Collinsville, Oklahoma, he stole a car because he needed a ride to the train station, thoughtfully leaving a note with directions to return it to the rightful owner 10 miles away, after which he "took a northbound train and has not been heard of since," according to the *Morning Tulsa Daily*.

Eventually, detectives traced him to Toledo, Ohio, where he was taken into custody for, among other things, "obtaining a diamond ring with a forged check." Returning to Claremore, Oklahoma, local photographers captured the dashing, young criminal in handcuffs and "dressed to the nines in a dark suit, white turn-down collar shirt, and multicolored silk tie. It is his second attempt to win a reputation as an artist in the bad check line," as reported in *The Tulsa Daily World*.

As it would turn out—and as would so often be the case during a 40-year career as a check forger, thief, huckster, and con man—the judge let Charles Howard off easy, citing the thoughtful note he had left in the stolen car. This time, however, he "suggested" the young man join other American patriots fighting in Europe during the Great War.

Chapter 14

Exploits, Perils, and Pitfalls

"Charles Howard" took the hint and promptly enlisted—this time as Robert Vernon Spears—but not before managing to pull off one final scam. After emerging from the Oklahoma City recruiting station, Spears struck up a friendship with Cecil Gilbert. The two were scheduled to ship out in days for basic training at the same time, so Spears suggested they celebrate, though he himself was short on cash.

"Not a problem," Gilbert responded and informed his new friend that he had the equivalent of $2,000 in his pocket. Together, the pair had a whirlwind of a time feasting on expensive meals, going to picture shows, smoking Cuban cigars, and frequenting peep shows. Exhausted after a night of revelry, the two finally collapsed in their hotel room at the end of the weekend.

But as one might guess, when Gilbert awoke the next morning, his wallet was gone from underneath his pillow, as was his new best friend, Bob Spears. The police quickly tracked down Spears—who was still keeping the party going. He promptly made a full confession and pointed them to what was left of the money, which he had hidden behind a cabinet in a pool hall.

Mr. Gilbert, however, missed his friend more than his money and begged the police to release Spears, telling them, "I guess I like the guy, and besides, I will be serving in the trenches with him." Within the hour, they were on a bus to Jefferson Barracks military base near St. Louis, with the *Tulsa World* summing up the story in an article entitled, "Lad Frees the One Who Robbed Him."

112 / Chapter 14

That was January 1918, and from there, Robert Spears took on yet another persona—that of an aviator sergeant in the 314th Aero Squadron, which was attached to the Royal Flying Corp—not a First Lieutenant and wounded war hero, as he later claimed. Two years later, he was exchanging rings with Ora Clayton. Just a couple of days afterward, he was preparing to court Dorothy Hayes with stories of combat, danger, and courage in the face of the enemy.

An inveterate fraudster, womanizer, and serial deceiver, a certain irony would strike Robert Spears' life shortly after he drove away into the night, leaving his newlywed wife Dorothy behind. Now without any marital entanglements, Spears was free to scheme and scam his way from Washington, Oregon, and California toward the other western states of Nevada, Utah, Idaho, and Colorado before ending up in Denver, where he met his next mark—a bright-eyed, curvaceous, and quick-witted young lady by the name of Laura Meyers.

She was everything Bob was looking for. Besides being easy on the eyes and even a bit sultry, it was obvious she had money and came from money. Less than a month after they met, they were married and preparing to leave immediately for an extravagant honeymoon.

Leaving his bride in the lobby, Spears made his way up to their fourth-floor room to gather their luggage. However, when he returned downstairs, his new wife was nowhere to be found. Nor was any of his money that she was graciously holding for the couple.

The *Denver Post* responded by running a headline that read, "Man Seeks Annulment on Grounds Wife Tricked Him to Obtain $1,000." Indeed, Robert was defrauded—this time just one hour after he had said, "I do."

Furiously and instantly, he filed suit in district court to annul his marriage "on the grounds that I was tricked into the ceremony for the purposes of accessing my finances. For that reason, my consent was not valid and was, in fact, given against my will based on fraudulent representations by my future wife."

Robert Vernon Spears had apparently met his match in Laura Meyers Spears, and there was never any report that she

Exploits, Perils, and Pitfalls / 113

was either apprehended or had his money returned. Humiliated and mortified at being duped and outplayed at his own game, Spears would redirect all of his energy from spontaneous and short-lived crimes—forgery, theft, mail fraud, and larceny—toward more substantial "long cons."

In 1926, Spears was trying to plot out his next big score. For that, he needed to assume his boldest identity yet—a multi-millionaire playboy heir who lived largely and took the world by storm: *Oscar L. A. Delano.*

Oscar L. Delano was, in fact, a very real person and a very, very real millionaire who lived in a veritable mansion in tony Westport, Connecticut. Having recently received an inheritance from his steel-tycoon father equivalent today to $55 million, the younger Delano—in the true decadent and hedonistic spirit of the "Roaring Twenties"—was squandering his fortune through wild parties that lasted for days and were the topic of awe and envy among every social circle.

Delano was the consummate Jay Gatsby of F. Scott Fitzgerald's famed novel—published just a year earlier—who filled bathtubs with prohibited gin and danced the nights away next to loosely dressed flappers with even looser morals. Having inherited grand homes in Manhattan, Miami, and a ranch in New Mexico, there was never a day without drunken excess or a night without a sexualized soiree.

For Robert Spears, the fashionable clothes, broad-brimmed hats, and sleek, European convertible sports cars were an almost irresistible alter-ego. Stepping effortlessly into the skin of the real Oscar Delano, he looked the part from the outset and soon had women of his own hanging on each arm.

As he would do years later in concert with Al Taylor, Spears—as affluent playboy Delano—began attending midwest conventions, usually fraternal organizations, to gather intel on a mark and then—impersonating them—wire home to their wives expressing that they needed funds quickly because they had lost their wallets. Without asking questions, the wives would respond—often requiring a loan from the local bank. The funds would be sent by Western Union, where Spears would collect them.

114 / Chapter 14

For two full years, "Oscar Delano" was a fixture at major events, along with his harem of beautiful and provocative girls whose job it was to glean pertinent information from the marks. However, the biggest payday would come at an annual Freemason conference in St. Louis that drew a nearly incomprehensible 50,000 registrants.

Consisting of only men wearing Homburg hats and drinking without interruption until they dropped, Spears enlisted several young girls of questionable intent to lure in unsuspecting conventioneers and earn a commission. "Like fish in a barrel," he would later say with a smile.

Spears also signed up another fraudster by the name of C. P. Weiler to partner with "the whales" to help coordinate their operations from their headquarters at the convention hotel. Soon, the pair had so many girls coming and going that the house detectives—common in those days—assumed he was running a prostitution ring out of the hotel. But it would turn out to be an irate husband who eventually prompted a raid.

Claiming that Delano was entertaining his wife during the nights and buying her expensive gifts, the police crashed through the door of room 147 at three in the morning only to find Spears "entertaining a number of women on a single bed who were wearing merely skimpy night clothes and claiming to be spending the night only after missing their ride home," according to the police report.

Excited by the charge, Spears never denied the accusations, but neither could the authorities prove them to be true. Eventually giving up, the cops and the hotel manager apologized for the inference and the interruption and meekly left the room. Little did they know, "Delano" was actually in the process of defrauding guests of tens of thousands of dollars as well as running a second, completely separate scam from the same room at the same time.

Spears had also been placing listings in the Classifieds section of the area newspapers advertising that a successful national manufacturing plant was about to open a new factory in the St. Louis area. They needed to fill several positions—from laborers, welders, and pipefitters to office workers and supervisors—and

Exploits, Perils, and Pitfalls / 115

were prepared to pay well above standard wages to get the operation up and running quickly.

The advertisement indicated that a job fair was being held in one of the exclusive hotel's hospitality suites. Persons would be signed on the spot as long as they had identification and proper experience, and paid an upfront broker's fee, which would be held in trust until the new employee showed up for work on the first day. The ad, in fact, read:

> To qualify for this connection, you must have personality, first-class references and $2,500 in cash as a fully returnable surety fee. This is a real bona fide proposition, and we invite the strictest investigation of our firm by all interested parties. This is a one-time offer, and this ad will not appear again.

A phone number was provided for potential employees to call and verify that the offer was legitimate. That number went to the line in the next room, which was manned by Delano's associate, C. P. Weiler, who quickly and professionally confirmed the legitimacy of the offer.

At some point—in a bit of a revelation—the St. Louis police began to field reports of men who had been defrauded at the Freemason convention while at the same time learning about the "Broker's Fee Scam." They made a mad dash to the hotel room only to find it deserted, the occupants having relocated to another high-end hotel across town to continue their grift and cons on a different group of conference attendees.

Fortunately for Delano, he had paid off members of the hotel staff to keep an eye out for the authorities, and by the time police arrived at his new room, it, too, had been vacated. "LA Delano" had bolted only minutes earlier—leaving a whopping unpaid room service bill.

This time, however, he had no time to pack his suitcases— one of which contained a collection of "photographs of beautiful women, each featuring on the back the woman's name, address, age, and telephone number. They also found lists of dozens of convention delegates complete with their personal information."

116 / Chapter 14

The St. Louis Police Department immediately issued a full-scale public alert asking citizens to be on the lookout for Oscar Delano: "A man in his early 30s who is good looking, a flashy dresser, well-groomed, tall and fair, and a favorite with the opposite sex. Delano, alias Robert Spears, has been accused of several crimes in the area. He drives a sport-model of an expensive foreign-made automobile called a Duesenberg."

By the time the all-points bulletin was being broadcast, Spears was long gone from Missouri and had already set up shop in Kansas, where he began working what was, perhaps, his most mind-bending and bizarre con. Having located an abandoned storefront on the outskirts of Kansas City, he went about transforming it into an exotic and mysterious shadowy fortune-telling chamber.

There, he performed under the incredibly colorful name of the "Eastern Mystic Kigab Gypterm." With a promise to "peek into the future and unlock your destiny!" customers eagerly lined up for a reading that would tell them who to marry, how to become wealthy, and gain the secrets to forever health and long life.

Complete with a jeweled turban, long velvet robes, beaded curtains, purple drapes, and a crystal ball, virtually every reading entailed investing in some scam or potion or elixir that held "the secrets of the universe and vitality."

After the mayor's wife came home raving about the supernatural experience she had had with Guru Gypterm, unfortunately, the mystic's next customer was a detective who had been on the fraudster's tail for some time. The law had finally caught up to him, and he somewhat proudly confessed that he was responsible for everything he had been accused of and extended his velvet-robed arms to be handcuffed.

As soon as he was apprehended, Spears admitted placing the fake "Help Wanted" classified ads in the St. Louis newspapers. He admitted to the conventioneer scams and wire frauds. He admitted that he was, in fact, the Eastern Mystic Kigab Gypterm of Kansas City. And he acknowledged, with a great sense of pride, that his latest cons had netted him the equivalent of $55,000 in less than a week in just three cities.

The federal government would eventually take over the case from the local authorities, and they prosecuted him on the more serious wire fraud charges. In March 1927, Spears pleaded guilty, and from there, he was off to Leavenworth Federal Penitentiary which would serve as his home for the next year and a half.

With that, Oscar L. A. Delano's name was retired from his list of aliases.

Ironically, however, it would not be the end of the real Oscar L. A. Delano's troubles. From prison, Robert Spears found himself nearly obsessed with the playboy extraordinaire's exploits, perils, and pitfalls. It was as if, from behind the bars in his darkened cell, he could vicariously live through the life of a truly wealthy and lascivious substitute. If so, some lessons could have been learned.

Shortly after Spears was incarcerated, the real Oscar Delano was, in fact, in a battle royale with his peroxided blonde wife Ruth of just two years. Although he could easily afford it, Delano had decided to focus all of his energy and resources on fighting the court judgment, which would deliver her the equivalent of nearly $200,000 a year in alimony.

In the rules of the day, Delano knew that the best way to reverse the judge's decision was to capture his wife in some compromising and morally impure situation, after which the hefty alimony payment would be tossed.

Enlisting the aid of Chicago "fixer" Moxie Eisenberg, Delano put him on Ruth's trail, expecting him to find any number of shady liaisons. When he could not come up with a single instance, however, Moxie decided to stage the evidence himself. Kidnapping her with help from a conspiratorial cabbie, he poured a knockout syrup down her throat and sequestered her in a New Jersey hotel.

There, he stripped her of her clothes and laid her sprawled out on the floor with scattered gin bottles and men's clothing on every side. Photos were snapped, but even more damning was the fact that Oscar Delano, several witnesses, and two detectives just happened to show up at the hotel room and reported catching Ruth "in the midst of a drunken orgy."

118 / Chapter 14

The only police chief not in Delano's employ, however, refused to buy the story and in an unexpected turn, had Moxie Eisenberg arrested. Refusing to flip on his boss, the fixer was convicted and sentenced to the New Jersey State Penitentiary while Spears was in Leavenworth. Ruth ended up getting her divorce with an even heftier annual payment.

Spears, however, became even more intrigued by the life of the millionaire gadabout who—even after being outfoxed by Ruth—did nothing to curtail his outrageous and degenerate behavior. Though he had abandoned his own Delano alias, Spears still was living through the exploits of the authentic Delano—appreciating the man's ability to slip the law and do as he pleased.

Later, he would be surprised to discover the names of Moxie Eisenberg and Oscar Delano back in the news. After serving nine years as Delano's henchman, Moxie was finally released from the New Jersey State Penitentiary and was instantly rewarded with a "thank you" present from Oscar equivalent to $75,000. Unfortunately, Moxie didn't think it was enough to serve nearly a decade of his life as a proxy for Delano. He demanded nearly twice that amount as he said he had been originally promised.

Saying that he was willing to discuss the matter, Delano invited Eisenberg to his Westport mansion. He promptly called the police, who were on his payroll, and claimed Moxie was coming after him for vengeance. The ex-con was immediately arrested for blackmail and returned to his cell in the prison.

Oscar L. Delano was never arrested and lived to be an elderly man in Tampa, Florida—not far from the center of all the drama surrounding the Flight 967 drama.

From his prison cell, however, Robert Spears had to smile. His alter-ego had gotten away with everything, and he vowed then that one day he, too, would become wealthy enough to place himself beyond the long arm of the law.

Chapter 15

The Case of the Violet Paste

For the better part of four decades, Robert Spears, under his myriad of aliases, would work more cons, schemes, and scams than authorities would ever discover as victims seldom wanted to risk the humiliation and ridicule of admitting to being defrauded and preferred rather to just swallow their pride and count it as a lesson learned.

However, it would be naturopathy—with the prestige of being called "Doctor"—where Robert Spears would ultimately choose to stake his claim to wealth and prominence. Well, naturopathy with a little abortion on the side.

And, in the 1950s, he would not be alone.

Abortionists, though widely condemned publicly, for the most part, provided an important and necessary service for society. Throughout history, hundreds of thousands of abortions were sought and performed each year. The leaders of society—from politicians and police to priests and pastors—knew it could not and perhaps should not be stopped. As a result, an underground network developed and flourished, operating in the shadows with a wink and a nod from authorities.

The more recent evolution of this practice in the twentieth century, however—with its greatly sophisticated medical procedures and sterilized operating rooms—was now more of an accepted surgical option. Still outlawed, it was nevertheless part of the American fabric for most of the 1900s.

120 / Chapter 15

As mentioned earlier, one of the prime movers in this more modern version was a felon dominating the headlines at the time. Already well-known in the underworld as a master forger, he had, by mid-century, begun to make a name for himself as an abortionist. Still, he initially had developed a reputation for creating and selling fake diplomas.

It was Faiman and the previously mentioned Robert H. Reddick who acted—knowingly or not—as a magnet for Robert Spears to view naturopathy as the ideal front for performing abortions. And clearly, the big, big money was in abortions.

In the early years of the 1920s—a time of unbridled wealth and excess—Charles Faiman was looking at the good life from the outside. Though he was nothing more than a lowly truck driver, the 24-year-old had a vision of making something of himself and joining the culture of the roaring twenties and striding to center stage as a "sheik"—the flapper's male counterpart with his baggy trousers, shiny, slicked-back hair, and shoes covered with spats.

That golden opportunity arose when a university fell into bankruptcy and their remaining assets were auctioned off. Faiman had no interest in the academic resources that were being sold for pennies on the dollar, but one item caught his attention—the name.

After taking over the legal name of the National University of Sciences, the first thing he did was give himself a PhD in microbiology. That—along with other elaborately engraved but phony diplomas and embossed, gold-sealed certificates—gave him an air of academia and legitimacy.

As bold as that was, his next step was perhaps even bolder. Printing up mass quantities of fine-linen diplomas—suitable for framing—Faiman launched a mail-order diploma mill of impressive proportions from his elegantly furnished office in Chicago. Taking it a step further, he created letterhead listing professors, department heads, deans, and a highly regarded university president—all fake, of course.

By all accounts, with diplomas selling between $500 and $2,500 in today's value depending on the gullibility of the victim, "Dr." Charles Faiman was soon extraordinarily wealthy. *For*

The Case of the Violet Paste / 121

a while. Within two years, his house of cards collapsed when he was arrested for supplying typhoid germs as a tool of murder.

The case was scandalous. The country was all aflutter over the mysterious murder of Billy McClintock—tabbed as the "Millionaire Orphan"—after the toddler inherited the equivalent of nearly $40 million in today's value.

According to newspaper reports, William and Julia Shepherd cultivated a friendship with the McClintocks solely to kill them and gain possession of their vast fortune. The father was the first to die mysteriously. William Shepherd—who was the family lawyer and a well-respected attorney in Dallas—served as executor of his will, which left everything to his wife, Emma.

Moving the widow into their Texas cottage home, presumably to care for the grieving woman, it wasn't long before Mrs. McClintock fell seriously ill after eating a bowl of soup and was given an elixir by a doctor friend of Shepherd's. Emma, distraught with grief, tragically died shortly after, as did the doctor himself, under mysterious circumstances.

On her deathbed, however, Shepherd frantically amended the will to name himself as guardian of their only son Billy, who would soon be the sole heir of the massive McClintock fortune. Then, the dying mother curiously added a special codicil that named Shepherd as the ultimate beneficiary should young Billy die before he was married. It would prove to be a poor decision.

The Shepherds indeed raised the boy—adopting him in the process—and then became disturbed when, at age 21, he fell in love with a pretty school teacher, Miss Isabelle Pope—who was once characterized as "a second Juliet in both beauty and charm." A February wedding was planned, and so, with less than two months until the nuptials, William and Julie Shepherd decided that the only rational thing to do was to murder the young groom, ensuring that they would become the heirs of the McClintock estate.

On the evening of December 4, Billy ate a plate of oysters and came down almost immediately with a raging, uncontrollable fever. As he lay dying, Billy begged his adopted parents—with marriage license in hand and Isabelle by his side—to find a minister who could join the two lovers in holy matrimony on his

122 / Chapter 15

deathbed. Unfortunately, the reverend apparently could not be located, and Billy was dead before midnight.

The coroner, Oscar Wolff, ruled that the young man had died of typhoid—the most dreaded disease of the time and he was buried immediately for fear of viral transmission. However, as Julie Shepherd began the job of moving her family into the expansive McClintock Mansion—which was supposed to be the future home of Billy and Isabelle—the courts decided to exhume McClintock's body as detectives began to suspect foul play. Cracking open the cement slab over the tomb and removing the brass casket, the case suddenly took a radical turn.

A renowned bacteriologist and medical doctor stepped forward to notify police that William Shepherd had contacted him regarding supplying him with an unusually virulent form of typhoid bacteria cells. At the same time, three other scientists and doctors admitted they had also been sought out by Shepherd for the same purpose. The only difference was that the bacteriologist agreed to the deal.

And that man, of course, was Charles Faiman.

William Shepherd was arrested almost immediately and charged with the unfathomable crime of murdering Billy, his adopted son. At the time, Shepherd was also described by the prosecutor as a "weak-willed, soft man completely dominated by 'Lady Macbeth,' a cold, purposeful, masculine woman who plotted for years to secure the absolute control of the McClintock fortune."

Chicago police, on the recommendation of a grand jury, next arrested Mrs. Julia Shepherd, his wife, and a trial date was set with Faiman at the very center of a media circus. The Shepherds, according to the indictment, murdered their son with typhoid germs to prevent him from marrying Isabelle and leaving the McClintock fortune to his young wife.

At trial, more than one hundred witnesses testified against the Shepherds. The prosecutor, in his summation, declared that for nearly two decades, the couple cultivated the trust of the McClintocks solely to poison everyone in the family and gain control of their fortune. It was also charged that Shepherd—incredibly—also fatally poisoned the prosecutor's own brother,

The Case of the Violet Paste / 123

who had been serving as a state investigator for the case, with cyanide.

This case caused a major sensation in gangland Chicago of the 1920s, a city fascinated with murder and mayhem. When the bodies of Billy's mother, father, and doctor were exhumed, they were found to contain enough mercury poison to have killed multiple people.

When his name was first connected with one of the more bizarre stories of its time, Faiman tried to promote himself as one of the world's top bacteriologists and thus was able to barter an immunity deal to build the prosecution's case. As a result, he moved from being one of the primary defendants to being the star witness against his co-conspirator.

Freely and proudly testifying that he provided William Shepherd with typhoid germs in exchange for a $100,000 payout, Faiman explained that he gave the murderer three test tubes filled with deadly bacilli. Despite that smoking gun, the Shepherds were found not guilty of the murder and, as a result, were awarded their adopted son's inheritance of $35 million in today's money.

However, there was an unexpected side effect for Charles Faiman in the story. Upon cross-examination, the pseudo-medical researcher was eviscerated by the savvy defense attorneys, and Faiman was exposed as a complete fraud. Intending to invalidate his testimony, the defense paraded nearly 30 witnesses to the stand who described Faiman as a fraudster, a forger, and a slick conman who sold fake medical licenses.

Faiman's empire was crumbling before his eyes as he sat in the courtroom that day. However—as is the case with all gifted grifters—just a half-dozen years later, he would emerge once again, this time as a naturopathic doctor and a backroom abortionist.

Moving south from Chicago to Dallas, Faiman reinvented himself as a physician while still churning out phony medical licenses and doing a booming business in abortions from his trendy new clinic in the Lakewood Hills district. The Texas sunshine, however, would not prove to shine brightly for long on

124 / Chapter 15

the con doctor, and his time there would be marked by a continuing series of run-ins with the law.

Having escaped a prison sentence when he was just 22 years old for a botched and fatal abortion procedure, Faiman was soon knee-deep in trouble again in Dallas for posing as a legitimate physician and operating yet another fake diploma and medical licensing ring out of Jacksonville. When he was arrested, the police found a trunk load of phony licenses and forged medical degrees—most of these intended for naturopathic doctors.

In fact, it was Charles Faiman—wealthy and entitled—who both inspired Robert Spears to seek a career in naturopathy/abortion and provided him with a model of what a rich, fake doctor could look like. At the same time, Spears was becoming intrigued with Baltimore psychiatrist Dr. Robert H. Reddick. The respected and quite legitimate doctor had become disillusioned with the medical community in America, believing it to be a monopoly which protected profits over providing patient care.

Though that perspective might have been true, Reddick took a left turn—once he was disgraced by his peers for criticizing them—and began selling fake medical licenses to naturopaths and homeopaths—or anyone with ready cash—to support himself.

Thus was the evil alchemy that delivered Robert Spears to the shady medical community, with Dr. Charles Faiman providing him with a university diploma in the field of medicine and Robert Reddick awarding him a medical license to practice in Maryland, which in turn was transferred to and subsequently approved, after a $50 fee, by the Texas Medical Board.

With that, Spears promptly opened his practice on 6116 Gaston Avenue—ironically just a few doors down from Faiman's operation, who was now fighting for his professional life and freedom. But Faiman's days were numbered.

Time magazine, in its October 18, 1948, issue, seized the opportunity to tell the tale of the discredited doctor and abortionist in a featured article, entitled: "The Case of the Violet Paste."

The article began with a paragraph that no doubt was stunning to its conservative readers: "Society has harsh punishments

The Case of the Violet Paste / 125

for a girl who gets 'in trouble.' If she is poor and ignorant, she may be driven to use concoctions offered by people like 'Doctor' Charles Faiman. When she accepts such 'help,' there is an excellent chance that she will never need help of any kind again."

The article went on to describe Faiman as "a stocky, baldish, well-dressed man with a neat brown mustache and a look of respectability. He lives in an exclusive section of Dallas, drives a brand-new green Buick, and has an attractive second wife. He has been supported in his pleasant position by panicky pregnant girls."

Just the week prior, Charles Faiman had begun a two-year prison sentence for selling "abortion paste" after years of criminal activity. Apparently born in Riga, Latvia, he was first indicted as an abortionist in St. Paul, Minnesota, nearly three decades earlier.

But it was just a few years after that, in 1925, that Faiman made headlines by admitting in a Chicago court that he had supplied typhoid germs to William Shepherd for the purpose of murdering his rich foster son, Billy McClintock. Faiman got off by turning state's evidence but a witness testified during the trial that Faiman operated an unsavory St. Louis "massage parlor" and was "Doctor in Chief" at a shadowy medical clinic in Detroit. On the run to Dallas to escape those charges, Faiman was eventually indicted for "the illegal practice of medicine" as well as assault on his first wife.

These legal troubles, however, did not seem to interfere with his wholesale drug business, which he called "Physicians' Prescription Products"—basically poison for young, pregnant girls.

In 1940, the Federal Food & Drug Administration was conducting a major campaign to rid the country of "abortion pastes." During a routine checkup, an inspector discovered that Faiman was selling a violet-colored, sweet-smelling paste called "Metro-Vac" containing a poisonous metallic element.

There was no doubt that it induced abortions, but the FDA quickly announced that this preparation was the most dangerous in existence. The results were devastating: if the drug got into the bloodstream, the patient always died.

126 / Chapter 15

Unfortunately, the existence of the substance itself did not break any of the extremely liberal Texas laws—and the state did not seem to care—so the FDA set about to prove that Faiman had violated interstate commerce laws. It was something they had failed to prove until late one night in January 1947 when an inspector tailed Faiman to a post office and watched him address a package to a Louisiana doctor.

When opened, it proved to contain abortion paste—a $5 tube, enough for three perilous abortions. Next, an FDA agent followed the package to its ultimate destination, seizing it upon arrival as evidence. Later, another package was trailed through the mail to Arkansas.

However, Dr. Faiman's two-year sentence seemed to worry him only momentarily. As he was being escorted to federal prison, he seemed to have regained his old arrogance. With a persecuted air, he complained: "There's someone out there who's out to get me."

At the same time that Faiman was moving into his new home in federal prison, the newly minted Dr. Robert Spears was on the ascent and ready to take on Faiman's cash-paying clientele which had earlier been exposed under a headline reading: "Cash, Not Brains, Bought Permits."

And so, the fashionably dressed, well-spoken, and garrulous Dr. Robert Spears—with his competition conveniently disposed of—was on his way to becoming the golden boy of a burgeoning new but slightly cockeyed, off-the-books medical industry.

Chapter 16

The Calm and the Storm

Over a decade had passed since the days of the disgraced and long-forgotten Charles Faiman and Billy McClintock, and Dr. Robert Spears had since made a large imprint on the naturopathic world—sometimes for the better, sometimes for worse. During the era, however, this medical field had grown significantly in both size and reputation.

With more than 20,000 naturopathic, chiropractic, and holistic practitioners in the United States alone, in the 1950s, this alternative medical group was seriously challenging the number of traditional physicians in the American Medical Association.

And Spears had grown along with the industry.

He had become quite financially successful—now boasting a two-story brick house in an exclusive Dallas community that he had purchased in August 1954. By that time, he had worked his way up to being named as president of the Texas Naturopathic Association. Soon after, he parlayed that position into assuming a similar role with the American Association of Naturopathic Physicians, followed by the international version of the same.

However, few reporters were familiar with this maverick healthcare brand and only became marginally interested because of its peripheral connection to this current story of epic proportions—the crash of National Airlines Flight 967 and the fascinating mystery of Dr. Robert Spears.

The press and public were undoubtedly captivated by the question of whether or not Dr. Spears might somehow be alive

128 / Chapter 16

and not a victim of the airline crash after all. Even more titil-lating was the suggestion that he may have passed along his plane ticket to his best friend Al Taylor, who, presumably, was now resting at the bottom of a fathomless trench in the Gulf of Mexico.

Readers couldn't get enough of the story throughout the Christmas season of 1959 and the early weeks of the new decade. Barely an edition was published without some mention, some new development, and some potential evidence coming to light.

The main propagator of content for the newspaper writers was, of course, Mrs. Alice Taylor, who was still vocally maintaining that it was her husband Al who had died on that plane and not Bob Spears, whom she had detested from the first time she met him. Having brought on attorney Robert Mann and enlisted the confidence of several *Tampa Tribune* reporters including Tony Schiappa, she had become the loudest voice in the story and was perpetually dishing out her opinions.

Not to be outdone, Frances Spears was being pushed hard by newscaster and consummate self-promoter Eddie Barker to tell her side of the story as well. Quickly making a name for himself in the Dallas–Ft. Worth area as the single source of all things related to the topic, Barker virtually moved into the Spears' residence and kept all other reporters at arm's length.

But it would be neither of those sources that would dig up some of the juiciest tidbits to date in this bizarre but ever-evolving tale of deception, betrayal, and perhaps murder.

When an out-of-town reporter began to snoop around Al Taylor's apartment building, The Georgian, his landlady would only say, "Mr. Taylor was a good tenant. There was nothing remarkable about him. He seemed a lonely man except, of course, for his one friend."

That "one friend"—described as "49, with auburn hair and well-preserved"—as it turned out, was a very close friend. The police had already tracked her down and interviewed her, and the reporter was now hot on her trail. Reluctant to talk and immediately suspicious, her first question was, "How did you find out about me?"

The Calm and the Storm / 129

Agreeing to speak only on the condition of anonymity—
though she was later identified simply as "Muriel" in FBI logs—
she added: "It would cost me my job if my name were ever
dragged into this thing." But speak she did, and soon, she was
talkative and forthcoming.

> I am personally convinced that Al Taylor is still very much
> alive. We met about two years ago in a diner. I suppose you
> think there's something wrong with that, but there wasn't. He
> was always kind and considerate. He is a fine man. We never
> went out together much. Neither of us had much money. We
> didn't even go to the movies, but we were close.
>
> I don't believe for one moment Mr. Taylor is dead. He wasn't
> killed in that crash and he didn't blow up that plane. He's a
> good man, a fine Christian man. I know you don't believe that,
> but to me, he was always very considerate. He respected me as
> a woman . . . a man of only the highest character.
>
> We confided in each other, but we never became involved
> romantically. Do you know, he's never even been to this
> apartment? Sometimes, he drove me home, and we talked. He
> worried about me and cared for me when I was sick. He also
> worked very hard. He was a good worker for his company.
>
> I have a daughter to raise, and I don't make much money,
> and he had his former wife and children to support. We
> never had much chance to think of anything else, you know.
> He seemed concerned about the future with the financial
> pressure he felt, and he seemed very preoccupied with
> something.
>
> He worried about his finances and money and told me that
> most of his money went to support his ex-wife and her two
> children, including one from a previous marriage—25% of his
> paycheck to each of those three people, leaving only 25% of
> what he earned for himself.
>
> Taylor's stepson Blaine had a plan to sell large painted
> murals and wanted Al to finance the project, so Al Taylor bor-
> rowed money for him, but Blaine failed to repay him. It created
> a hardship, but he was generous like that.

Then the reporter asked the key question, "Did Al ever talk
about Dr. Robert Spears?"

130 / Chapter 16

"Not really. He never talked of his past. Mostly, he talked about the children and how he was worried about them, and his worries about money. The last time I was with him was just a week or maybe two before he disappeared. After that, I heard from him just once, you know, a few days before. . . ."

Her voice trailed off as she relived the moment and the conversation.

> I wasn't feeling well and I called him. I asked him, "Honey, what are you doing?" He was real sweet and he told me he was going over his books, working on his accounts, and I told him, "Honey, you shouldn't work so hard." I was concerned for him because he seemed stressed, but other than that he didn't express any other fears or appear depressed. That was a little odd because he was always happy in my company. We'd just laugh and giggle at something or nothing at all. We got along real well together.
>
> And like I said, I myself don't believe anything has happened to him. I think I'd know if it had. I'd have a feeling, you know. After all, can't a man just go off by himself without it being a crime?

The headline the following day would read: "Confidant Doubts Taylor Dead. Says Wasn't on Plane."

In a touch of humor, the FBI interview with Muriel, Taylor's neighbor and would-be girlfriend, included an item that never made it into print that had been related by a friend to one of the special agents: "Al told me once that he took Muriel on one occasion to the Wedgewood Restaurant in St. Petersburg, Florida and the following morning he commented that he would have to starve for a few weeks to make up for the money he had spent the night before on dinner."

At the same time that reporters were in a stir about Al Taylor's secret relationship and the identity of this mystery woman, far away in Minnesota, another group of journalists was uncovering yet another strange tale of relationships—this time regarding Robert Spears. And it would be, as they say, a doozy.

The Calm and the Storm / 131

Shortly after Spears and his partner in crime, Al Taylor, were released from the Maryland State Penitentiary in 1940, Bob headed to greener pastures in Minneapolis, Minnesota, where he heard the new art of naturopathy was beginning to take hold. Always attracted to the medical field for its inherent status, he wanted to learn more and felt it was a good place to reinvent himself yet once again—possibly even go straight.

Locating a boarding house—a common option in the era for single men—he was known as smart and charming and a perfect gentleman, according to his landlady, Mrs. Ella Saatz.

"He was a handsome big fellow, a sharp dresser and well-behaved. He wasn't a doctor then, but he was a journalist. Wrote stories for the Methodist *Wesley News*. He was very modern with a typewriter, and his own telephone in his room. I never saw him go to church. He just wrote about church people. He was also involved in the arts community."

At one of those arts meetings, Robert Spears—a relatively new use of a name for him—met a graphic artist who created designs for wallpaper. At that time, Bob was a writer for a national religious publication, having been given the job based on a largely phony résumé. Not making a great deal at his position, he also worked as a salesman selling various household cleaning items and elixirs.

Based on his well-groomed skill as a storyteller, he was even invited to deliver occasional Sunday sermons at the highly respected Minneapolis Wesley Methodist Church—one of the denomination's most revered congregations. Broadcast over the radio, his messages reached thousands and sparked a desire in him for such a platform. Ironically, one of his sermons was entitled, "The Calm and the Storm."

Indeed, a storm was soon coming.

However, it was a pretty, sophisticated secretary who caught Bob Spears' eye, and soon, they were appearing arm-in-arm on the streets of downtown St. Paul. Bonita Foster—"a charming lass with a sweet disposition"—was in her early 30s when they met. She was instantly impressed by his stories of dogfights in

132 / Chapter 16

the skies over Europe as a fighter pilot, as well as his years as a war correspondent and traveling journalist.

With the blessing of her mother—impressed by his sincere commitment to his Christian faith—the two were soon engaged. By the first week of November 1941, the couple were readying to become husband and wife as the final preparations for the formal wedding were being done.

The night before the ceremony, manager Nicholas Pappas of the New Bridge Café—the couple's favorite hotspot—threw an engagement party. There, the two, with great fanfare, signed their marriage license as they were showered with confetti and serpentine from adoring friends.

By the next morning, he was gone.

"He paid his bill in full, including the phone bill, and when I saw him coming down the stairs with his suitcase for the last time, I just asked why on earth he was leaving. Especially being engaged to Bonita, that sweet thing. He answered that his daughter had been in an auto accident in Cleveland, and he had to rush out there. Then he got into that rattletrap of a car and left. I ain't never seen him again."

Apparently, immediately after his "rehearsal dinner," Robert Spears responded to an advertisement in the Classifieds section of the *Minneapolis Star* placed there by a Mr. Leo Schertzer. It said he and his mother were traveling to California, and they had room for a passenger willing to pay $15 to help cover the gasoline, which was soon to be rationed for the war effort.

Literally leaving Bonita Foster weeping at the altar, Bob Spears was soon on his way west. She would never see him again, though she would, one day, read his name in her local newspaper as a potential mass murderer a full 20 years later.

As the sun began to rise over the midwestern plains, Spears was cramped into the backseat of Schertzer's two-door 1940 Chevrolet coupe, sitting next to 21-year-old Adam Novack, another paying passenger, and beginning what was to be a nearly two-thousand-mile journey. In the front was also the driver's mother, 59-year-old Mollie.

The Calm and the Storm / 133

Spears was leaving the midwest for good—and his bride-to-be Bonita in the process—ready for a fresh start in sunny California where jobs were plentiful, movie stars walked the streets, and there were a million transplanted Americans with their pockets stuffed with money.

As the quartet headed south toward Oklahoma—from where they would head west toward Burbank—trouble began to erupt. Tensions began to rise in the cramped quarters. Soon, young Adam, who had a police record, and 47-year-old Bob were rubbing each other raw.

Then, 40 miles outside of Oklahoma City, something went sideways. Hidden in a section of his knapsack, Spears had tucked away some cash—$485 that he had "borrowed" from Bonita for wedding purposes.

Digging around, he suddenly couldn't find it and immediately accused the annoying Novack of stealing the cash. The kid responded as might be expected, and soon, the two were in a tussle in the back seat as Leo, the driver, swerved along Route 66. Mollie screamed while grabbing the steering wheel to pull the Chevy over to the side of the road.

Uncharacteristically livid and out of control, Spears shockingly next pulled out a loaded .38 Smith and Wesson revolver from his sack and pressed it up against Novack's forehead. Forcing everyone to get out of the car at gunpoint, he marched them into a cornfield, where he tied them up and began searching each one. Finding nothing and becoming even more frustrated, he began digging a hole while threatening to kill or wound them and throw them in the ditch.

Changing his mind after grabbing all of the meager cash the combined riders could produce, Spears inexplicably put the group back in the car with all three wedged in the back seat. Then, in the strangest twist to date, he soaked a blanket with ether—a bottle he had taken from his salesman's kit—and placed it over their heads.

Demanding that they inhale deeply until they pass out, the three soon lost consciousness. Spears was on his way to California—probably without any clue as to what he would do next.

134 / Chapter 16

Later, he would claim that his only goal was to turn them over to the police for stealing his money.

Then, just as the Chevy rolled onto Main Street in the downtown of tiny, rural Weatherford, Oklahoma, the two young men began to regain consciousness and threw the ether-soaked blanket over Spears' head as he was driving.

That was when all hell broke loose.

The result was what newspapers would come to call a "weird gunfight saga" in which several people were seriously wounded and countless cars demolished. Spears ran wildly down Main Street, spraying bystanders with tear gas—also from his sales kit—including the town's mayor.

Eventually, two of the original Minnesota group would end up in the hospital—Leo Schertzer was shot directly through the chest and barely lived. Spears was behind bars with a bullet hole through his left hand and part of one finger missing. This time, however, his legal situation was more serious.

Spears' crime—first-degree robbery and attempted murder—happened to be a capital offense in the state of Oklahoma, which meant it carried a sentence of hanging. For some odd reason, the weird nature of the case attracted the attention of attorney Albert Darnell—an Oklahoma state senator—and he agreed to take on the defense. Incredibly, through his connections—or under-the-table negotiations—Darnell managed to plead the charge down to second-degree robbery, though that still carried a four-year sentence.

Robert Spears would forever be infuriated by the incident and would never get over it—well reflected when he filled out his intake form at Oklahoma State Penitentiary and was required to write the cause for his incarceration. It only took one word for the delusional Spears as he scrawled, *FRAMED.*

Chapter 17

Lighting the Fuse, Running Like Hell

Twenty long years and hundreds of crimes after his release from Oklahoma State Penitentiary, Dr. Robert Spears was safely tucked away in William Turska's desert hideaway and should have been sequestered from all of the news that was swirling around about him in virtually every newspaper in the nation as well as every major city around the globe. *But he was not.* If anything, he was becoming obsessed with following himself in the press.

Unafraid of being recognized, he would regularly venture into Phoenix and its surrounding suburbs to gather newspapers from every major city at newsstands and stand there gawking at his photos on the front pages of the various editions. A true narcissist, his interest in himself was insatiable. Bill Turska was also feasting on the fact that he was now harboring the most sought-after man in America. These were heady times for the two.

On a cold Saturday morning—January 16, 1960—Bob Spears got up and poured himself a cup of freshly percolated black coffee. Sitting at the Formica-topped kitchen table in one of the mismatched yard sale chairs, Spears casually clicked on the radio and began reading one of the papers he had picked up previously. Scanning it for relevant news, he was suddenly drawn to the breaking news alert on station KPHO.

136 / Chapter 17

> An FBI report that has just been released in Miami Beach by the Civil Aeronautics Board maintains that one of the passengers on National Airlines Flight 967—Dr. Robert Spears, a Dallas, naturopath, ex-convict, and accused abortionist—may actually still be alive.

The alert continued on to explain that the FBI was refusing to elaborate on the report, which was said to contain a letter the Bureau had sent to the Civil Aeronautics Board. The letter, which had been read at a CAB hearing, quoted Julian Blodgett, chief investigator of the Los Angeles District Attorney's office, as saying that Spears may have had someone travel for him to collect a large insurance policy and naming his wife as beneficiary.

According to the newscast, the FBI was speculating that the person who was listed as "Spears" on the flight's manifest may, in fact, have been his good friend and drinking companion William Allen Taylor, a salesman who had been missing since the night the plane took off. The breaking news ended with a sobering statement:

> An all-points bulletin has now been issued nationwide for a 1957 Plymouth sedan with a coral-and-cream, two-toned exterior that belongs to Taylor but is now believed to be in the possession of possible fugitive Robert Spears. All citizens of Phoenix are asked to be on the lookout for that automobile with Florida license plates reading 3-65205. If spotted, police suggest approaching with caution.

The news was incredibly concerning, and Spears needed to steady his hand to not spill his coffee. For the first time, a reliable report—based on FBI findings included in a soon-to-be-released Civil Aeronautics Board report—was announcing that Spears, in fact, may be alive and may have tricked his good friend into taking his place on a plane that he himself may have doomed by unwittingly carrying a bomb on board.

With the FBI putting the pieces of the puzzle together, the gears in Bob's brain were churning on overdrive as he desperately tried to determine his next move. Despite the relative safety of the secret New River compound, Spears' anxiety was

Lighting the Fuse, Running Like Hell / 137

already getting the better of him. Should he bolt and go on the run? Should he lay low and just let all of this blow over? But would it ever?

It didn't take long for Spears to suggest to Turska that they hit the road to learn more about this troubling development and to deal with Taylor's car that was still tucked away and out of sight in Ely, Nevada. Both men had been confident that their secrets were safe in the desert, but now there was a legitimate cause for concern. The car was most definitely the one thing that could connect them to a much bigger crime.

Discussing the situation, the two agreed that they needed to retrieve Taylor's now very recognizable '57 Plymouth and they jumped in Turska's Mercedes to make the eight-hour drive to Nevada. With every stop, the men checked the newspaper racks to see if there was any mention of the CAB report, but so far their secret was safe. The news had apparently yet to reach the late editions of newspapers in the West.

After retrieving the Plymouth in the middle of the night, they made their way back under the cover of darkness and arrived by dawn at Turska's New River home. After a few hours of sleep, Spears decided that the car—as much as he loved it—had to be destroyed. Driving it into a ravine at the far end of the property, he removed the Florida license plates, filed off all of the identification numbers, removed anything from the interior that might tie him to the vehicle, and drove it into the deepest rut.

At first, he felt that it was sufficiently hidden among the brush to avoid detection, but the farther he walked away, the more the shiny coral-colored paint seemed to reflect like a beacon under the midday sun.

There was only one other option.

Pulling out several sticks of dynamite that he had brought along, Spears slid them under the chassis, lit the fuses and ran like hell. The explosion sent car parts flying in a tower of dust as Turska and Spears drove away along a makeshift trail, laughing like the drunken madmen they were.

Still concerned about the Civil Aeronautics Board report that had hit the radio airwaves, however, the pair next drove into nearby Cave Creek to see if the news had yet reached the

138 / Chapter 17

local newspapers. While Spears was filling up the tank of the Mercedes, Turska wandered over to the office to give the man three dollars and caught him with his nose buried in the Sunday edition of the *Arizona Republic*.

The headline blaring from the front page read: "Ex-Convict Linked to Gulf Crash." Going over to the news rack, Turska bought every copy. Seconds later, with gravel flying, the dubious fugitives were spinning out of the service station and back onto the main road.

But before they were even halfway to New River, another plan began to develop inside Robert Spears' head. He knew he needed to act quickly. He knew he needed to do one more thing before his face was plastered on the front page of every newspaper in America.

Whipping the car around in the middle of the road, Spears pointed it in the opposite direction—heading into the heart of Phoenix. There was one more job that needed to be done. After driving for about 30 minutes, Bob Spears unexpectedly pulled the car to the side of a busy street and tossed the keys to Bill Turska without explanation. Getting out and instantly blending in with the Sunday afternoon pedestrians along a crowded sidewalk, Bill wondered if he would ever see his friend again.

With Mexico only a few hours away, it would make sense that he might want to disappear into another world with a new identity and start a new family. It certainly wouldn't be unreasonable. Or perhaps there was some other nefarious purpose for Spears' quick exit. Purchase some guns and ammunition, maybe? It could be that he anticipated a shootout at the compound and didn't intend to go down quietly or at all.

Whatever it was, Turska decided to sit tight for an hour or two. He'd make his way over to a newsstand that he knew was around the corner and grab a copy of the *LA Times*, the *Dallas Morning News*, the *Houston Chronicle*, and the *New York Times* if it was in. That should give him a clear picture of what stories were out there about his guest, Robert Spears. He, too, was more than curious. Bob hadn't said much.

At the same time that Bill Turska was pushing a dollar bill across the corner of Stanley's Tobacco Shop with an armful of

Lighting the Fuse, Running Like Hell / 139

newspapers and a pack of Chesterfields, Spears was crossing the street at East Highland—head down, overcoat collar turned up, hat pulled down low, hands jammed in his side pockets.

Patiently waiting at the red light, a woman in her early thirties—her head wrapped in a pink scarf, wearing an Angora sweater—was listening to Marty Robbins sing about El Paso. Tapping her fingers on the steering wheel, she considered making it crosstown to visit a friend.

It was then—right then—that she spotted someone who looked hauntingly familiar. She couldn't see his face, other than the dark, heavy-framed glasses, but his stride and chunky body—that lumbering style—was oh so familiar. Her eyes followed him as he reached the middle of the crosswalk, where he stopped dead in his tracks. Turning slowly, he stared directly at the woman, who quickly lifted her sunglasses to her face.

That was when she knew exactly who he was—a face from the past.

It had been some time since Annette Turska had walked out on her much older husband, who had turned out to be a kook, a drunk, a carouser, and an inveterate ne'er-do-well. She thought the man had such promise when they first met—he was a doctor, after all, with a thriving downtown practice. Then, the booze, the uncontrollable anger, and the constant life on the edge of the law finally got the best of her, and she had had enough. Long before Spears had shown up on the doorstep at New River, she had slammed that door for the last time.

Now divorced and presumably done with him forever, seeing Spears brought back that unhappy world in a flash. The two couples had been friendly years earlier—even vacationed together—and she knew both Bob and Frances well. Annette also had been reading the newspapers and knew that this man— Robert Vernon Spears—was being sought by the FBI. Sought by the Feds for, of all things, a connection to a plane crash to fake his death and collect insurance money.

Could it be true? Could it be him? She didn't think he recognized her—she had dyed her hair since they were last together and cut it shorter. Still, she intuitively slinked down in her car seat slightly. And then the light turned, and she gunned the gas

140 / Chapter 17

pedal to take herself far away from that man—and her ex-husband if he was involved—and the world where she used to live.

After just a few blocks, Annette pulled over to the curb and tried to steady herself. Her heart was racing, her hands trembling. She knew she had to make a decision. Cutting short her errands on that day, she pulled back out into traffic and breathlessly rushed home. There she sat for a few moments in front of her telephone, afraid to pick it up. Afraid not to.

Going back to her living room, she grabbed her copy of the *Arizona Republic* one more time and began to read. She needed to confirm that the story she remembered was, in fact, true. More so, she needed to convince herself that what she was about to do was the right thing.

And when she was convinced that it was the right decision, she picked up the receiver and said, meekly, "Operator, the police station, please."

Bob Spears eventually returned to the Mercedes parked alongside the downtown Phoenix street with Bill Turska now napping, his hat over his face. Sliding into the driver's side seat, Spears started the car without saying a single word about what he had been doing. Turska never asked. Such was their relationship. Don't ask, don't tell. It was as simple as that.

Nearly an hour later, they had settled into the New River hideout and were once again feeling confident in their strategy. If anything, they felt as if they had dodged the bullet—even with the ever-widening exposure to Spears' potential role in the Flight 967 crash, no one had come close to figuring out where they were or what they were up to.

"Always one step ahead," Robert had said with numbing regularity. "Always one step ahead." He popped the bottle cap off an amber beer bottle he had just pulled from the ice chest. Settling into a ragged Naugahyde chair, he lit a cigarette and closed his eyes. It had already been a long day, and he needed a moment to gather his thoughts.

"Wadda ya think that's all about?" Turska questioned while running one hand through his thick brown hair. "What's all the ruckus on the main road? They're kickin' up a helluva lot of dust out there."

"No tellin'," Spears responded with disinterest. He didn't bother to open his eyes to look out the large picture window in the front room. However, Turska was almost pressed up against it, scanning the scene outside.

"Hey Bob, I think we got company." And that was when Spears jumped to his feet.

Chapter 18

Plastic Palm Trees and Peril

Over the past two hours, Bill Turska had noticed an unusual amount of traffic on the road that fronted his house some two hundred yards away. That meant only a car or two every 20 minutes, but still, that was an oddity in their desolate neck of the Sonoran Desert.

Robert Spears had joined him at the window as his friend picked up a pair of field glasses. Trying to follow one of the cars, he became instantly concerned. "They're all black Buicks. All the same, just going in opposite directions back and forth on Old Black Canyon Highway. They're law enforcement, but not local. Bob, I think they might be FBI."

They were, in fact, the FBI.

J. Edgar Hoover, the infamous director of the Bureau, had decided to turn his attention to what was increasingly appearing like an outrageous, unimaginable crime and had issued strict orders that, if captured, Hoover himself wanted to call a press conference to announce that Robert Spears had been arrested. The fugitive was considered a jewel in the Department of Justice's crown.

The "traffic" continued for the next few days with cars regularly driving by slowly and deliberately and then turning around as soon as they drove out of view only to retrace their course.

Spears and Turska were convinced that it had nothing to do with the Flight 967 controversy, but rather, word had

144 / Chapter 18

somehow gotten out about the new abortion clinic they had set up in the back room of the residence. Using the equipment they had retrieved from both Los Angeles and Dallas, they had constructed a rather advanced operation and had already been serving several young women each day.

The only possible explanation was their word-of-mouth advertising had unfortunately fallen on the wrong ears. They knew, however, that unless they were caught in the act—including photographic and testimony evidence from shamed patients—they could skirt any arrest. They had done it dozens of times already over decades. There was nothing about this that was of much concern. A few greased palms here and there always solved the issue.

However, just to be sure, Turska managed to spot the plate number on the back of one of the cars and had a friend run the license. Sure enough, it came back registered to the FBI. This was no abortion sting—that was always a state crime. No, this was about Flight 967. There was suddenly no doubt about it.

And so, as Robert Spears continued to track the movements of the string of black Buicks outside, Bill Turska packed bags for the two men. In moments, they slipped out the back door, jumped in the Mercedes, took off along an obscure, rocky desert trail, and disappeared into the inky blackness of the moonless desert.

In the early morning hours of Tuesday, January 19, Turska strolled into the tropically decorated lobby of the nearly new Bali-Hi Motel on Grand Avenue in Phoenix and explained to Dolores Carlson at the front desk that he was a physician who was checking in a friend who was ill and pre-paid his $8 room fee.

After being directed to room 208, Turska and "George Rhodes"—a favorite alias of Spears—had a conversation about what they might do next. There was much to consider. Before he left, however, Turska gave his friend a big hug and reminded him of their pact never to turn on each other.

Then, he left him with the words, "You can trust me, Bob."

Less than 30 minutes later and five miles south of the Bali-Hi, William Turska walked through the doors of Aaron Kinney's

Plastic Palm Trees and Peril / 145

law offices. He explained that he needed to talk about an uncomfortable situation in which he had found himself embroiled.

As George Rhodes was settling into his room on the second floor to take a nap, Turska was simultaneously told that there were severe penalties for harboring a fugitive and was strongly advised to contact the FBI and fully cooperate with their investigation. Suddenly sitting up in the bed, Spears had what he called a "hinky feeling" and decided he might need to make a move.

Bob did not completely trust Bill Turska, though he was one of his best friends. He began to pack his bags and make his way back to the plastic palm tree-lined foyer. As Turska was trying to distance himself from Spears, Spears was doing the same. He was convinced that Turska—who had serious legal and criminal issues of his own—might choose to flip on him to resolve some of his own problems.

Eyeing the cocktail lounge at the far end of the lobby, Bob picked up a magazine from a coffee table and pretended to read it as he made his way over to the pay phone booth in the corner.

First buying a drink, he sipped at it as he leafed through the yellow pages until he located the Hotel Desert Sun just a half-mile down the road. It was best to switch hotels as quickly as possible if Turska was up to something—his visit now feeling more and more like a Judas' kiss of betrayal.

At the same time he called a taxi to pick him up and take him to the Desert Sun, he saw some strange men entering the lobby wearing sunglasses. To him, they looked like G-men. Approaching the front desk, they spoke in soft tones to Miss Carlson. She shook her head, and they left.

From his view in the least obtrusive seat in the lounge area, Spears' heart began to pound. His alias may have saved him. Returning to the pay phone, he made a second call, this time to an old friend. The friend agreed to help but couldn't swing by until the following morning.

After a sleepless night—his luggage still packed and now haphazardly tied together with a section of rope so that he could haul it all in one trip—Spears returned to the lobby with an overcoat collar turned up and wool newsboy cap pulled down low over his eyebrows.

146 / Chapter 18

After finding a chair at the edge of the room, he did not move for the next several hours, reading every magazine in sight, some more than once. As he read, his eyes nervously glanced around the room—was anyone watching him? Did anything feel out of the ordinary? Did anyone seem out of place?

But with his anxiety and paranoia building exponentially, Robert Spears was now the one out of place.

"I think he read just about every magazine we had in the lobby," manager James Pentkowski would later relate to eager reporters. "He just sat there the whole time wearing that heavy overcoat and cap, which seemed odd. It seemed like he was waiting for someone but trying to hide at the same time."

Unfortunately, the motel's shiny new coffee shop was also a favorite among local cops. Spears fretfully noted officers coming and going throughout his lobby stay. Then, even more concerning, around noon, he heard a police walkie-talkie squawk: *Be on the lookout for a pink and white two-toned 1957 Plymouth with Florida tags. If located, do not apprehend subject. Contact FBI immediately and indicate whereabouts. Subject may be armed.*

Spears realized, with that police bulletin, that the search for him had significantly escalated. He had a serious problem now. With Mexico within reach, he just needed to get out of the Bali-Hi to someplace where he could devise a plan. He needed to buy some time. Needed to think.

Feeling that the heat was now too great and the room was closing in on him, Robert Spears decided to head back upstairs, dragging his collection of luggage, which was still tied together. Standing in the far corner of the motel balcony, he scanned the parking lot for police activity and along Highway 60 in the distance.

Shortly after one o'clock—to his dismay—Spears sighted two automobiles that looked suspiciously like unmarked police cars. As four men emerged—dressed in black suits and ties—Spears realized that he had to act quickly. In just a matter of minutes, they would undoubtedly be on the second-floor balcony in full sight of him.

For Robert Vernon Spears, it was now or never.

Plastic Palm Trees and Peril / 147

Clutching his rope-bound baggage, the fugitive deftly dropped one loop around his neck so that a suitcase was hanging from each of his sides. Picking up another bag and his briefcase, Spears bolted and stumbled down the back stairs of the motel and re-entered the lobby through the cocktail lounge entrance.

From there, he waddled over to the front desk and requested that Dolores call him a cab—it was an emergency, he explained. He needed a ride immediately. In minutes, a taxi screeched into the motel turnaround. Spears tossed a 10 dollar bill on the counter to cover his room—though not leaving until he got $1.20 in change.

Then, in a mad and desperate rush—still yoked by his luggage collection—Spears scrambled for the open-glass front doors as he screamed and waved at the cabbie. Unfortunately, motel manager James Pentkowski was in his path, and he went flying. The man would later crow, "His actions were those of a man who realized his capture was imminent."

The commotion, unfortunately, also caught the attention of the two men in the black suits—who had only intended on getting an afternoon cup of coffee in the lounge and had nothing to do with a stakeout. They quickly jumped up and turned.

Pentkowski would later describe the chaotic situation to reporters. "Spears didn't wait for the cab driver to pick up his luggage from the lobby after he checked out. Instead, he had his two bags tied together at the handles and flung them around his neck and went running pell-mell down the driveway when the cab started to pull up.

"Next, he tossed the roped-together bags into the trunk before the cabbie could even lend a hand. He was yelling, as loud as he could, 'Phoenix International Airport!' Then, as he got into the back seat, I heard him say, 'Rio de Janeiro, Brazil. I'm going to Rio and am late . . . step on it!'"

For the first time all day, Spears felt that he could breathe a sigh of relief.

As requested, the cab driver began to pull out from under the striped awning over the entrance to the Bali-Hi with every intention of slamming his foot down on the gas pedal and flying out onto Highway 60 toward the airport.

148 / Chapter 18

He would have done exactly that had not a man dressed in a black suit with a black tie and matching fedora stepped in front of his taxi with a single arm and open palm outstretched in his direction. Seconds later, both back seat doors were yanked open. One of the suited men pulled Robert Vernon Spears out of the car and pushed him down to the curb.

The second man—both FBI agents—clasped handcuffs on his wrists.

It would prove to be an inglorious ending to the chase of America's most famous fugitive of the era. Just two short months had passed since National Airlines Flight 967 exploded in mid-air—claiming every life aboard—and before it plummeted to the deepest part of the Gulf of Mexico.

Still, though it would be the end of the chase, it would be far from the end of the story of Robert Vernon Spears, for the consummate con man had a few tricks up his own sleeve.

Chapter 19

The Look of a Worthy Adversary

In Washington, DC, shortly after 3 pm, J. Edgar Hoover stepped to the podium in the FBI briefing room and tested the microphone before making an announcement. "As of today, January 20, 1960, Robert Vernon Spears is in police custody in Phoenix, Arizona. He was apprehended as he attempted to flee from an area motor lodge by four agents and is currently being questioned regarding several potential crimes. We will have more details as they become available."

As soon as he finished speaking, a roar went up from the crowd of reporters who had packed themselves into the relatively small room. With a sea of arms waving in the air—there were hundreds of questions that still needed to be answered—Hoover paused briefly and then exited the room in a huff.

Ironically, only a few miles away on Capitol Hill, the Senate Aviation Subcommittee was meeting with Civil Aeronautics Board members to discuss the latest findings on the fate of Flight 967 and the possible role of Robert Spears in its catastrophic failure.

Also at the same time, Robert Spears himself—now stripped from his George Rhodes persona—was seated in a cold and sterile interrogation room at the Phoenix offices of the Federal Bureau of Investigation located just a few miles from the Bali-Hi. As he fiddled with an unlit cigarette in his hand, his mind was racing. He had fabricated so many stories in his lifetime that he had become an expert deceiver, but this would be his truest test.

150 / Chapter 19

Oddly, he was excited for the challenge.

When he first arrived at the FBI offices, Spears was patted down for any weapons—there were none. Then, the contents of his pockets and jacket were placed in an envelope. The agents thought it was significant that he was carrying the equivalent of $20,000 in cash and a passport—an indication that he was prepared to go on the run.

The Feds wasted little time drilling Spears about his recent movements and the mystery of his name being listed among the dead on the doomed airliner. Settling in for what they expected to be a long battle with a cagey opponent, the investigators were surprised to find their suspect affable, gracious, and even overly forthcoming. It was as if the man had been looking forward to the moment, at least to the sparring.

And for the next three hours, that is exactly what the agents got.

Offering up a tsunami of words, it appeared, however, that Spears was saying little. He was prepared for the battle and enjoying every moment of the exercise. Still dressed in a suit and tie—as he most often was—he looked like a worthy opponent. The interrogators quickly learned why the man had been such a smooth, successful, confidence man for more than 40 years.

Spears' story for the agents was a simple and straightforward one, as if it had been practiced and rehearsed for some time.

He and his good friend, Al Taylor, had met in Tampa a few days before to discuss possible business opportunities in Dallas. Taylor was anxious for a fresh start, Spears explained and wanted to escape the nagging clutches of a demanding ex-wife and a self-absorbed stepson.

Spears had a successful naturopathic practice in Texas. That had opened many doors—some that potentially might benefit Taylor. The original plan was that Spears would fly from Tampa back to Dallas while Taylor would drive there in his '57 Plymouth so that he would have his car available.

According to Spears' account, they met at the Tampa airport to have a drink and discuss those business opportunities one last time before they were both on their way to Texas. Shortly before the midnight flight, however, Al started complaining about a

The Look of a Worthy Adversary / 151

sore neck and arm—he supposedly had been wearing a neck collar over the previous days—and was dreading the long drive through the night.

It was at that point that Bob—gracious to a fault—offered to turn over his airline seat to his buddy, and he would drive the car to Dallas. It was what a good friend does. Taylor gladly accepted, of course, and Spears only requested that when he arrived, he deliver a box to his wife that contained $2,400 in cash. She needed it right away. Since he wouldn't be arriving in town for a couple of days, that would be a great favor to him.

Taylor responded that it would be no problem. Handing over the package—wrapped in brown paper and tied with jute string—the two shook hands and said goodbye for what would turn out to be the last time ever. It was all tragic, of course, and the guilt would weigh on him forever—Spears explained mournfully—but it was just a twist of fate that was somehow written in the stars.

It was at some point the following morning that he heard about the plane crash and was distraught over what he feared was the loss of his best friend of 30 years. Driving along heartbroken and guilt-ridden, it was then that he began to consider—perhaps—that the Fates were offering him a new beginning. Maybe this was a golden opportunity to escape his federal abortion charges in Los Angeles—with an almost guaranteed prison term—and disappear.

It would undoubtedly be devastating to his lovely wife. Still, he would connect with her at some point—apologize profusely and beg her forgiveness—and then reestablish a home somewhere, probably in Mexico, with their two children and more than one million dollars in insurance money—which was, of course, a whole lot of pesos.

The agents were befuddled by Spears' nonchalant tale and the ease with which he delivered it. There was no sweat on his forehead, no shifting of the feet, no glancing eyes, no stammering or awkward pauses. The man was masterful, and for the first time, the trained FBI agents felt outmatched.

After Robert Spears finished his thorough and completely feasible explanation of his non-role in the crash of the airliner,

152 / Chapter 19

as well as the tragic loss of his closest friend, the interrogators began to realize that they had little substance to hold him on.

Although they felt that their own theories were undoubtedly correct, at the moment, they had nothing to back them up. Still, the idea of releasing a suspect who potentially downed an airplane full of innocent passengers to fake his own death and collect a million-dollar insurance payout was especially galling.

At the point that they were preparing to cut him loose, however, one of the agents happened to ask about Taylor's 1957 Plymouth that Spears had admitted to driving from Florida to Arizona. *Where was it? What happened to it?*

"Well, I drove it to Phoenix. I had a friend here in town, and I thought that would give me some time out of prying eyes to figure out what I was going to do . . . maybe go to Mexico."

"Did Mr. Taylor give you permission to drive his car to Arizona or, possibly, to Mexico?"

"Well, no, not exactly. I said I was going to drive it to Dallas and meet him there and he agreed."

"I understand, but did he ever say it was fine with him if you drove on through to Phoenix? Just asking for my notes here. . . ."

"No, he never said anything about that . . . not that he would have minded. . . ."

"Well, Mr. Spears, I guess we won't ever know that, will we? Because the airplane he was probably on is now at the bottom of the Gulf of Mexico."

"I suppose not."

"So, in that case, Mr. Spears, I'm placing you under arrest for violating the Dyer Act of 1919. Please stand and turn around and place your hands behind you."

As Robert Spears was being handcuffed and notified of his rights under the law, his face reflected the shock that the agents hoped they'd see. *The Dyer Act of 1919?* The Feds had, in fact, outfoxed their adversary, leading him into a trap without any awareness on his part. It was a sweet reward for three hours of hard work.

They had employed a strategy that had worked successfully on scores of suspects since Al Capone—underworld gang boss of a massive Chicago crime family. The mobster had been

The Look of a Worthy Adversary / 153

tripped up for the relatively minor oversight of not reporting revenue on his income tax return. The tax evasion charge was sufficient to get the gangster behind bars until they could sort out his other sordid crimes.

Similarly, the FBI was able to nab Spears on the barely known Dyer Act, which made it a crime to transport a car across state lines without the expressed permission of its owner. The law was originally enacted to collar members of stolen car rings but, to anyone's knowledge, it never had been applied to a case where someone had been handed the keys to a vehicle by a friend and welcomed him to drive it—especially in a situation where the car was never reported as stolen nor was there any complaint filed.

It was a unique angle, to say the least.

Still, though the charge might not stick—it was a bit of a technicality they knew—it was designed to buy the Feds enough time to dig deeper into the case and perhaps get one of his associates to flip or to work out some kind of a plea deal in exchange for the truth. There were 42 families, after all, who were grieving and hoping for some answers.

The press, which had surrounded the Bali-Hi and the plaza in front of the FBI Phoenix offices, clamored for information and news of the Dyer violation quickly made headlines.

Attorneys across the southwest dismissed the charges as silly and predicted that the Federal Government would ultimately be humiliated by their shortsighted decision. But the one thing that the FBI knew was that they had their man in custody. They would deal with the next steps as they unfolded.

Wasting no time, Spears was publicly perp-walked to an office down the street that was set up to serve as a temporary courthouse where he was to be formally arraigned for transporting a vehicle across state lines without permission. Mobbed by reporters as the contingent moved slowly along the sidewalk, one of the writers called out, "Hey, Bob, did you plant a bomb on that plane?"

With a look of shock—captured by press photographers—Spears yelled back over his shoulder, "No, oh my gosh, no!" The reporter wouldn't give up and asked, "Well then, where's

154 / Chapter 19

your friend, Al Taylor?" Slowing for a second, Spears replied, "I'll explain everything tomorrow. You'll hear it all tomorrow." Then, the authorities pushed him forward before the conversation could continue.

Once he arrived at the makeshift courtroom, Robert Spears stood before Commissioner Carey Wilson who had been pressed into action because of an overload in the federal court system. Wilson was tasked with the responsibility of determining whether or not there was enough of a basis to further hold Spears or release him.

"Mr. Spears, do you understand the charges being brought before you today? That is, a violation of the Dyer Act, which makes it a crime to transport a stolen car across state lines. Do you understand that, sir?"

Spears smiles politely and responds: "That's right, sir. Yes, I do understand that."

Wilson next asked Spears, "Sir, have you ever been convicted of a crime before in this state or any other? A state crime or a federal crime?"

"Well, yes, I've been in some trouble before." Spears nodded pleasantly as he responded.

"I see here, Mr. Spears, that the District Attorney has asked for a rather significant amount as a bond. $100,000, in fact. That implies you are a flight risk. Sir, do you think you will be able to make a bond in this amount?"

"I don't think so, sir. I don't believe I'll be able to make bond at this time."

"Well, I'm inclined to reduce that amount, Mr. Spears. You seem to be a good citizen, and this is a relatively minor charge for a bond of that size. I'm going to reduce it to $35,000. I could be wrong, but I hope you won't make me regret this act of compassion."

"That's all right, sir," Spears replied with a hint of a chuckle. "I doubt I could make bond even if you knocked off $30,000." Wilson smiled in return as his gavel came down. Spears was then returned to the Phoenix city jail, where the next round of interrogations began.

The FBI agents knew they probably had just a limited time with their suspect and wanted to get as much information as possible before some lawyer or family member got him cut loose.

Oddly enough, Spears didn't seem as concerned about the court proceedings as he did about getting a hold of some medicine seized in one of his suitcases. Demanding that it be returned to him immediately, he explained that he had a serious health condition and required the medicine regularly. The agents had no knowledge of this concern, but his request was dismissed and what would turn out to be a six-hour interrogation was soon launched.

Spears would eventually be ushered into a cell where his investigators would begin a time-proven technique called "stress interrogation," which involves allowing the alleged criminal to sleep for a few hours and then rousting him at odd hours for more questioning. Designed to rattle the prisoner into telling the truth, an officer recorded this note in Spears' file:

"The prisoner seems to be eating and sleeping well and showing no signs of nervousness despite being rousted up for four to six-hour rounds of questioning by teams of agents working in relays. The prisoner apparently remains unfazed by the activity."

Incredibly, this interrogation technique would continue for a very long two weeks. Spears was no worse for the wear. If anything, he seemed to be enjoying the cat-and-mouse chess match that it had become, perhaps even energized by it. His file would include the note: "The man is unruffled. He is sticking to his story, and there seems little doubt at this point that anything will change."

And they were correct.

Nothing would change for some time. The only person who appeared to be getting any mileage out of the entire affair was the teenage desk clerk at the Bali-Hi, who had become a small celebrity of sorts by continually retelling her story of Robert Spears' dramatic arrest—often reenacting it upon request.

Dolores Carlson, indeed, was the girl of the hour as reporters feasted on her recollections of "George Rhodes" dashing

156 / Chapter 19

through her lobby with suitcases hanging from his neck—bowling over motel manager James Pentkowski—and diving into the open taxi door. "Yep," she bragged with pride. "It was Mr. Rhodes, all right, and he went right through that very door!"

A photographer snapped her photo, but not before she took a moment to primp.

Photo 1 U.S. Army Airman— Robert Spears, age 24, served as a sergeant in the U.S. Army Air Service and was assigned to the 314th Aero Squadron, stationed at Stonehenge, which was attached to the Royal Flying Corp. *March 1918.*

Photo 2 Robert v. Spears Mugshot—Upon his arrest in March 1927 for mail fraud and then subsequently for forgery, a smartly attired Spears was sentenced as inmate 33914 to two years at the State Penitentiary in Jefferson City, Missouri. *October 4, 1928.*

Photo 3 William A. Taylor Mugshot—Arrested at the same time for running a fraud scheme with Robert Spears, Al Taylor (head shaved and in work clothes) is photographed as inmate 34323 at the Missouri State Penitentiary. *October 4, 1928.*

Photo 4 The Best Man—On the day of his wedding to Frances Massey, Dr. Spears, left, is shown with his best man Allen Taylor, who later rode the "Death Plane," as it was called in *Life* magazine, in Spears' place. *December 22, 1950.*

Photo 5 No Embezzlement—Dr. Robert Spears, former president of the Naturopath's Association of Texas, tells House investigators that he had only $8,200 in his Legislature Fund, not $56,000 as reported, and that he misappropriated none of it. *March 7, 1957.*

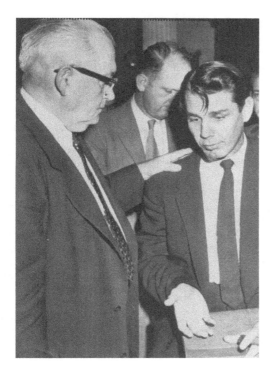

Photo 6 Out of My Hands—Dr. Robert Spears, former president of the Texas Naturopathic Assn., left, tries to talk with Rep. John Lee, member of the House Bribery Committee from Kermit, Texas. Rep. Lee said he would propose a motion to cite Dr. Spears for contempt in refusing to answer questions. *March 21, 1957.*

Photo 7 National Airlines—Flight 967 was a DC-7 (N 4891C), owned by Delta Air Lines and operated by National Airlines under the command of Captain Frank Eugene Todd, Copilot Dick Sheridan Beebee, and Flight Engineer George Henry Clark, Jr. *January 1959.*

Photo 8 Tampa International Airport—Opened in 1952, TIA was built to service three major airlines and the regional airport was considered one of the most modern at the time. It was instantly popular and opened up traffic to destinations from Los Angeles to New York. *November 1952.*

Photo 9 Ill-Fated Flight—Passengers board the first leg of a National Airlines JetStar flight in New York on their way to Miami. The flight was intended to continue on to Los Angeles through New Orleans and Dallas but went down shortly after takeoff from Tampa. *November 15, 1959.*

Photo 10 Airport Insurance—Vending machines selling flight insurance were familiar signs in the early 1950s. After a rash of airline accidents, pilots associations lobbied against the machines out of fear that they encouraged sabotage and by 1961 they had disappeared. *Circa 1958.*

Photo 11 Arizona Hideout—Robert Spears lived in this small desert home north of Phoenix, owned by William Turska, for about two months after being reported killed in the Gulf of Mexico air disaster. *January 1960.*

Photo 12 Voluntary Witness— William Turska puffs on a cigarette as he talks to newsmen in Phoenix after a four-hour session with FBI agents about the Robert Vernon Spears case. Turska requested the interview, later saying, "We just had a chit-chat." *January 23, 1960.*

Photo 13 Wants Answers— Mrs. Alice Steele Taylor talks to newsmen in her attorney's office while looking for answers regarding her missing former husband, Tampan William A. Taylor, who is believed to be among the passengers of a no-survivor plane crash. *January 22, 1960.*

Photo 14 MGM's Loomis—"There's nothing like exercise to make you feel young," says Charley Grapewin, right, a veteran actor who exercises daily under the direction of Donald Loomis, left, of Metro-Goldwyn-Mayer's physical education department. *September 9, 1967.*

Photo 15 Missing Man—Dr. Robert Spears, head down and wearing a wool cap, is guided by an agent out of the Phoenix FBI office to face awaiting newsmen. He was the missing man who was listed as a passenger on an ill-fated National Airlines plane. *January 21, 1960.*

Photo 16 Walk of Shame— Covering his face to protect his identity, Dr. Robert Spears, after his arrest at the Bali-Hai Motel in Phoenix, is escorted by FBI agents to the courthouse for arraignment on stolen car charges. *January 21, 1960.*

Photo 17 Inconsolable—Mrs. Janet Frank, widow of Julian Frank, an air crash victim who carried $900,000 worth of life insurance, hugs her two children, Andy, 2, and Ellen, 4, with her mother, Mrs. Karl Wagner at their home in Westport, Connecticut. *January 14, 1960.*

Photo 18 Abortion Tools—Lt. Herman "Bud" Zander of the Los Angeles Police Department's "Abortion Squad" reveals tools of the illegal trade as discovered under a cabinet during a raid. *Circa 1957.*

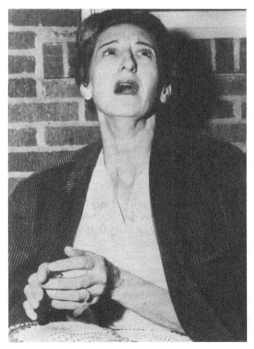

Photo 19 Back from Dead—Frances Spears, wife of "mystery man" Robert Spears, cries as she talks to newsmen after learning the FBI located her husband who was thought to be aboard a doomed airliner and presumed dead in the crash. *January 20, 1960.*

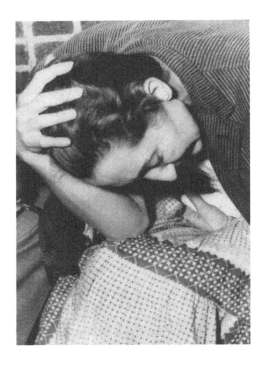

Photo 20 Shocked—Mrs. Robert Spears breaks down while talking about discovering that her husband, who she thought was dead, has been found by the FBI living under the name of George Rhodes in a Phoenix motel. *January 21, 1960.*

Photo 21 Confession—Mrs. Frances Spears, here with her attorney Charles Tessmer, admits that she saw her husband, Dr. Robert V. Spears, in Dallas after the plane crash in which 42 died. Mrs. Spears told newsmen that a prison crony of Dr. Spears, William Taylor, took his place on the ill-fated plane. *January 22, 1960.*

Photo 22 Sentenced—Well-dressed but solemn-faced Robert Vernon Spears, center, is handcuffed to other prisoners as he is led to U.S. District Court in Phoenix today. Spears, central figure in a suspicious airliner crash, was sentenced to five years for interstate transportation of a stolen car. *February 15, 1960.*

Photo 23 Guilty Plea—Robert Spears walks along a Phoenix sidewalk with other prisoners to his arraignment in federal court on a charge of interstate transportation of a stolen car. He pleaded guilty to the charge while still under investigation for the air crash that claimed 42 lives. *January 21, 1960.*

Photo 24 Mystery Man's Wife—A somber Frances Spears, wife of the mystery man in a suspected airliner crash, walks with two FBI agents toward a plane at the Phoenix airport after visiting her convict husband in jail. *March 4, 1960.*

Photo 25 Terminal Island—Inmate Robert Vernon Spears poses for picture taken by reporter Edmund Barker, during one of his interviews with Spears at the Terminal Island Federal Correctional Institution at San Pedro, California. *February 6, 1962.*

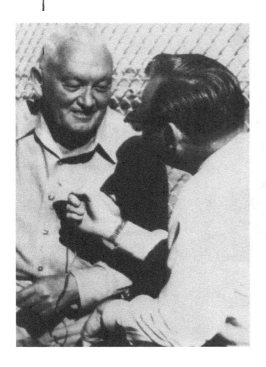

Photo 26 Bomb Plot—Robert Spears, left, is shown as he gives a taped interview to Edmund Barker of KRLD News Dallas, telling of a bomb that was carried aboard a National Airlines flight from Miami to Dallas by his former cellmate William "Al" Taylor. *February 3, 1960.*

Photo 27 Prison Boss—Olin G. Blackwell, warden of Alcatraz during Spears' incarceration, was a loose-lipped, fast-living, heavy drinker, nicknamed "Gypsy" by the guards and known as "Blackie" to his friends. *October 4, 1961.*

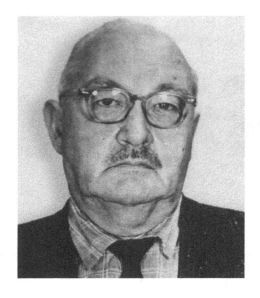

Photo 28 Dynamite—The FBI photograph of Dr. Robert Spears, taken for its picture file, following his arrest. This photograph was used for identification purposes by witnesses during the Bureau's extensive investigations. *January 21, 1960.*

SPEARS ASSOCIATE WARDENS RECORD CARD

Offense NMVTA
Sentence 5 years Begins 2-15-60
Date Imp. 2-15-60 At Phoenix, Ariz.
Date Rec'd 3-6-61 fr Terminal Island
Par. Elig. 10-14-61
C.R. 10-23-63 Max. 2-14-65
Comm. Fine G.T. 480 days
PREVIOUS RECORD:
Jails 2 Ref. 2
Pens. Fed. State 3
Detainers: Fed. State 1
Escapes: Fed. State
CUSTODY:
Crimes Involved: (Enumerate)
Using Mail to Fraud 2
Larceny & False Pretense 2
Armed Robbery 1
Abortion Criminal 2
Forgery & Parole Viol. 2
Aliases:
Robert Howard; Logan Hunter; Robert Lane; Lionel Ryan; Robert Buchanan.

Race White Age 6-26-94
Married yes Deps. 3
Citizen USA Relig. Prot.
Physical Cond. No Report
Mental Cond.
Education: S. A. T.
G. R. IQ 129
PSYCHOLOGICAL & APTITUDE TESTS:
Occupational Status: Subject claims to have been a doctor for many years. (Naturopath & Homeopath)
Avocational Interests: Hospital work
History of Occupational Experience
Occupations | No. Yrs. | Verification of Performance | Quality | Dependability

Springfield

Number 1493-AZ Residence Dallas, Texas Occupations

SPEARS, ROBERT VERNON

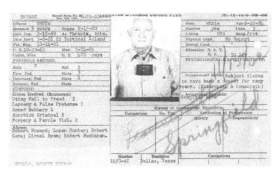

Photo 29 Alcatraz File—An identification card attached to the folder on Robert Vernon Spears, Alcatraz inmate 1493, which contains his personal information. *November 15, 1964.*

CRIMINAL HISTORY

NAME	NUMBER	CITY OR INSTITUTION	DATE	CHARGE	DISPOSITION OR SENTENCE
Logan Hunter	14822	Kansas City, Mo.	8-12-26	Con man	Rel to Fed. Officers
Robert V. Spears	24309	St. Louis, Mo.	3-29-27	Mail fraud	18 mos. LK
Robert Spears	33914	SP Jeff. City, Mo.	10-4-28	Forgery	2 Years
Robert Lane	63006	SP Columbus, Ohio	12-12-30	False Preten	1 to 7 Years
Robert Lane	13481	Asylum & D.C.Jail	4-8-33	Larc. af trust	
Robert Buchanan	7679	PD Ontario, Canada	5-18-33	False Pretense	1 Year
Robert Spears	27730	SO Miami, Florida	3-9-36	False Pretense	1 Year
Robert Spears	30718	SP Balto., Md.	3-8-37	Forgery	5 Years
Robert Spears	44201	SP McAlester, Okla.	3-18-42	Robb. 2nd.	4 Years
Robert Vernon Spears	25716	SO Dallas, Texas	12-12-58	Att abort.	$1000 Fine

(Please furnish all additional criminal history and police record on separate sheet)

Photo 30 Criminal History—The far-from-complete federal "rap sheet" for Dr. Robert Spears that was included in his prisoner file after he was arrested in Dallas for an attempted abortion at the Alamo Plaza Motel on March 3, 1958. *December 12, 1958.*

Chapter 20

From Out of the Sea!

Sweet pony-tailed teen Dolores Carlson was not the only one who was talking. Far from it. It was quickly obvious that anyone who had a part—major or minor—to play in this melodrama that had thoroughly captured the attention of America, was now ready to speak their mind and grab their share of the spotlight.

Suddenly—to the delight of reporters outside of that exclusive circle—others began to throw their hats into the ring of public opinion. If anyone had seen Spears—or whatever name he was using at the time—along his drives from Tampa to Phoenix, from Phoenix to Los Angeles, from LA to Vegas, and then later to Yuma, Eastern Nevada, Dallas, and who knew where else, soon they were coming out of the woodwork.

Still—through this rapidly developing story—Alice Taylor and Frances Spears were engaged in a caustic verbal interstate slugfest of their own, aided by their newspaper corner men. Words were flying between them constantly, and those in their camps fired up their emotions with every chance they got.

However, one day, in particular, would change everything and it would soon be Frances who would grab all of the headlines instead of Alice.

On the afternoon of January 20—at the same time as the chaotic scene at the Bali-Hi—newsman Eddie Barker of radio station KRLD and one of his photographers stopped by to see Frances and snap a photo of her holding up a picture of her husband to use for promotional purposes. None of them had heard any

158 / Chapter 20

news that day, nor was anything yet being reported from Phoenix, and they were all just chatting lightly while sipping coffee.

At some point, the maid walked in and announced that there was a call for Mr. Barker from his newsroom. Taking the receiver, he nodded a few times, asked, "Are you sure? Absolutely sure?" and then thanked the caller. Turning to Frances, his face solemn, he stated firmly, "Mrs. Spears, your husband is alive."

The shock of those words physically pushed her back into her seat as her hands flew up to cover her face. Then, appearing numb and dumbfounded, Barker related, "She got up, walked around, and said, 'What can I say? I told him it wouldn't work!' About ten minutes later, she seemed to break down. She cried for some time." The photographer was snapping photos throughout, capturing her agony.

It was an emotional scene. However, it was the phrase that Frances had used that caught Barker's attention: *"I told him it wouldn't work."*

The implications were obvious. First, Frances had spoken to her husband after the crash and knew full well he was alive. Second—and this was even more disturbing—the entire episode now appeared to have been orchestrated in advance. Barker shuddered at the thought. *Could this have been a fake death insurance plot?* However, he knew he had to keep this secret under wraps. The story of his lifetime, he felt, was about to get much better.

Frances quickly clammed up, and the men departed to develop the photos and to prepare for the evening broadcast announcing the fact that Robert Vernon Spears had been located in Phoenix and was now under arrest by the FBI. And, most importantly, Eddie Barker will have scooped them all. Soon, based on his reporting, a Dallas newspaper headline in large, bold type read, "'Dead' Dr. Spears Arises from Out of the Sea!"

Shaken to the core and clueless as to where to turn next, Frances quickly realized that she needed a lawyer. In part, he could help her manage the news of her husband's reappearance, but also the criminal charges and the questions that would surface regarding her claim for a million dollars in life insurance benefits—which she filed just two weeks after the crash.

From Out of the Sea! / 159

But there was one more thing. She knew almost from the beginning that Bob was alive, and she had elected not to notify the police or share that truth with anyone. She had read enough novels and seen plenty of television court programs to know that she could now be charged as an accessory to his crimes and be guilty of harboring a fugitive. Those were serious charges that could leave her two babies as orphans.

Panicking, she made a series of calls to try and locate Charles Tessmer, the family attorney, who was several hours away in Austin at the time. When she was finally able to reach him the attorney left his dinner in haste and rushed back toward Dallas.

In the meantime, Eddie Barker—inexplicably—had managed to convince Frances to go out onto her front porch to face some reporters, but really to get more photos of a distraught and confused woman. Contorting her face in agony as she sobbed, she ultimately collapsed, burying her head in her lap as a newsman wrapped his coat around her in the chilly January weather.

The excruciating series of photos from that event made the front page of nearly every newspaper.

Trying to avoid the sea of flashbulbs, she finally faced the throng of reporters and whispered in a raw, husky voice, "I'm numb. I have no comment. I have nothing to say. I don't feel anything. I don't know anything." When the newsmen pressed for more comments, Barker pushed them away with a hand, saying, "Leave her alone. Her kids have to have a bath."

More than annoyed by one of their own keeping the star of the story away from them, one of his fellow reporters yelled out derisively, "Are you going to give it to them, Eddie?" *Time* magazine, covering the case, in their next issue, said of Barker: "To the angry Dallas newsmen, Edmund Barker, news director of the local CBS outlet, seemed a traitor to the reportorial trade."

Frances was not complaining, however. From that point on, she referred to Barker as her press advisor.

Well past midnight, Tessmer eventually made the turn onto Gaston Avenue and was shocked to see blocks of the usually quiet neighborhood filled with vehicles of all kinds. Despite the early hours, there was a carnival atmosphere around the house.

160 / Chapter 20

"I recall thinking as I parked the car as close as I could to the house," the attorney would later recall. "That I'd never seen so many newsmen, television cameramen, newsreel men, and reporters gathered around the front of that structure."

The automobiles and trucks with their special press credential license plates were spread almost as far as the eye could see—parked haphazardly all around the area with no regard for either passing traffic or the lawns and driveways of the neighbors. "I was reminded at the time of a child's sandbox with the toy cars temporarily scattered and forgotten by their young owners," Tessmer would add.

Lights inside the house caused it to glow with warmth, but outside reporters and newsmen who had now swarmed the front yard were huddled in the cold, frustrated and angry not to get more access to Frances.

Some, holding their cameras, sat on the steps of the house. Others stood anxiously on the lawn, facing the house and fixed on the front door, desperately hoping for another speck of news before they had to rush off to meet morning deadlines. Around the neighborhood, people were hanging from windows, not wanting to miss a minute of the action.

As soon as Tessmer was spotted, people sprinted from all points to surround him in a giant circle, pushing microphones in his face and yelling out questions simultaneously.

"You know more than I do," Tessmer protested with a touch of humor as he strode up the sidewalk while trying to make some progress toward the house.

"Tell her it's for her own good to talk to us. She looks pretty broken up right now. We just want to get her side of the story. If she doesn't talk, it makes her look like she was part of it. Makes her look guilty."

Brushing them back, Tessmer replied, now a bit annoyed by the unrelenting pressure, "I am sure she will hold a press conference shortly. And I'm sure you will agree this has been a tremendous shock for her and her family. Let me talk to her. I'll see what I can do."

The flash bulbs popped, and strobe lights flared as the door opened to let Tessmer into the house. However, it closed quickly

From Out of the Sea! / 161

again, leaving the reporters even more frustrated. When the attorney entered, however, it was a concerning sight—his client was seated at a small table next to a man with a rolling portable tape recorder between them.

Tessmer stared hard at the bespectacled young man with the crew cut who rose as he entered. The lawyer knew him well. He was Eddie Barker, of course, the news director for radio station KRLD, who had been camping out with Frances for some time.

Although his client appeared unsettled, she was far from hysterical. Despite the late hour, she thanked him for coming so quickly from such a distance and then offered him a cup of coffee.

"Mrs. Spears, you have absolutely nothing to fear," the lawyer said reassuringly. "You knew nothing about it, of course."

"But she did know," Eddie Barker said proudly. "She told me all about it."

Tessmer immediately turned and glared at the reporter with daggered eyes and began shaking his head. "My first thought was how could I get this jerk outta here," he later confided. "The guy had the potential to blow up the case before it was even underway. He was such an idiot!"

In short order, the attorney was disturbed to find that Frances had been pouring out her heart for hours to someone who might not be acting in her best interests. With just a cursory listen, the lawyer realized that she was sharing far too much—especially to a member of the press—and was revealing information that could put her in jeopardy.

Equally concerning was that even at this early morning hour, newsmen were still camped outside, and the attorney had no idea who else she might have spoken to. Something needed to be done, and Tessmer went into damage control.

While shooing everyone away, the reporters still clustered outside expressed their unhappiness when the attorney told them that a press conference would not be in the immediate future. Next to go was a wounded and furious Barker—who had been discussing the situation in detail with Mrs. Spears "over a period of many hours from around four in the afternoon until a

162 / Chapter 20

little past three o'clock the following morning when her attorney finally arrived."

After Barker was given the door, speaking to his client alone until the sun began to come up, Tessmer encouraged Frances to take the sleeping pills her doctor had prescribed and get some much-needed rest.

Still wanting to stay in the good graces of Frances—and protect his exclusive position with her—Barker took it upon himself to send a telegram without her knowledge to Robert Spears in the Phoenix jail: "The babies and I are well and thinking of you." Tessmer later shared that Barker signed it with a message so personal, so inappropriate, that he would not reveal it to anyone.

Nearly 1,200 miles away in Tampa, Florida, as Frances Spears was trying to recover from the shock of discovering that her husband was in FBI custody and after being harshly lectured by her attorney for talking too much, another wife in this melodrama was attending a morning tea.

Alice Taylor had come from prestige and money and would carry herself with the sophistication of a society matron throughout her life. Not that the Taylors had money and not that her husband had ever come close to making them rich—though there was no doubt he was a hard worker—but Alice's roots went deep. She always had an air about her regardless of her personal situation.

On this particular Wednesday, Alice was surprised to find her house surrounded by news vans and reporters when she pulled into her driveway. Something must be up, she assumed, but she really hadn't a clue what it might be. As soon as she put her Cadillac in park, the reporters crowded around her door—some with microphones, others with notepads and pens.

"Have you heard? Have you heard the news, Mrs. Taylor? Any comment for us?" a reporter from the back of the crowd called out. "Have you heard that Robert Spears is alive and has been arrested in Phoenix?"

Alice's first words in response were interesting: "Of all the times not to be home!" she replied and then added, "But I'm

From Out of the Sea! / 163

overjoyed that they finally found Dr. Spears—what a character he is! I loathe him! The finger of scorn has been pointed at my husband Al for so long, but in all the years I've known him, he was never a bad man."

Inviting the reporters into her home—being the perfect hostess that she was raised to be—she calmly answered questions. However, she never held back when it came to displaying her hatred for the man she believed long ago perverted her husband and ruined their home. For some time, she ranted on about the evils of Robert Spears and maintained she would pray that he would get the maximum penalty that the law allowed for downing an entire airliner.

"All along, I've had the premonition that Mr. Taylor was aboard that plane, and I've never deviated from it," she told the assembled writers in her cultured, measured voice. One reporter would later comment that "there was almost a steely gleam in Alice's eye as she spoke." She continued imperiously, "I am waiting for Dr. Spears to tell me what happened to Mr. Taylor. I suppose they will get a confession out of him."

Reporters took note that she never commented on the fact that the appearance of Robert Spears meant, in effect, that her own husband was now probably officially among the dead. It appeared to be a secondary issue.

Eventually, Alice politely ushered out the newsmen and headed to her room to gather her thoughts. This had indeed been a monumental day, and she tried to take stock of the significance of it all. Foremost in her thoughts was the relief that she had been vindicated.

After weeks of arguing that it was Spears who placed Al in that seat on Flight 967 to fake his own death and work an insurance scam, it was finally her version of the story that proved to be the truth.

And now that bitch Frances Spears could shut her mouth for good.

But Alice Taylor was far from done. Committed to making the most of her moment of triumph, before she said farewell to the reporters, she announced that she would be holding a press conference at the offices of her attorney on the following day. At that time, she would provide further details on the days that

164 / Chapter 20

preceded the fatal crash concerning her husband—information that had never been previously released.

The next morning, a large contingent of reporters eagerly gathered at the downtown offices of Robert Mann, crowding the corridors in anticipation of hearing a now-unfettered accounting of events by Mrs. Taylor. Alice hadn't proven to be the publicity hog that she saw Frances Spears as—steadfastly refusing to allow any photos taken of her. However, she would now be unleashed after the FBI nabbed Spears.

Arriving well in advance of the announced time, the journalists began to become concerned when nothing happened as the hour lapsed. Then, Robert Mann, dressed smartly in a gray, pin-striped suit, stepped out and spoke. "I regret to inform you that we will not be having a press conference today."

There was an immediate uproar. Mann was soon inundated with a barrage of questions from angry reporters demanding an explanation.

"Mrs. Taylor has consented to an exclusive interview with *Life* magazine, and she needs to have her hair done by a stylist in anticipation of providing a photograph for the story." The reporters were incensed by the obvious slight. They were the ones who had provided Alice Taylor with the platform she so desired and now they were being shunted for the national press.

Alice would never recover the goodwill she had so enjoyed from the press prior to this decision.

In an attempt to get back in their good graces, however— and to counteract the front-page coverage Mrs. Spears had been receiving in Dallas—Alice ultimately began to dish out her highly anticipated "back story" about the days leading up to the doomed flight and the activities of her husband about which no one else, to this point, had become aware.

The morning following the *Life* interview, Alice Taylor began her story with the events that had occurred just two days before the date of the crash when her husband received a call from Spears saying that he had recently arrived in town and was staying at the Hillsboro Hotel. Inviting Al to join him for dinner, the two had a good time—several diners remember the pair laughing together—and then left to drive over to nearby St.

Petersburg to meet with a friend. Oddly, she noted, they didn't return until the next morning.

This meeting, on Friday the 13th, and the identity of the person—who was referred to in correspondence only as "the fellow"—would remain one of the great unsolved mysteries in the case. Investigators would always believe this individual held some significance to the eventual crash of Flight 967.

Chapter 21

Zombies and Aliens

An in-depth review of the FBI records regarding this aspect of the mystery, however, may provide some insight into Spears' activities at this time, especially as they relate to Al Taylor and the St. Petersburg "fellow." That in turn could also reveal some of the most important pieces of the puzzle that may explain exactly what was building up during those last fateful days and hours before Flight 967 exploded into a million pieces, taking 42 innocent souls with it.

This chapter of the Spears saga seems to have kicked into gear when the doctor and his best friend came into possession of a recipe for something they called "the gook."

It would appear that the pair had finally located a formula for creating a pharmaceutical concoction that had the potential to change the face of the abortion industry in America and around the world. More importantly to Spears and Taylor, it would make them wealthy beyond their wildest dreams.

According to the FBI's investigation, it's reasonable to assume the plot—if it can be called that—unfolded during the week before Flight 967's scheduled departure.

Taylor, it would appear, had stumbled across an individual—a mad scientist in the world of abortions—who had created a formula for a substance that, when applied vaginally, would cause the mother to abort her fetus up to almost any point. This had him seeing dollar signs unlike anything he previously had imagined.

168 / Chapter 21

After sharing his discovery with his best friend Bob Spears, the two were anxious to grab hold of a business opportunity where Spears could create a product—or have it made for them—and Taylor could distribute it, thus bringing the two good friends together in a venture. It's not unreasonable to surmise that "the St. Pete fellow" was the chemist who had literally cooked up the perfect recipe, and Spears had canceled a well-advertised speaking engagement in order to spend a day and night with him.

Robert Spears, in fact, was quick to brag about this new business venture and not shy about boasting of its potential. In a letter to Frances, written just shortly before Flight 967 was scheduled to depart, he addressed this poultice as "the gook."

> Have been cooking gook since last night and it should be done by noon tomorrow. Then my work will be done as soon as I get it dished up. The folks want the recipe, but I don't want everyone to know what I put in my stew. At first, I thought I'd let'em have it, but decided not to.
>
> I found out one thing, however, if I do very much of this I'll have to get a steam cooker in order to save time and have every batch come out the same. It will be simple to have an electric cooker that can be plugged into any wall socket so that I don't have to stand over a stove for hours.

In a first interview with FBI agents, Frances maintained that she did not know the name of the person Dr. Spears was to contact in Tampa to cook and distribute his "gook." In a follow-up interview, however, she amended her statement to say that she "could not divulge the identity of the person who was contacted by Dr. Spears," implying she knew the man's name.

When it was pointed out by the agents that on several prior occasions she had furnished conflicting information as to whether or not she knew the identity of the doctor who her husband was involved with in the "gook" project, "she claimed that if agents misinterpreted her remarks to conclude she knew who this individual was, that was a mistake and she vigorously claimed she did not know the identity of the doctor. She then

Zombies and Aliens / 169

declined to discuss the matter and refused to make any further comment about it."

Clearly Frances Spears was being obfuscative regarding the topic but it did not mean that she was sharing more with her husband. During those final ill-fated days in Tampa, Robert somewhat mysteriously wrote three letters to his wife just prior to the National Airlines flight and sent them by airmail to their Dallas home.

Eventually, the FBI obtained these and were surprised to find that the "gook project" was at the center of much of that correspondence. Robert Spears had written to his wife:

> It appears that this deal will work out better than expected. The income from this source should amount to $1,000 or more a week [$10,000 today] with just what I can work up by myself. We should do quite well with this.
>
> Have been cooking up batches of "gook" since the previous night and it will not be ready until noon tomorrow. I should be all wrapped up by Saturday and then on my way home on Sunday to see you and the kids.

Frances Spears would later explain to FBI agents that her husband would often be "cooking something like gook on the stove in the kitchen, trying to find the right recipe." My understanding was that the cooking of gook is necessary for making an abortion paste, and that other doctors familiar with abortion activities do not know about the cooking process.

"I want to be clear that I don't know all of the components or ingredients of 'gook' but I have, at times, observed my husband boiling down soap, which I believed to be Lilly soft soap. He would need to boil it for long periods of time to reduce it to a paste. I do not know what he put into the soap before or after to make what he calls 'his gook.'"

In an attempt at transparency, Bill Turska would provide more information on the process of making gook. "The base for the 'gook' was a green 'soft soap' which was commonly placed in opaque white dispensers for use in public restrooms. This material is no longer carried in the American market, but Spears

170 / Chapter 21

had access to thirty-some barrels of the stuff. He said he could make a fortune on it.

> Spears told me he got a hold of his soap supply from a doctor out of Massachusetts who had it and that he paid $5,000 [$50,000 today] for the gook formula from a German fellow. I have no actual knowledge as to the effectiveness of this "gook" and I've not used any myself. I've never actually heard of any "foolproof" formula which would induce an abortion, without the use of Instruments.
>
> I did hear, however, that the preparation of KY Jelly, mixed with the right proportions of potassium iodide, is effective for abortion purposes. KY Jelly—a jellied, glycerine-based product—can be obtained practically anywhere. Once Spears suggested, or indicated in some way, that dynamite could also be boiled down to obtain a glycerine which could later be used in the preparation of the "gook."

Dr. Wenton Welch, another friend of Spears in Dallas and a successful osteopath, later noted for FBI agents that Spears, around this time, stated that he had just gotten some "hot news" from a friend of his in Florida named William Allen Taylor.

> Approximately two weeks after this phone call, Taylor came to Dallas and stayed at the Statler Hilton Hotel. He was coming for the purpose of arranging to have Spears "cook up" a medicine to be used in abortions. According to Dr. Spears, a product known as Lilly Soft Soap, which has been recently withdrawn from the market, is the main base for making this abortion medicine.
>
> He told me Taylor, who was engaged in the business of selling this medicine to unknown individuals in Florida, had been unable to acquire any of this type of soap or a similar type soap. Spears had informed him that he could obtain a similar type soap which could be used for this abortion medicine.
>
> Spears and Taylor then formed an agreement to split any profit from this operation fifty-fifty, and Spears had estimated they could gross at least $1,000 a week [$10,000 today] through this cooperation. Spears said he had a contact where he could get this soap and then manufacture the medicine and Taylor would sell it.

Zombies and Aliens / 171

It was decided that since there was a risk involved in shipping it interstate that Spears would come to Florida and manufacture the medicine from this soap and would then turn it over to Taylor for sale while he himself returned to Dallas. I believe this type soap that Spears had access to came in eighty pound kegs and is the type used to make liquid soap such as is used in public washrooms.

The FBI were flabbergasted when they heard Dr. Welch's testimony because it filled in several gaps in the story, suggested a possible motive, and hinted at a potential cause of the explosion that brought down Flight 967.

Two things were now distinct possibilities.

First, since Spears was convinced that this new gook represented a million-dollar product, he was now faced with sharing the income in a 50/50 split with Taylor. Al might have been his best friend, but Spears—since his youngest days—was infected with greed and an aversion to work. It was entirely possible that he had decided that he was not anxious to split the revenue. The fact that his friend often said, "I want to disappear," didn't hurt.

Second, it had always been problematic that someone could bring sticks of dynamite onto a plane without it being noticed. They would have been both heavy and bulky especially when combined with a timer and the necessary wiring.

But now, Turska had introduced the idea of boiling down dynamite—as crazy as it might seem—into a glycerin or gelatin-like substance which would be light and easily moved. In fact, the FBI brought in an explosives expert, Mr. John Bilderback, to test this theory.

"In this reduced, gelatinous form, the substance is known as nitroglycerin but commonly referred to by thugs as 'jelly.' The jelly is detonated by a cap or fuse. It is a common method for blasting Texas oil wells where 'nitro' is ignited with a blasting cap and a timer. The cap can be triggered by something as ordinary as a flashlight battery."

Then he added: "Nitroglycerin is extremely dangerous and extremely powerful but it is also extremely volatile and it can easily be set off by simply jarring a container."

172 / Chapter 21

Next to add to the evolving story was an interview with Bessie Price, a relative of Frances, who worked at Texas Instruments in downtown Dallas. Her company, interestingly enough, built and sold electric timers, often to be used in photography. In a short matter of time, the FBI had located places around Dallas where Spears could have purchased dynamite for easily transported nitroglycerin, a timer, and blasting caps, and wiring such as was found in his home during the search.

Things were starting to fall into place.

On Saturday—the evening before the National Airlines plane was scheduled to depart—Robert took a break from cooking gook to meet with Al Taylor at the Rib Room in the Hillsboro Hotel—this time along with Al's 18-year-old son, Junior—to celebrate their upcoming venture. As the meal ended, the trio went up to Spears' room to further their conversation. Junior would later share more about that meeting with Art Smith of the *Tampa Tribune*.

"They were in good spirits and jovial, I'd say. It seemed to me like they were celebrating something—toasting and cheering—as if a good thing was about to happen, something real big. I found it odd that my father was flashing a lot of cash because, well, he usually didn't have that much. He showed me $600 [around $6,000 in current value] and was kinda waving it around boastfully."

Alice, however, according to her recollection of this time, said that the next day something was wrong. "Al drove to see me and Junior, but my son wasn't home at the time. Al kept checking his wristwatch and looked anxious to leave," she recalled. "He couldn't wait—he took off like a teenager. He was nervous and agitated—very disturbed. When he left in his car, he took off so fast I wondered what on earth was wrong."

Al wasn't gone long before he called back to the Taylor house on Jefferson Street in Tampa and checked again to see if Junior had returned. He hadn't. Two more, nervous and unsettling calls followed. Al very much needed to speak to his son, he explained. All of this upset Alice, who, by this time—based on Junior's comments to her about the meeting at the

Zombies and Aliens / 173

Hillsboro—was convinced that Bob Spears was responsible for her husband's strange behavior.

"I was so angry that I went right into the kitchen to call Spears at the hotel and give him a piece of my mind," she confided. "But I was told that the guest in that room had already checked out. That was at 3:05, I remember, and it made me think that perhaps that was the reason my husband was in such a sweat. My feeling at the time was that he needed to get down there to the hotel before checkout time to pick up Spears.

"Then, around seven that evening, I got a final call from Al. That's when he told me that he was on his way later that night to go to Atlanta about a job. For some reason, he told me not to tell Junior about the trip." Unbeknownst to Alice, Al next called his boss at Pioneer and got permission to take off the next morning, Monday, November 16, saying that he would probably be back at work after lunch.

"That was odd," she later told a reporter. "Because he had told me he'd be flying back from Atlanta the next night and then would call me. The whole thing seemed more and more strange. Al had never said anything about an out-of-state job interview, and it made no sense because he made good money at Pioneer and lived close to us in Tampa. Also, Christmas was just around the corner."

That same evening, several patrons at Morrison's Cafeteria—just down the road from the Tampa Airport—spotted Taylor. In fact, a waitress remembered having a lengthy conversation with him.

Florence Holcomb, the head cashier, would cause quite a buzz when she revealed to reporters that on that night—just an hour and a half before Flight 967 was to board—"He was eating alone, but I remember he was heading to Dallas because we had a waitress now living in Fort Worth, and I said he should look her up. He just laughed and paid his bill. He also told me he was in a bit of a hurry because his flight was leaving soon. He left the diner at about 10:30, I recall."

As Sunday evening, November 15, 1959, rolled past midnight, Taylor—"a man in a light brown suit"—was seen rushing to the insurance vending machine to purchase a one-way flight

174 / Chapter 21

policy. He provided the key information—National Airlines Flight 967—signed the form, then dropped in six quarters to receive a policy worth $37,500 and made his son the beneficiary. The transaction was time-stamped at 12:16 am, and the flight was in the air by 12:32.

Several at the airport that night remember him carrying a brown paper-wrapped package—"like a shoebox"—under his arm that day.

Al Taylor's car should have been in the airport parking lot that evening, but it was not. Clearly missing, the authorities would eventually put out an all-points bulletin for it. "The fact that my husband's car was found in Dr. Spears' possession delights me no end," she told the assembled reporters. "It gave the FBI a basis to hold him in custody. Thank goodness for the Dyer Act!"

All of this deeply reinforced that she had been right all along about the evil influence of Robert Spears since the first day she met him. Alice would never pass up the opportunity to demean and discredit him and lay the blame for everything that happened at his feet.

She also went one step further. "I also believe that Dr. Spears may have hypnotized my husband, and that's why he boarded the plane with a package handed to him by the doctor. Spears was a known hypnotist—an expert, I am told—and it only confirms my suspicions about this evil man."

Reporters would later track down hypnotist Melvin Powers of Los Angeles, who admitted to teaching Spears some of the dark arts with what he termed "my hypnotizing disk." Spears would, in fact, hypnotize his wife during her two childbirths and admitted with pride that he used it from time to time in his medical practice. This was supported by the fact that police found more than two dozen books on hypnotism in Spears' home.

More surprising was the fact that the FBI located Bessie Price, one of Spears' in-laws, who stated that he would on occasion demonstrate his hypnosis prowess at family reunions. After hypnotizing Frances, he was able "to stick a needle deep into her

Zombies and Aliens / 175

hand and she would have no apparent reaction whatsoever to what should have been great pain."

Frances later confided in Bessie that "this was no parlor trick, it's just hypnotism." With a bit of a bite, Mrs. Price added: "He would do this just for the entertainment of the members of the family who were present at the time."

Special agents also were able to secure witness testimony that revealed Spears' took regular trips to Florida over a four-year period to develop his hypnotist skills from an advanced practitioner there. Interesting to the agents was the fact that Al Taylor accompanied Spears on the last of these visits, only days before Taylor boarded that ill-fated National Airlines plane. This lended some credibility to the popular theory that Taylor had been hypnotized to think he was, in fact, Robert Spears when he boarded the flight.

More importantly, Alice Taylor, in a single interview, had now planted the seeds of a delicious conspiracy, and the papers were quick to run with it. Over the two-day period when Alice began to talk following the announcement of Spears' arrest in Phoenix, *more* than two thousand articles were written and published in newspapers across America.

At the same time that outrageous science fiction movies featuring zombies and aliens were delighting movie goers in theaters and drive-ins throughout the country, the idea of a hypnotized, stumbling, mindless, bomb-carrying plane passenger was simply too tasty to resist.

Chapter 22

The Story of a Strange Love

Because readers were generally taken by Alice Taylor's sophisticated and measured dialogues, Tony Schiappa and Art Smith of the *Tampa Times* knew they had a gold mine as the go-to journalists whom Alice most trusted and who guaranteed that her message would always be delivered accurately.

A little more than a thousand miles away, Eddie Barker knew he had his work cut out for him. In a fight to the death for column inches in the national press, the Dallas broadcaster needed to counter the inroads Alice, Tony, and Art had recently been making on his turf. So, he reloaded his journalistic guns and launched a salvo with a story that came to be headlined, "Doctor's Wife Shocked, Sedated Over Story."

Turning to blatant emotionalism, Barker began to turn to heartbreak as his new approach. With photos of a sobbing wife and mother accompanying every article—Frances' face often hideously wrenched and contorted—the story now centered around the woman's unfathomable pain. Oddly, in this case, she had discovered her husband was alive and not at the bottom of the sea.

Barker also introduced the idea of the persecution of this simple mother of two babies at the hands of a callous FBI. In a featured and syndicated newspaper article, the sensationalist newsman related her sad tale of woe. The opening paragraphs cast an odd shadow over the entire story:

178 / Chapter 22

> This is the story of a strange love. Frances Spears is 29 years younger than her husband. Severely thin and tall and one of 10 children, she perhaps had little male companionship when she was a young lady. You get the idea, after being around her, that here was a woman who needed affection and love.
>
> Dr. Spears evidently gave Frances Spears that affection and love. Tearful, bewildered, and distraught—Frances is standing by her husband as any good woman would. But the real story is in the full measure in which she returns it.

The article went on to state that she "closes her eyes to his 33-year record of fraud, forgery, vagrancy and armed robbery," at the same time that the FBI is also investigating if Dr. Spears had a hand in sabotaging the National Airlines plane that crashed in the Gulf of Mexico.

"He was so good to me and to the babies," sobs Mrs. Spears in the article. "He was such a good husband. I know if there was a bomb on that plane, Bob Spears didn't do it. He is just not that kind of a person. He is kind. He loves his children."

Ed Barker explained that he asked her once if she still loved her husband. "Love is not something you forsake just because somebody is in trouble. I'll stick by him as long as I can." In the radio broadcast, Barker added that Spears was sought in eight states for eight indictments.

Barker held the position in his article that it was difficult to see Frances Spears as anything other than a troubled mother and even more difficult to believe she had any inkling of the fantastic role her husband had lived.

"She was a 25-year-old secretary, and he was a jovial and successful, middle-aged man of nearly 60 when they married in 1950," Barker explained. "The family pictures she showed me reflect her happiness then and her joy as the children arrived. In the furnishings, the family pictures, the children, and the very atmosphere of their beautiful two-story brick house is told in the story of a normal, happy family.

"In them all, you get the idea that this is what Frances Spears wanted all along."

A radio and television broadcast accompanying the newspaper article lasted over an hour and a half. In it, Barker recorded

The Story of a Strange Love / 179

an emotional interview with Frances Spears and the stress and depression of her current realities eeked through. She began by apologizing.

"I'm sorry, but I guess I'm still recovering from what happened earlier today," she explained penitently. "FBI agents woke me up before dawn while I was still in a deep sleep induced by sedatives my doctor had prescribed for me. They had me sign a letter of consent for them to search my home, which I agreed to. Then they removed my personal letters and address books and appeared particularly interested in Bob's collection of several dozen books on hypnosis."

Then the interviewer asked the question that everyone had been wondering if not voicing aloud: "Frances, I must ask, did you try and get your husband to turn himself in?"

Without pausing even a second, she replied, "Yes, desperately so. I begged him to call Mr. Tessmer. I had been in such pain just wanting to contact the authorities while he was in Dallas weeks earlier, but at the same time, I had a strong desire to protect my husband.

"I decided I had to wait until someone in authority either contacted me or I made up my mind to contact someone in authority. I needed some time. Robert had protected me all my life. It was the only thing I could do under the circumstances. I just simply couldn't turn him in. I just couldn't at that time."

As the interview drew to a close, Barker asked Frances if she still loved her husband after all the trouble he had brought on the family. She smiled forlornly and replied softly, "I've always loved him. I still love him . . . you don't blot out ten years of your life just because someone's in trouble."

Frances Spears had glossed rather quickly over the search of her home on January 21—which was both extensive and time-consuming and produced a treasure chest of important evidence including what was listed as "bomb wiring," assorted timing devices, packing material and a number of items relating to the practice of abortions.

These included, according to FBI reports, extension lights and cords, one medical tool manufactured by "Dittmar Stainless," a medical tool which appears to be a long needle-like tool

180 / Chapter 22

with an eye on one end, medical forceps, a "used" porcelain pan, small yellow plastic sheets, and one tube of "Abbocillin-DC" with a syringe and needle.

Interesting, too, was a supply of towels stolen from the Maurice Hotel and the Alamo Plaza Courts motel. After the FBI left, they notified Mrs. Spears that she was not to leave her house nor be in contact with anyone other than her lawyer and her doctor.

Later that evening—and less than 24 hours after her husband had been arrested—Frances saw herself on the local CBS station and buried her face in shame. Her sick children by her side, she heard herself talk about her virtually impossible situation:

> I have told the authorities everything I know about the case. And I admit that I have been untruthful with the reporters. I did meet my husband at the Lakewood Hotel some weeks ago after Mr. Turska came to my house and delivered a handwritten note from Bob. At first I thought it was a trick. But I had to know. I hope people understand. . . .
>
> I asked him, of course, about what had happened, and he told me that he had driven Taylor's car so that Al could fly here to have his injured neck repaired. Once Spears learned of the airliner crash he saw an opportunity—I guess you could say—to leave me and the babies with some financial security. He felt he had been a burden on us, and it was a chance to free us of that burden.

"But why wouldn't your husband contact you from the road to put your mind at ease, to keep you from grieving so terribly as you did?" It was a question everyone in America was undoubtedly asking.

"Well, Bob told me when we met that he had blacked out after he heard the news about the crash of the National Airlines jet, though he somehow was able to keep driving. It wasn't until he arrived in Benson, Arizona—about three hours south of Phoenix—that he started to recall everything that had happened. That made sense to me."

Eddie seemed—or acted—confused by her statements and odd explanations and said, "Mrs. Spears, I have to ask . . . why in the world would Al Taylor just up and go to Dallas without telling anyone? It makes no sense."

It would be Frances' response to that question that would once again light the fires of fury and vengeance in Alice Taylor watching the same broadcast a thousand miles away.

"Well, Mr. Barker, my husband told me that Al's ex-wife was giving him a rough time, and he wanted to get away from her. He said she was a mean woman and terrible to be around. Personally, I have little use for Al's wife as she gave him a 'dog's life' for many years."

With that bit of cattiness delivered by her nemesis through a national platform, Alice Taylor was ready to explode.

Chapter 23

Heroes in the Spotlight

After the wives of the two principal characters in this bizarre mystery had proven that it was possible to become celebrities for inexplicable reasons, William Turska—consummate self-promoter and eternal entrepreneur—was not about to let such a golden opportunity pass him by. Even if it was for his own tainted involvement in this sordid affair, at the moment, he saw himself as the brightest star in this ever-evolving drama, and he expected to play it for all it was worth.

In fact, after thinking it over carefully, he decided to edit reality and make himself the hero of the tale. Now, it was Turska himself who helped capture the most wanted man in America. Now, he was the source of information that the press was clamoring for.

Instead of being an accomplice and harboring a fugitive, Turska—in his new telling—was the one working with authorities to bring a criminal, and the suspect in a heinous crime to justice. It would not be an easy transition—Spears, after all, was one of his best and only friends—but the challenge was exciting, and the payoff immeasurable to his ego.

Turska contacted the media himself and offered to provide them with the "true story"—the one in which he is the star—and he quickly became a literal quotation machine. The first bombshell he dropped was the fact that blasting caps—dynamite—were found in Spears' possession when he was arrested. This was a stunning turn, and immediately, reporters made the

183

184 / Chapter 23

connection between an explosive-toting fugitive and an airliner that was downed by the detonation of a bomb.

Next, Bill Turska was proud to reveal that it was he, in fact, who had contacted the FBI after visiting with his attorney. Once he had Spears safely checked into Room 208 at the Bali-Hi under the alias of George Rhodes, Turska explained that he went to the Feds immediately, wanting to do the only right thing. It was he who delivered the conman to the FBI.

The more he talked, however—and he talked a lot—the more he began to develop an uneasy feeling that he might be actually incriminating himself. His intuition was correct, and, as a result, he spent the better part of the following day in the Phoenix offices of the Federal Bureau of Investigation. The interrogators pressed hard in an attempt to better determine Turska's role in the entire puzzling affair while he continually shifted in his seat and tried to recall what he had already said.

Eventually released—and having thoroughly confused the investigators—he realized that the best thing he could do was argue his case through the media. Reporters had been waiting for hours outside of the FBI doors, where they hoped to finally be rewarded when he emerged. That moment came in the afternoon when he stood on the front steps, smug and imperious.

Then, making a bit of a show of it—though pausing long enough for photographers to snap his photo—Turska began to sprint down the sidewalk to escape the mob and build the suspense. As soon as he was in the clear, however, he immediately called several reporters and welcomed them—as the chosen ones—to an "exclusive press conference" to be held at his home.

As dusk began to settle on the New River outpost, Bill Turska—dressed nattily in a brown fedora with matching suitcoat and polka-dot bow tie—and the contingent of newsmen gathered at the rather shabby clapboard ranch house, which prominently featured peeling paint, dying cactus, and a rusty water heater alongside the front door.

"I barely knew Robert Spears, to be absolutely honest with you," he began as reporters scribbled on their notepads. Smoking an unfiltered cigarette down to the nub, Turska continued to glory in his moment in the spotlight. "I really only knew him from our common interests as naturopathic physicians. We served on boards and committees at the association level, that sort of thing."

How did Dr. Spears happen to come to your home while he was on the run? The reporters want to know.

"We had passed at one of our annual conferences some years back, and I, you know, told him if he was ever in the area, to just look me up. He was always welcome. It was really nothing more than that. Frankly, I was quite surprised to see him."

What was the man like? Did you ever feel afraid of him or feel uneasy around Dr. Spears?

"Hell no, it was as easy going as it ever was. Bob loved to make cornbread, and it was delicious, too. He'd mix it up, then bake it, and then had to slice it up just so, and turn it so it wouldn't steam up. He helped me put in a new bathroom and build a patio. Even paid for a section of water piping to the new bathroom out of his own pocket. You couldn't ask for a man to be more generous with gifts and gratuities."

Did he ever talk to you about the downed Flight 967 jetliner or explain his connection to it?

"No, not at all. He never once talked about it. In fact, I never even knew about the plane crash until I heard it on the radio or TV some days later. We don't really get any newspapers out here, you know, we're away from all such things. I'll tell you, though, it struck me like a bolt out of the blue when I heard it!"

So, what did the two of you do? What did you talk about? How did you spend your time?

"Well, it was just a casual, easy-going time. We mostly chit-chatted about medicine and the state of naturopathy, and some business opportunities connected with that. He was a good cook so we had some real nice meals, I'll tell you. He was never anxious or nervous or anything. He missed his family and spoke of them often. No one ever came by, and anyone else that tells you otherwise is lying."

Tell us about the dynamite you discovered. Where was it? How much was there?

"When he first arrived, he said he just came by to get some rest and relaxation in the desert air, but then one day, I found

186 / Chapter 23

a 50-pound crate of dynamite in a small shed back around my house, and I wondered how the heck it got there. I didn't find it until after he was gone, though. When I did, I told the cops about it straight away. I have a medical clinic and don't want no explosives anywhere near the place!"

There are reports that Dr. Spears had learned hypnotism and was an expert in the practice of it. Any comment on that?

"Oh yes, Bob Spears was quite proficient in hypnotism. Modern medicine—which is a monopoly and a conspiracy, by the way—dismisses such things, but there are many keys to health, and hypnotism is surely one of those."

When did you grow concerned about Spears' activities, or when did you begin to think something might be up that made you want to contact the authorities?

"I'm not really sure. I began to hear some rumors when I was in town once about something to the effect he was being sought for questioning. I wasn't really sure what it was about—so I contacted my lawyer to see what he might advise. He said to get the man out of my house and then call the police, actually the FBI. I signed the motel register for him because he was a very sick man at that time. He was suffering from flu and bronchitis."

Though the interview would hit the national wire services and quickly spread, reporters were almost instantly dubious. William Turska was a known entity in and around Phoenix, and he was only viewed as a shady character at best. After a quick check, he was discovered to be under indictment for practicing illegal abortions. Furthermore, he was despised by nearly all who knew him as a liar, a cheat, a blowhard, and a pompous ass.

With just a little sniffing around, in fact, reporters began to turn up dirt on the so-called doctor. It slowly dawned on Turska that it might have been better for him to keep his mouth shut, something that was, apparently, quite difficult for him to do.

In short order, locals stepped forward and readily shared that they regularly visited the Turska's homestead to drink and dine with him and his "gray-haired, husky, older companion" by the name of George Rhodes. It was not uncommon to see them around, everyone agreed, as they often ventured into downtown Phoenix, where scores of people saw the two together.

Specifically, Levi Chatwood—an elderly rancher living nearby—responded to a writer's question by saying, "The old man, you mean? I thought maybe he was Turska's father or something. We'd just say hello when I'd go over to get water from the well, and that was it. I never learned his name. You could hear 'em both laughing and carrying on well into the night, though."

Mrs. Floy Kilbreth, owner of the local store, went even further. She soundly contradicted Turska's claim that he'd never heard any news about the plane crash. "Turska or his friend George Rhodes came into my store every single day to pick up things but especially to get the morning copy of the *Arizona Republic*," she stated unequivocally. "One or the other never missed a day. Not a lone day because they had to get that paper. And they'd talk about it too. Talk about the plane crash an' all."

Turska's story of heroism and civic duty was rapidly falling apart, and the Feds were keeping a close eye on all of his activities and statements, knowing they could be used in a court of law. Along with his crumbling story and massive inconsistencies, reporters were also digging deeper into his past—something that was an unexpected and unwanted development on his part.

To say his past was checkered would be an understatement. That might also be said of his present as well.

As soon as Robert Spears' name and photo surfaced in the press, several young women came forward to say that they had been "treated by a Dr. George Rhodes at Dr. Turska's clinic," who now looked suspiciously like the man in the newspapers. All commented anonymously—they received more than "treatments" there—but the picture of an active and successful abortion practice operating out of the New River compound was being solidified. Turska could feel the heat.

Not that he hadn't felt it before.

Just a few months earlier—at the same time that Spears and Loomis were being collared in Los Angeles on abortion charges—William Turska was also facing an abortion case of his own in Phoenix. As more and more girls stepped forward—many now with debilitating health issues—the image of Turska

188 / Chapter 23

as an abortionist, rather than a naturopath was beginning to take shape.

Digging deeper, reporters discovered, in fact, that the Arizona State Board of Naturopathic Examiners had revoked his license to practice years ago because he had never completed the necessary education and training courses. As a result, in little time he was charged for practicing medicine without a license, though it failed to slow him from doing so.

Advertising as a specialist in "female disorders and situations," he continued to see "patients" but only to "offer advice and supply nutritional supplements and address the diets of clients."

It was not the first time that he had been stripped of a medical license and, in fact, it was soon revealed that Turska—while serving as a naturopathic doctor in Oregon—had been arrested for operating a significant marijuana farm in his backyard a decade earlier in 1949, for which he received a five-year suspended sentence and probation.

At the same time, he had his medical license revoked by the state's medical board for also failing to complete his required education courses and "acting with habitual intemperance and unprofessional conduct."

Stories on William Turska began to pop up the following day in newspapers across the country—some touting his outrageous claims, others on his less-than-legal exploits. The man was a conundrum, but a fascinating and colorful character and the press loved him.

Unfortunately—from his perspective—he had to share column space with the two loudest voices in the story: Alice Taylor and Frances Spears. At this point, each of the two wives was locked in a public relations battle, and the war of words had all the attraction of a catfight. That left little oxygen for Turska with the added challenge that much of what they were saying refuted the naturopath's testimony.

Chief among these issues is the fact that Turska had depicted his time with Spears as passing in the night with virtually no relationship and never leaving his home. All of this was far from the truth, of course, and now his lies were beginning to catch

Heroes in the Spotlight / 189

up with him—especially his covert trip to Dallas to arrange the meeting between Spears and his wife. It was a key element in the overall story—and a major deception on his part. The FBI was now following his words closely as an accessory to a crime.

Obviously, Turska was well aware of his guest's connection to the downing of Flight 967 and his midnight run to Dallas for Spears to see his wife—"probably for the last time ever"—made him complicit in the cover-up. So, he did the only thing a serial con man does: *He made up an entirely new lie.*

Calling an impromptu press conference a day later "to set the record straight and clear some misstatements on my behalf," Turska concocted a revised version of the events of the past months.

The front desk clerk at The Lakewood Hotel in Dallas—Rev. Joseph Estep—publicly identified William Truska and "George Rhodes" as the persons he registered weeks back. This time, Turska admits that he and Spears were there shortly after the start of the new year.

"He was desperate to see his wife, and I thought it was the Christian thing to do to let them reunite for a few minutes because I knew Bob was planning to go away soon and probably for a long time. It was an emotional meeting, but to be totally honest, I think there were probably some dramatics there as well. I was just trying to be a good person."

This "good person" persona would become the core of Turska's newly revised version of events that would recast him as a responsible citizen and reasonable friend. Spears' arrival in Arizona and their subsequent activities now took on a new twist.

Their trip to Ely, Nevada, was because it was the closest enclosed place they could find to store Al Taylor's car—he wanted to protect it for his friend and out of the blaring Arizona sun.

And, yes, it was true that Robert Spears had confided to him that he gave his seat to Al Taylor because he was suffering from a bad neck and back and was going to Dallas to see a specialist. Then, he now recalled, when Spears heard the news about the plane crash—with his name on the manifest—he just couldn't resist getting a new start under a new identity, sidestepping the

190 / Chapter 23

abortion charges in Los Angeles, and providing for his wife and kids with the massive insurance payout.

"It's something anyone would have done," he added circumspectly.

"He was devastated over the loss of his good friend, but the opportunity to escape all of his legal troubles was just too good to pass up." In an interview with a *Life* magazine reporter, he went on to say, "I can't condone Spears' decision and, in fact, I tried to talk him out of it. He wanted to change his character, change his fingerprints, change everything. I argued with him. I told him you couldn't change the character you'd been building all those years. But he just wouldn't listen."

Once again, the good friend and responsible citizen was hard at work spinning his story to anyone who would listen. "He is so different than what he seemed to be when he was first with me. Believe me, I didn't have the slightest inkling of the kind of trouble he was in," said Turska. "I think it's a grievous thing to take advantage of a friendship that way. What a Dr. Jekyll and Mr. Hyde he turned out to be!"

The FBI had already concluded that neither of the men in their scopes was what they were portraying themselves to be. They knew by now that William Turska had been intimately involved with their fugitive not only since last November but for many years. They were, as one agent understatedly put it, "as thick as thieves."

The Bureau had also determined that Turska had given Spears a heads-up to clear out of the Bali-Hi Hotel as soon as he gave the signal—promising his friend he would give him at least a 24-hour head start—which he did. Turska might have turned him in to protect his own hide, but he still didn't want his good buddy to get in serious trouble. That was why Spears was waiting in the hotel lobby on that fateful day instead of hiding in his room or at the second hotel he had booked further down the road.

The puzzle pieces were finally falling into place. Both men, despite their outward protestations, could feel the noose tightening around their necks.

Heroes in the Spotlight / 191

The FBI decided to bring in Turska for another round of questioning to see if his story might change once again. This time, they grilled him for the better part of four hours and gleaned some additional intriguing information. After he emerged from the interrogation, he was again met with flash bulbs and the screams of reporters—something he craved.

Hey Doc, what went on in there? What did they ask you?

"You might say we just had a chit-chat to find out just how much and exactly what I might tell you people. As you know the full details in this situation cannot be told."

There are rumors floating around out there that when Dr. Spears came to your house, he was not alone. Any comment on that mysterious person? Was it Al Taylor, maybe?

The question startled Turska a bit . . . he did not want to be connected in any way to Al Taylor. That was an uncomfortable subject. "All I will say is that I know Spears had a traveling companion when I first saw him," Turska said abruptly. "Other than that, I have no comment." The reporters noted the change in tone and moved on to another lighter subject.

Is the FBI maybe thinking they can get a confession out of Dr. Spears by using hypnotism?

"Oh, I don't think anybody could hypnotize him," Turska responded with a grin. "He is too strong-willed. He's like a bull." He was clearly enjoying his newly fashioned role as the go-to source for reporters.

As he should, for that preferred status would not last forever.

Chapter 24

A Burning, Searing Secret

The Spears' home on Gaston Avenue in the Lakewood community of east Dallas had become a tourist attraction as cars passed slowly with windows down to snap photos of the two-story brick house with the hope of seeing Frances or the kids in the front yard.

Eddie Barker, however, had her under lock and key to preserve his golden egg and keep the other reporter poachers at a safe distance. The FBI was also clear about the matter. Other than her doctor, her attorney, and her press agent Eddie, no one was to visit and she was not to leave the premises. At the moment, she was still considered a "person of interest" concerning a possible conspiracy charge with her husband and an "aiding and abetting" issue.

However, being sequestered did not mean, of course, that Eddie Barker couldn't spin gold from his perch in the Spears' living room, where he would often spend the night on the sofa. In fact, to show his generosity to his fellow press members, Barker chose to disregard the FBI's directions and invite reporters into Frances' home for a formal press conference.

In fact, 37 reporters and photographers—including television news crews—crammed into the home where they stood shoulder to shoulder awaiting Frances' entrance with Barker acting as an emcee for the staged event. When the moment came, Mrs. Spears emerged from a back room dressed like a celebrity in her tailored brown suit with matching alligator heels and a

194 / Chapter 24

string of pearls. Her opening words launched a hundred flash bulbs.

"He is a model husband. To know him is to love him."

That phrase would be the first line in nearly one thousand articles posted in newspapers around the world with photos of a long-faced, droopy-eyed Frances Spears. But she was not done.

> The reason he came back here was that he couldn't go through with it. He couldn't stay away from me and the babies. There was never any doubt in my mind that this scheme wouldn't work and that he would eventually be found, whether in Phoenix or Timbuktu. My husband was devastated that Mr. Taylor was in his place. He repeatedly has told me, "I just wish it had been me."
>
> The fact of the matter, though, is that Al Taylor simply wanted to escape from Alice. He had made arrangements to leave the country to get away from his ex-wife, who was just really hard on him. My husband told me when we met at the Lakewood Hotel that he didn't just want to leave the state but to leave the country to be away from her.
>
> Al Taylor was always having trouble with his wife or the Taylor children—he had a troubled stepson named Blaine—and often broke down and wept about his troubles at home in Tampa. It was not an uncommon sight when he visited us.
>
> I also want to be clear that once I found out that my husband was alive, I had no intention of touching the life insurance money. I told Bob the only thing I could do was to get a job and allow the insurance money to stay intact so it could be returned at some time. I never had any idea of taking any money that did not belong to me.

Then why, if you knew your husband was alive, did you hide it from the police and the press? Why didn't you just turn him in?

"Well, when we first met, he'd said, 'Let's sleep on it.' But the second time—the following Monday—he then told me it was his only chance to get away. I admit that I misled all y'all, but I swear I never misled the police. If I had ever been asked by them, I was ready to be truthful. I tried to keep my nasty secret to myself until the proper authorities contacted me. That's the God's-honest truth."

A Burning, Searing Secret / 195

Eddie Barker's carefully manufactured press conference continued for hours and dragged on long into the afternoon. Frances, eventually exhausted and irritated, was being pushed on by Barker's drive to make this the story of the century with him at the center.

Having changed into a new outfit—oddly adorned now in a leopard-print gown—after a while, she sat on the floor with a semi-circle of reporters gathered around her. Taking a long drag on her cigarette and blowing out the smoke dramatically, she nevertheless continued with her story.

> If my husband is innocent, I want him proved innocent. If he's guilty, let the chips fall where they may. This thing was burning my insides out, just waiting for the telephone to ring, saying they had found him or they had caught him. When I was interviewed first, I had to stand there and tell you things that weren't true. If I had told you what I knew, newspapers would have had a heyday. I've been awake night and day for two weeks with this thing.
>
> My God, I'm telling you that you just can't live with something like this. It was burning the heck out of me, and it had to be stopped in some way. I finally decided not to keep it a secret anymore because it won't do me or him any good.

And that would be the end of it for this long, and somewhat tortuous day.

Frances had finally run out of words. Recognizing this, Eddie Barker began shuffling reporters toward the door and thanking them for coming. It would be their job now to whip this story into a national frenzy. As Eddie stood on the threshold, Frances unexpectedly joined him to deliver a final word for the remaining members of the press. It came with a sweet, endearing smile. "All I really want to say is that my husband really is a lovable man."

Barker's theatrics and Mrs. Spears' candid comments instantly earned her an invitation to visit the FBI in their offices. After dinner that evening, Frances was escorted by scowling agents to FBI headquarters in Dallas for additional rounds of questioning.

As Alice Taylor was reading the latest edition of the *Tampa Tribune* she was burning with anger. Her counterpart

196 / Chapter 24

had grabbed center stage and stolen the spotlight. Incensed at being out maneuvered, worse yet, people were now beginning to question her version of the events—that Robert Spears had orchestrated the entire affair to duck abortion charges and get a fat insurance payout all at her husband's expense.

Frances Spears' comments that Al Taylor was trying to escape the grip of his shrewish ex-wife made her furious, and Robert Turska's aspersions were salt in the wounds. It was enough already, so Alice decided to pull out her ace in the hole to once again gain the upper hand. Now it was her turn to push that damn Frances Spears back into the shadows.

Preparing to go on the offensive, Alice called her attorney, Robert Mann, and had him schedule a press conference. After having earlier spurned the press at Mann's office to have her hair prepared in anticipation of the *Life* interview, the reporters were reasonably skeptical, but they nevertheless showed up en masse on the following day.

Alice would not disappoint. Dressed to outshine Frances Spears, she strode out to the gaggle of men looking resplendent in a fashionable gown with a majestic hat and a slightly larger string of pearls. Photographers who had, to this point, been forbidden to take a photo of the elegant woman were now welcome to do so, and the flashbulbs temporarily blinded her.

The first thing Alice chose to address was Mrs. Spears' allegation that Al Taylor was trying to escape her clutches. It clearly had infuriated her, and her voice was spiked with irritation.

"He had been asking me to marry him again, you know, so we could make a better home for the boy," she pronounced in her usual imperious manner. The press was almost instantly puzzled. The boy, in this case, was Junior, who was now an adult and had joined the Marines.

"My husband has always been a quiet, decent man who was a hard worker and a good citizen. Unfortunately, he was betrayed by a person he considered his friend and by Frances Spears, who was in this scheme for the insurance money. Al had no reason to run or even to seek a new job. This was all part of Dr. Spears' plan."

A Burning, Searing Secret / 197

The reporters were not convinced. It wasn't long ago that Alice was telling them that Al was unhappy and restless, even encouraging him to seek a new position in Atlanta. "This may be a new beginning in your life," she said at the time. "I hope this helps you get on the right track."

She went on to dispute the claim that her husband had a sore neck and was seeking treatment in Dallas. "There was nothing wrong with Al that would require special attention. He complained several times of pain in his shoulder, but it was nothing serious."

Again, the reporters grew suspicious. They had earlier uncovered the fact that Taylor had indeed suffered a serious back injury as a result of a 1950 auto accident and wore a neck brace for more than a year while he was still married to Alice. During that time, it was well-documented that he had gone to Dallas to spend the better part of a year with the Spearses and, in Frances' words, "to get away from Alice and the kids."

Sensing that the tide was turning and the press were less likely to be inclined to take her stories at face value, Alice Taylor furiously pulled out her ace in the hole. Smiling with delight, she held up a sheaf of papers and waved them victoriously in front of the assembled mob.

"Well, then, perhaps these might convince you that I'm telling the truth!" Her tone was indignant, her voice sharp and annoyed. The patented poise had suddenly dissipated.

In fact, Alice Taylor did indeed have something in hand that would shake up the story, and she was well aware of it.

She revealed that over the years—but especially leading up to that fateful day on November 15, 1959—her husband and Dr. Spears had been in close communication. Both were voluminous writers and it was now she who was in possession of those letters. Once again, waving them in front of the newsmen, she was taunting them with her secrets.

Attorney Robert Mann was cautious, concerned. This catfight between his client and Mrs. Spears was quickly spinning out of control, and he was understandably nervous about Alice introducing information that might eventually be considered evidence.

198 / Chapter 24

Despite that uneasiness on the part of her lawyer, however, Alice pressed forward in her unacknowledged but very real competition with Frances Spears and—to the delight of the newsmen now crowded tightly around her—prepared to read one of the letters.

"As you can see, gentlemen, this is a handwritten letter from my husband, Al Taylor. I can assure you that this is his script. This is correspondence from Robert Spears, and what I will read to you is Al's response, written on the reverse side which was very common for the two of them to do." Slipping on her reading glasses, Alice proceeded to read from the sheet of paper.

"They just delivered the box you sent with your shirts and shoes. It's sure going to help so they are much appreciated. I'm still wearing the other shoes I got from you back in '51, so you can see I don't spend much for what I put on my back or feet. But you forgot that I wear a 15½ dress shirt, so I'll have to get the ones you sent altered. No problem, still very thankful to receive. Respectfully, Al."

Alice paused to explain that, even though Al could afford to buy his own clothes, he seemed to glory in receiving used clothing from his mentor and idol, Bob Spears. He preferred to have those altered at some expense just so, she maintained, he could be wearing the same suits Spears once wore. In a sick form of adulation, he literally wanted to walk in the older man's shoes.

The reporters were lapping up this kinky and titillating bit of trivia and straining to read portions of the letter itself as Alice held it out prominently in front of them. Even the fact that the pair shared the same sheet of stationery—recording their every thought regardless of how insignificant—felt somehow unsettling. The reporters wanted more, and Alice quickly pulled another page from the many sheets in her hand.

"As you can see, gentlemen, this is a handwritten letter on the engraved letterhead of the Maryland Homeopathic Medical Board with Dr. Spears name at the top with an MD after his name which, of course, he was not. Nor was that Board legitimate for heaven sakes." Alice snapped off each of the last words with a bit of a bite.

A Burning, Searing Secret / 199

"My dear Al, I am writing while sitting on a plane and preparing for landing at Los Angeles International Airport. I'm getting the hell out of Dallas for good. It's nothing more than a cow-town with nothing left but dry cows. No more milking to be done there, I'm afraid. San Pedro is a port city in California and I think the prospects there are quite promising. Well, the plane's getting mighty rough now, so I'll close. Sincerely, Bob."

While the reporters were still scribbling on their notepads, Alice explained that it was Spears' custom to write on lifted stationery from hospitals, medical centers, legal firms, and elegant hotels, whether or not he had even stayed there, to elevate his position to her husband. Al would then respond on the back of that sheet as well as make comments in Spears' original missive. It was an odd and unique form of correspondence.

"But now, gentlemen, I would like to read you a most interesting letter from Dr. Spears to my husband that was written from his home in Rolling Hills, California, on November 5, 1959—just a little more than a week before the fatal plane crash." Pausing for effect, she once again lowered her readers.

My dear friend, I understand your frustration with not being able to get ahead financially. You feel like you aren't getting anywhere, no matter how hard you work. A $5,000 debt [$60,000 today] is no laughing matter. You mention you are consumed with constant thoughts of depression.

I believe I might be of some help. I am wondering if things wouldn't be a lot better if your thinking was more positive. A professional might be helpful, and our group consists of some of the best psychologists and hypnotists in the country. With your permission, I'd like to set something up on your behalf with one of my colleagues.

In November, I'd like to come out to Tampa and talk to the doctors about setting up a clinic to treat deafness. Maybe pick up a few hundred bucks. I know you're worried about Alice finding out about your jail records, but I wouldn't worry about that. I used to be afraid that that might hurt me, but when I got all that publicity, only a few familiar friends shied away. In some ways, my credit was better after the news came out!

200 / Chapter 24

> While I'm in Tampa, I also plan to come and see a fellow in
> St. Pete. Many thanks for your offer to stay at your apartment,
> but I'm afraid it would be an inconvenience to you. Anyway,
> I've got to spend some time in St. Pete.
>
> One more thing . . . please don't put my name on the enve-
> lopes of any future correspondence, but rather use F. Massey
> at the Dallas address from now on. That was Frances' maiden
> name, and she will know to hold all letters for me that come
> to that name.

At that point, Alice held up the letter from which she had
been reading and pointed to the fact that the Spearses had circled the name F. Massey in red for emphasis. Flashbulbs popped
once again.

> And so, gentlemen, as you see, just days before my husband
> and Dr. Spears met in the Tampa airport on that terrible day,
> the duplicitous doctor was clearly up to something. These let-
> ters talk about hypnotism, secret meetings, an alias, money
> issues and setting up a "deafness clinic"—which was their
> code word for abortion.
>
> I also want to note that when Dr. Spears says my husband
> was complaining about debt, I find that hard to reconcile. I
> know for a fact that he was making about $8,000 a year at Pio-
> neer [$90,000 today], and he lives in an inexpensive two-room
> apartment, rarely buys new clothes and avoids extravagance.
> His expenses are minimal. I suspect that he has been hiding his
> money away somewhere.
>
> When I combine that with the nervousness and extreme
> anxiety Al was expressing on that final day, along with lies
> to me and his work about going to Atlanta, it leads me to the
> only logical conclusion which is that Robert Vernon Spears
> was somehow manipulating if not controlling my husband
> who worshiped him and was in some way doing his bidding.
>
> I believe that trust, in the end, cost Al Taylor his life, and
> thus Dr. Spears is nothing at all like the good and decent man
> that his wife makes him out to be.

Though Alice was sure she had taken the final shot, it turned out
not to be as headlines in Dallas read: "Dr. Spears' Wife Shuns
Mrs. Taylor."

Tampa reporters, now sympathetic to the grieving Alice, picked up her cause and carried it forward. "The Dallas naturopath emerges as a powerful father-advisor in the life of the salesman. Taylor, on the other hand, seemed a tortured, troubled man not happy in his job or his lonely existence. Spears was constantly pushing Taylor to look for greener pastures.

"The doctor regularly played the role of a successful, patronizing elder statesman, passing along his advice and counsel to a poor, mentally depressed friend who was looking for a way out. Perhaps they were both looking for a way out."

Frances Spears returned that volley with, "Bob is a very kind person. He was always very kind to me, kind to everyone."

Alice Taylor quickly countered, "Al was an honest, hardworking man whose reputation should not be smeared. As to Mrs. Spears, she has never called me, and I hope she never does."

She never would.

Alice also would never reveal to the press one letter in particular that Al had written to Dr. Spears about her son, Blaine, just days before the plane crash which claimed her husband. It was up to the FBI to discover this one:

> Dear Bob,
>   Received your letter yesterday. Please let me know definitely when you will be here, where and what time. I went to the airport on Tues nite at 9 and plane was late, so waited until 10:30 and of course you didn't show.
>   Blaine is getting ready to take off for New Orleans then to Carmel, Cal. Looks like I'm stuck again and if he was alone I'd do something about it but I can't afford to have his wife and baby on my conscience.
>   Sincerely, Al

The FBI, regarding this letter, noted: "She was asked if she thought the second paragraph of the letter implied that Taylor may possibly have been intending to kill her son Blaine—possibly in an airplane—but that he did not want to also kill his son's wife and children. She made no comment about this statement."

Chapter 25

A Side Trip to the House of Love

While the general public was consumed with the ongoing and increasingly entertaining, verbal warfare between the wives, the FBI was doing the hard work of trying to reconstruct the last days of Al Taylor and Robert Spears before their fateful meeting at the Tampa Airport. They were convinced that a clue was hidden out there and were determined to find it. The loss of all 42 souls on an airliner virtually demanded justice.

But the investigators seemed to be running into more dead ends than open doors. More bizarre twists and left turns than was reasonable to expect. One of those—and introducing yet another odd duck of character—was when the FBI got a call from an anonymous source suggesting they look into "Mahdah" at the Universal Temple of Love.

The agents were used to a menagerie of characters in this melodrama, but they certainly weren't prepared for the All-Glorious, All-Seeing Source of Enlightenment that was the Mahdah.

The FBI was cognizant of the fact that from the time Dr. Spears—along with his co-conspirator Donald Loomis—had been arrested for operating an illegal but lucrative abortion operation, the slippery naturopath seemed to be on the move in what appeared, at least, to be an attempt to cover his tracks and make him hard to locate.

The investigators now knew from the correspondence between Taylor and Spears, which Alice had brought forward, that he had taken several trips during that time. First, there was

203

204 / Chapter 25

the unexplained flight to New York to visit with attorney Julian Frank in his Manhattan offices while secretly connecting with Taylor, who was there under the guise of escorting his artist stepson. Frank, of course, would die not long after Taylor in a bomb-stricken plane crash of his own.

As soon as he was released on bail there were several unexplained flights and stays in New Orleans, Dallas, Los Angeles, Miami, Phoenix, and Chicago in a whirlwind of travel that left the investigators' heads spinning.

However, on November 7, 1959—again referencing Alice Taylor's unearthed letters—the agents knew Spears had planned a trip to Florida, though they were not clear what that was about. It seemed, however, to hold some key to the mystery. Then the cloud of mystery began to dissipate when one of their offices received an anonymous tip from a female caller.

Perhaps Mrs. Bonnie Bantz was second-guessing herself when she let her phone handset settle back into its cradle. Perhaps not. Lighting up a cigarette, she blew the smoke high into the air away from her makeup. Having just turned 51, she was more conscious of maintaining herself. But now, recently relocated to Tampa to retire with her husband, she was wondering if she hadn't made the mistake of a lifetime.

Taking a big breath, she wondered if there might not be consequences.

Spears had been friends with Dr. Robert Love for many years, and he appreciated both their personal and professional relationships. As a prominent doctor of osteopathy in the twin cities of Tampa/St. Petersburg, Dr. Love had grown quite wealthy over the years and was looking forward to eventually retiring to a life of fishing and spoiling grandchildren.

After a divorce, he was happy to find love once again—this time with Mahdah, a beautiful woman 30 years his junior. Friends saw the situation a bit differently, however. One friend later explained to the FBI that Mahdah had a habit of locating wealthy, elderly men, marrying then and then—in every single case—having them die two to three years later. In some of those cases, her husbands were somehow cajoled into changing their wills to make her their sole heir and cutting off the rest of the family from any inheritance.

And thus, true to form, it was no surprise when the May–December romance only flourished for two years before Robert passed away in 1955 in much the same way Mahdah's previous three husbands had—with unexpected massive headaches, convulsions, and seizures for which there was no known cause. A house guest at the time said Mahdah refused to call a physician and Dr. Love subsequently died, followed by a quick cremation. And Mahdah was instantly even wealthier than before.

Born as Eli Griffin, this lovely bride was quite the free thinker and spiritualist and had been an evangelist for exploring the celestial and inner realms to find lasting peace, fulfillment, and enlightenment. In the process, she changed her name to "Mahdah" primarily because it sounded mystical. She would no doubt have been disappointed to discover the name in Arabic means "plain and flat."

But to her credit, her married name would now become Mahdah Love—the perfect moniker for a spiritual guru, healer, hypnotism-enthusiast, and diviner of the stars. Also fortunate for her was that upon her husband's death, she inherited his vast financial estate, including his massive and elegant mansion.

Mahdah almost immediately converted their stately home into a spiritual sanctuary and renamed it the Universal Temple of Love. Simultaneously taking on the titles of both Reverend and Doctor—a doctor of naturopathy, in fact—she then began to create an enlightenment center for spiritual retreats not unlike the communes that would later come to represent the era of the Flower Children and even later on, the New Age Movement.

The Temple—informally known as the House of Love—soon became a destination for seekers of all stripes from mysticism and psychic explorations to a safe place for alien watchers and alternative lifestyles.

All of this, of course, fit in quite nicely with Dr. Spears' eclectic medicinal perspectives and his openness to all things out of the ordinary. It also didn't hurt that Mahdah was flush with cash and adored him as a silver-haired mentor and father-figure.

206 / Chapter 25

For that reason, as one of the nation's most well-known naturopathic practitioners, he was always welcome to give lectures, offer clinics, and peddle his wares at the House of Love. In fact, when he called in late October to mention he would be in Mahdah's area on November 7, she eagerly jumped at the chance to offer him a slot in her ongoing lecture series. Dr. Spears—flattered and looking forward to "picking up some C's" (hundreds), as he said in his letter to Al—accepted her kind offer.

It was also clear to investigators that Spears, while he was out on bail for his LA charges, intended to set up a "deafness clinic"—code for abortion—in the area. It is reasonable to assume that he was discussing pulling his debt-ridden friend Al Taylor into this lucrative venture, perhaps even the Mahdah herself.

Spears was preparing to heavily market his new and improved "Go-OK" product—an oral abortifacient which almost instantly was in demand. His proprietary formula was "guaranteed to relieve uncomfortable female issues" and promised that "everything would *go okay.*" It was gaining momentum and was designed to be the next chapter in the naturopath's life and career. There was evidence that Al Taylor had been signed to handle national distribution.

Dr. Spears had, in fact, developed over time a brilliant form of shipping his self-aborting products—Euro-Clear, Metro-Vac, Go-OK—to avoid detection from postal inspectors who were always on the lookout for contraband making its way across state lines.

FBI records indicate that Spears had created a national network by connecting area businesses—perhaps unwittingly, perhaps not—so that his customers could pick up packages under the radar without their mailman showing up at their front door.

As examples, FBI records named several businesses in the network and described how the system worked. For instance, at the time, cross-country bus companies—Continental Trailways in this case—would accept packages from non-traveling customers who would use them as a parcel delivery service.

Neil Shietal of Continental Trailways, in fact, explained to the field agents that it would be easy to ship a package or

A Side Trip to the House of Love / 207

luggage without the sender accompanying it. After all, anyone could purchase a ticket under a false name and check the luggage through to the point of destination and then have someone else simply claim it using that name at the receiving end.

And that was exactly what Spears and his associates would do to distribute their illegal abortion concoction. Buying a bus ticket under a fake name and then checking their "luggage" at the terminal, it would be carried across the country and finally left at one of their depots in the name of the passenger. That person in turn would go to the luggage counter and retrieve the parcel that had been checked in his name—no identification was required in the 1950s—and retrieve it without question.

Listed by name in the FBI report were also numerous companies that Spears regularly employed—probably paying them a small fee—including service stations, dry cleaners, apartment complexes, department stores, grocery chains, opticians, and a variety of small town businesses that would receive shipments under false names.

When the cops went to the places and showed them names to whom packages were addressed, they responded that they had never heard of that person. Nevertheless, someone by that name had retrieved the package and then disappeared.

Clearly Dr. Spears had a flourishing mail-order business— the 1950s Amazon of abortion creams—and by all appearances he was luring Al Taylor in with the promise of earning big money. At the same time he was flashing "before and after" pictures of women upon whom he claimed to have performed facelift surgeries in California for exorbitant fees. It was all a lie.

The fact that "Go-OK" and the other ointments were ineffective at best and dangerous or lethal at worst was not an issue for Spears as he knew no customer would ever complain to authorities, or family members would be forced to seek out some other surgical solution. Women desperate for an abortion always moved on to the next option until the situation was finally resolved.

But with all these business opportunities swirling around the mad doctor, it appeared to be the special speaking engagement that most excited him as Mahdah guaranteed him a huge crowd

208 / Chapter 25

for the event, which was being regularly advertised in the *Tampa Tribune* and open to the general public.

So excited was he to regain the spotlight during what was a darker period in his life that he reached out to Al Taylor to have him contact Mahdah Love and ensure she was promoting the event effectively. A large crowd was important for both his pocketbook and ego. Taylor, of course, did as he was told and subsequently assured his friend that all was going well and a large crowd was anticipated.

Mahdah was especially intrigued with the doctor's insights on the power of hypnotism to control the mind and body as a way to open "the doors of perception"—as writer Aldous Huxley described it—and to conquer negative character traits. During the upcoming visit, he promised to show her how to develop similar skills including a personal demonstration on a friend of his. Thrilled with the offer, both of them were now eagerly anticipating the November 7 visit.

All of that was what made the next development so confusing.

Just days before the heavily marketed event, Al Taylor called Mahdah Love to say that Dr. Spears regretfully would not be coming to the House of Love "due to unforeseen circumstances." Mahdah was immediately taken aback—in part because it was so odd that the doctor himself wouldn't have made that call. She later admitted that she had become suspicious that "something strange was up."

Taylor, however, reassured the spiritual healer that all was well and that Spears very much wanted to reschedule the event for a future time. When she pressed further, asking where Spears was and if it was possible to speak with him, Taylor had no answers, adding to the confusion of the moment. But as one of his devotees, she chose to let it go.

By all accounts, Dr. Spears was in the Tampa area on November 7, as promised, just not at The Temple. For some reason, he had decided to lower his profile—a fact that investigators found interesting. Even more puzzling was that Alice told the FBI that her husband—despite the lecture cancellation—was supposed to still pick Spears up at the airport, but Al reported that his friend had never showed up when he actually had.

A Side Trip to the House of Love / 209

The agents had a different take on the whole matter and were pursuing it diligently. They believed the lecture story was just a cover for a clandestine meeting between Taylor and Spears and someone who was only referred to in the letters as "the fellow in St. Pete." It was all too much of a coincidence to be overlooked and virtually begged for deeper investigation.

Mahdah Love, however, had moved on and would not think about her dear friend again until she unexpectedly received a Christmas card just a month later from Frances Spears, heart-breakingly announcing that her husband had been killed in the tragic downing of Flight 967. "She told me about the plane crash and said things were sad in her house because of Spears' death. Frances was clearly in grief."

And, as was always the case with Robert Vernon Spears, it would be just a few weeks later that Mahdah would be shocked to hear of her friend once again. This time, it was a *Tampa Tribune* headline proclaiming that he was indeed still alive, had been arrested by the FBI, and was under investigation for participation in the bombing of the airline that supposedly had carried him to his death.

Inviting reporters and camera crews to her Temple, Mahdah vigorously defended Spears' name and announced that she refused to believe the horrible implications being cast about one she called "a delightful person with a cheery spirit and a charming, gentlemanly nature. No allegations will change my mind about him. I wrote to Mrs. Spears in Dallas just the other day and told her that when this is all over, she could come and stay with me. What has happened recently wouldn't change that."

As much of America was trying to sort through the mystery of Flight 967 and the sudden reappearance of Dr. Robert Spears from among the dead, the district attorney in Phoenix was preparing to go to trial on the stolen car charge. Meanwhile, the FBI feverishly tried to pin him to the airline disaster.

And, in the greatest of ironies, from the quiet of her own living room after having just moved from Minneapolis to Tampa, Bonnie Bantz—formerly Bonita Foster and the one-time fiancé of Robert Spears—was pondering what her former husband-to-be was now up to. Having been jilted, robbed, and left at the altar

210 / Chapter 25

20 years earlier, she had arrived in Florida just weeks before the mysterious plane crash.

But on January 22, 1960, she picked up her morning copy of the *Tampa Times* and saw the line that rocked her world once again: "Robert Spears—Mystery Man."

And that was when she decided to pick up the phone.

Chapter 26

Twists, Turns, and Accusations

On the first day of February in 1960, Robert Vernon Spears—dressed nattily in a sports coat, white shirt and tie—stood respectfully in front of Judge David W. Ling in the Federal Court of Phoenix. His wife, Frances, watched solemnly as her handcuffed husband was marched into the courtroom by U.S. Marshals. This was to be the first hearing of his case, followed by the setting of a trial date.

Looking up, Judge Ling was surprised to see Spears sitting alone at the defense table. "Mr. Spears, where is your defense attorney? You realize that if you cannot afford one, a public defender will be appointed for you."

The smiling, almost radiant defendant responded politely. "Yes, your Honor. I've elected to decline legal counsel and represent myself."

"Are you sure about that, Dr. Spears? These are quite serious charges you are facing. You are accused of violating the Dyer Act, a federal offense. But it is your choice, of course. And so, in that case, how do you plead today?"

For all the build-up to this day, all the newspaper column inches that had been dedicated to this story, and all the whispers and allegations that were being bandied about, no one on earth expected this hearing to be anything other than perfunctory and mundane.

Legal analysts around the country had loudly predicted that nothing would ever come of these charges that were undeniably

211

212 / Chapter 26

weak and felt trumped up at best. Clearly an arrest for crossing a state line in a friend's car—that no one could prove he hadn't been given permission—had no chance of standing up.

Everyone knew that the purpose of the collar was to buy the Feds some time to dig up anything on a possible connection to Flight 967. However, during the weeks that the prisoner was being held, the Bureau hadn't come up with a single piece of incriminating evidence. They had their suspicions, but they were stymied. Thus, the accused naturopath felt more than comfortable representing himself in court.

But then Robert Spears did what he had done so many times in his lifetime—turn everything on its head.

"Again, Dr. Spears, how do you plead in regard to the charges brought against you today?" Judge Ling was growing impatient with a courtroom full of radio and television newsmen, reporters, and interested observers.

"Your Honor, I will enter a plea of *nolo contendere.*"

The gallery immediately fell quiet. A plea of *nolo contendere* meant that the defendant in a criminal prosecution accepted conviction as though he was guilty but did not admit guilt. This was an unexpected twist when all involved assumed it was a forgone conclusion that *Not Guilty* would be the obvious plea.

Even the judge was stunned and looked up with a puzzled expression. The plea was completely unanticipated, and Ling seemed unprepared for the move. Gathering himself, he asked, "Dr. Spears, are you sure you don't want to seek the counsel of an attorney? One can be provided for you. . . ."

Before the judge could finish, Spears spoke up loudly, "I do not, your Honor."

"Well then, I need to inform you that, unfortunately, sir, a plea of *nolo contendere* is not an option here. You must plead either guilty or not guilty."

Shrugging his shoulders and allowing a grin to crawl across his face, Spears offhandedly replied, "Oh, all right then . . . guilty."

Judge Ling, unconvinced that the defendant fully appreciated the gravity of his situation, once again asked Dr. Spears if

Twists, Turns, and Accusations / 213

he might want to get the advice of an attorney before he made such a surprising plea.

However, the doctor didn't hesitate for a second and said simply, "I want no counsel." With that, the gavel came down, and Judge Ling promptly stated that sentencing would be announced in exactly two weeks, February 15.

Newsmen and reporters immediately rushed for the doors in a mad sprint to make their afternoon deadlines, and the courtroom was almost instantly vacant and quiet. Only two lawyers who had been following the case closely remained behind.

"That man is crazy. He has a fool for a lawyer and a client." Both attorneys laugh, but the second sees the strategy quite differently.

> Crazy like a fox, I'd say. Think about it. He'll probably only get a year, more likely six months. He can do that standing on his head and maybe even get it cut by a third for good behavior. Three square meals and a bed isn't all that bad. He's maybe spent half his life in prison. He'll do just fine, and then he will be back on the street doing whatever he does.
>
> Of course, he still has to face the abortion charges in Los Angeles, but he'll only get two or three years for that—Loomis is pretty connected out there—and that sentence will be served concurrently, so with good behavior, I bet the whole thing will add up to 18 to 20 months max . . . a piece of cake.
>
> But I'll tell you the real reason I think he pleaded guilty . . . I bet you the Feds threatened him with charges related to the airline crash unless he entered a guilty plea on this lesser charge. This will be just minor jail time. The other thing would come with the death penalty.

The retired attorney's thinking was sound. Spears knew he'd get next to nothing for "borrowing" a friend's car. Perhaps even probation. And that was more than enough reason to pass on legal counsel and stand before a federal magistrate with an ear-to-ear grin.

Robert Spears is pleased enough with the outcome that he is photographed whistling as he walks down the sidewalk escorted by marshals. This is merely a bump in the road, and

214 / Chapter 26

with his new non-surgical abortion formula selling like wildfire, he was confident that the future was nothing but bright.

Two weeks later, on February 15, 1960, Spears stood once again respectfully before the bench of Judge Ling, this time to find out his sentence. "Spears was easily the most distinguished-looking person in the Federal Court," one reporter wrote. "He had both the confidence and the arrogance of a man who knows he has gamed the system."

As was the custom, the judge asked if the convicted man had anything he'd like to say before his sentence was handed down. Spears, leaning forward and speaking clearly, answered, "No sir."

Then, with every eye trained on him, Judge Ling shocked the legal world and Robert Vernon Spears by delivering the maximum possible sentence the law allowed—five years in a Federal Penitentiary. An audible gasp could be heard in the courtroom as Spears staggered a half-step backward.

Trying to take it all in—Spears was clearly unprepared for this moment—he immediately asked the oddest of questions:

"Can you tell me if my wife will be eligible to receive my social security benefits? I'm of retirement age now, and I'd like for them to be able to get my checks." His head-scratching response to finding out that he had just received the harshest possible sentence for the least imaginable crime was to ask a judge about the intricacies of government entitlements.

As Dr. Spears—once again a felon—exited the courtroom in handcuffs, he glanced back and threw a kiss to his beloved, who had been patiently and supportively in the courtroom gallery throughout the proceedings. With tears in her eyes, she acknowledged her husband's gesture. Then, she watched him disappear into the corridor where he would be escorted back to his Phoenix jail cell to await extradition to California to face the abortion charges there.

However, the tears wouldn't last long. Frances Spears—a staunch defender of her husband—decided to go on the offensive, and she knew exactly what to do next. A phone call from a court pay phone to Eddie Barker launched what would turn

Twists, Turns, and Accusations / 215

out to be the next chapter in this now-serious drama and one in which Frances will bare her teeth.

Convinced that Robert Spears is being dealt with unfairly and prejudicially, she refused to take this sentencing lying down. She decided then and there that if her husband went down, then she'd make sure a few others went with him.

Eddie Barker was rubbing his hands in delight. The readers and radio listeners were positively giddy over the thought that Frances might strike back.

Meanwhile, Dr. Robert Spears was sitting in the jail's rec room playing poker with matchsticks and smiling like a Cheshire cat.

Only a few days had passed after sentencing before Barker was touting breaking news on his February 20 evening broadcast. With ratings reaching new heights, listenership was virtually guaranteed as the microphone crackled as Barker came on the air.

"Tonight, ladies and gentlemen, I am bringing you a very special guest. In an exclusive interview, Frances Spears—wife of the recently sentenced Dr. Robert Spears—will be revealing some news that is guaranteed to shock the nation. You will not want to move from your radio sets for the next hour, or you will be in danger of missing out on the most stunning revelation yet to be shared in connection with this ever-evolving case."

Frances Spears cleared her throat before speaking and then said, in a more aggressive voice than usual, "It is a fallacy in the United States that when a man has paid for his sins, the debt is resolved. My husband is being severely punished for a minor offense, and it's all because they think he did something else that he did not. There are people out there who are committing far worse crimes in the name of the law and getting away with it!"

Far worse crimes in the name of the law?

Her choice of words was intriguing, and Eddie Barker—who knew full well what was coming—allowed them to hang out there for a minute before speaking up. This was, after all, what the promised "stunning revelation" was all about.

216 / Chapter 26

The next day, the numerous newspapers summarized the contents of Frances' on-air interview, and it was everything that was promised and more.

> The wife of Robert Vernon Spears said Saturday night in an interview with Radio Station KRLD that her husband was involved in a large-scale abortion racket in Los Angeles. She said payoffs were regularly made to the police there.
>
> In the recorded interview Saturday night, Mrs. Frances Spears told News Director Eddie Barker that a well-known Los Angeles criminal attorney served as the middle man between abortionists and police in the California city. She said her husband told her that the police officers involved included "one of the top law enforcement officials and those that worked under him."

According to Mrs. Spears, the criminal attorney was a go-between who collected money from abortionists and then passed a share of it—a set percentage of each fee that was paid—along to a squad of detectives who had the ability to pick and choose the individuals and places to sweep and which to overlook. She refused to name names.

Responding to the accusation, Los Angeles Chief of Police William H. Parker said such a claim had never been communicated to him, adding: "I think we ought to know exactly who it is we're talking about. We have 6,000 employees in the department—4,600 officers alone—and I'm not in a position to just pick names out of the air. We have always vigorously investigated anything with relation to the conduct of our employees," Parker continued.

"If the people at the Dallas radio station have information, they should be specific. I don't care who they give the information to—the district attorney, grand jury, or us—they should be specific. If they are going to mention officers, I think they ought to name them."

Ed Barker went on to say that Julian Blodgett, chief investigator for the Los Angeles District Attorney's office, visited Spears on February 4 in his jail cell in Phoenix. Barker suggested the possibility that Blodgett's visit had to do with the investigation

Twists, Turns, and Accusations / 217

of the police racket in Los Angeles. However, Blodgett subsequently told the Associated Press: "We have developed no evidence to substantiate the allegations at this time but the investigation is continuing."

In the interview, Frances never mentioned any officer by name—nor would she ever—but for those in the Los Angeles area, and especially those detectives assigned to the Abortion Squad Detail, this was quite unsettling and unwelcome news. It didn't take long for there to be whispers, finger-pointing, accusations, and premature "retirements."

More than a month after Robert Spears—described at the time as "a paunchy 65-year-old"—first appeared in court on the car charges, he was still sitting in the downtown Phoenix jail waiting for his transfer papers to come through, which would send him to California to face the earlier abortion charges there.

Frances had returned home shortly after the sentencing to launch her public relations campaign on his behalf, but now—in total shock—Robert was being alerted to the fact that Frances was waiting for him in a visiting room. Both surprised and pleased, he was excited to see his wife as he was ushered through the door to the small, windowless room.

But she was not alone this time.

Apparently since she had last been interviewed by Special Agent Emmet Murphy in her home, Frances had begun to change her mind about having a "heart-to-heart conversation" with her husband. "I've been thinking about such a trip all weekend but I'm getting very confused.

"At times I want to see him but I don't know if I can stand it. I know that the only thing that can be accomplished by the trip—if Bob confesses to this terrible thing—will be that I will put a knife to his throat! I'm afraid of finding out the truth in this case and if I confront my husband and I get that answer. . . ."

Frances couldn't continue for a moment, but, after gathering herself, continued.

"I can't understand why Bob is doing this to me. I don't understand why he refuses to discuss any of this matter if he were not involved in the crash of the airplane. Or why he would allow me to undergo interrogation over all of this. I don't know

218 / Chapter 26

why he wouldn't talk to me about his activities, especially if it resulted in 42 lives lost in a plane crash."

She then began to sob, almost uncontrollably, overwhelmed by the possible implications of her husband's heinous actions.

"I tell myself that the Bob Spears I know as my husband and my children's father couldn't have done anything like this, but in view of everything I have been told and everything I have learned since this thing happened, I am afraid he did have something to do with the crash."

And then, in the typical blame-shifting behavior so often exhibited by an abused person, Frances ended her statement with, "I also believe I may have forced him into doing this by hounding him about his abortion activities, while at the same time my desiring to have a high standard of living and picking at him."

Days later, Frances Spears was at Love Field along with FBI escorts to surprise her husband with a visit to find the answers she felt she needed.

Now sitting on either side of Frances in a jailhouse room were special agents looking stern and business-like. The men got right to the point, explaining to Spears that he had a wife and young children who would be bereft and penniless without him. This would be his one chance to look out for them, to care for them from afar while he, in all likelihood, spent the rest of his years in prison. All he needed to do was tell the truth about Flight 967.

It was a tempting offer, but Dr. Spears wouldn't bite.

Speaking directly to Frances, he spoke softly in a whisper, "Darling, I know things, but I can't talk. It's better that you don't know what I know." She nodded, whether or not she understood. Dr. Spears was not willing to give up any information on the circumstances surrounding the plane crash, knowing that it could be used against him.

After allowing the couple to have some private moments and a long farewell hug, they said their sad goodbyes. Frances was escorted back to the airport and placed on a return flight to Dallas. While she was waiting to board, a reporter who saw

Twists, Turns, and Accusations / 219

her called out, "Mrs. Spears, what's your role in the case?" She replied shyly, "I'm just trying to do what's right."

Seeing the FBI agents on either side of her, the reporter asked, "Are you in protective custody? Are you under arrest?" The humiliation of it all and the sad turn of her life, felt almost unbearable. "No," she replied with her head down as she prepared to board the plane, "I'm only trying to do all I can. Whatever I can."

Waiting on the tarmac as Frances deplaned in Dallas was, of course, opportunistic newsman and self-promoter Eddie Barker. Fearful that any of his competitors might get the scoop on her trip to Phoenix with FBI agents, Barker cornered her inside the terminal and immediately clicked on his ever-present tape recorder.

Pushing his microphone in the face of the weary and broken woman caught in a world of regret, he asked brusquely, "Mrs. Spears, did you learn any information from your husband that might help solve the mystery of Flight 967? Anything at all?"

Looking up at him with her long face and drooping eyes, she answered, "I know he could go a long way toward clearing it all up—maybe not overnight, but in time. He knows things. . . ." Barker jumped on this and pushed further. "Do you believe he is keeping some things from you?"

With a weak smile, she answered, "Yes, there are some things he feels he has a reason for holding back, even from me. He gave me his reasons, and he has given them to others, and that's all I will say about the matter."

Then, with a wave of a hand, one of the agents opened the door of the car that had been brought for her, and she slid into the backseat.

Frances Spears was ready to see her babies.

Chapter 27

The Rock and the Role

Robert Spears was eventually shipped out to California. By April 1960—less than a month after Frances' visit—his new home was Terminal Island Federal Prison just off the coast of San Pedro. In one of the great ironies of his lifetime, he was only five miles from his former luxe estate in Rolling Hills—a community reserved exclusively for the wealthy and prestigious—where he was a neighbor of his current co-defendant, Donald Loomis.

At Terminal Island, he quickly became a popular inmate and enjoyed a robust correspondence relationship with Frances—exchanging letters almost daily. Robert Spears—in an odd development—was also cleared for correspondence with just one other individual: Gene Rembert, a 46-year-old used car salesman that he said he knew nearly two decades earlier in Dallas.

That was strange because there was no record of a Gene Rembert ever being in Robert Spears' life. In fact, there was no record of a Gene Rembert ever existing at any time at all. According to the talk, the mystery friend was the pseudonym for an FBI agent who was assigned to continue the attempt to gain some info on the Flight 967 disaster. Believing Spears knew something, the Bureau refused to ever give up.

So, finally, almost a full year after he was first indicted for providing illegal abortion services, Dr. Spears was again standing in front of a judge. By this time, he had become so familiar with the process that he could literally direct court officials on proper procedure.

222 / Chapter 27

Expecting to be standing next to his old pal and current co-defendant Donald Loomis, Dr. Spears was surprised to find that the former-MGM abortionist had already accepted a plea deal. Having performed as many as 3,000 abortions during his career, Loomis happily agreed to plead guilty in exchange for a sentence of one year in county jail and a fine. Apparently, his contacts—or his threats to reveal what he knew—in the end, worked out just fine.

In a way, the sentence was encouraging for Spears. He had only been charged with one abortion count and could reasonably expect little more than probation based on his partner's deal. As a result, he announced to Judge John Barnes that he, too, would be pleading guilty and begging the court for mercy.

There would be no mercy for Robert Vernon Spears, however.

In a head-snapping decision, the judge unloaded on Spears by sentencing him to the maximum allowed by law—five years in Federal Prison and, worse yet, his incarceration would be served consecutively, not concurrently as federal guidelines suggested. With his Phoenix conviction, that added up to 10 years in prison—something no one could have ever predicted.

To his shock, his time would not be served in the relative comfort and freedom of Terminal Island, as he had a right to expect, but rather the most feared prison in the country—Alcatraz. It was a horrifying outcome from what he had come to expect—little more than a slap on the wrist—based on the Loomis' sentencing.

As with all federal prisoners, inmates were required to fill out an intake form upon arrival. True to Spears' generally sarcastic tone, he simply wrote of his past crimes: "Drove car across state lines. Hadn't oughta."

It wouldn't be long before the 67-year-old naturopath was settling into the life and routines of his new home—he had, of course, been in more than 10 prisons at this point in his life. So, within the first week, he contacted the warden with a request, perhaps to determine his standing.

"I've been engaged in the practice of medicine for several years," he wrote. "And in order to keep up with my studies, I would like to request that a medical reference book be added to

The Rock and the Role / 223

the prison library. I believe it would be an essential resource." The warden did, in fact, reply quickly with a note: "So that you will not get off on the wrong foot with me, please refrain from diagnosing, prescribing, or advising while you are here. Request denied."

With that rejection, Spears had a clear understanding of his status in Alcatraz.

Frances also had a more realistic view of her future with this latest development. Within another week, she had filed for divorce and sent what she knew would be a heartbreaking letter: "You don't know how difficult it is to write this, knowing that you will probably consider this to be your 'Dear John' letter, but honestly, Bob, I've got to make a change in my marital status."

Her husband responded in an understanding tone but confessed that this came as a terrific shock, adding, "Please keep me informed about the children, and if you choose to remarry, I hope it will be to someone with a good education and not addicted to alcohol. If their stepfather is good to them, there will never be any trouble from me."

As he had done so many times before, Spears began to adjust to his new world. It was a stricter and more regimented one than he was used to, but prison held no fear for him—it was merely a different address for a specified amount of time. As was virtually always the case, he quickly became a favorite of both guards and inmates. Renowned for his cooking abilities, he became a bit of a master chef in Alcatraz and developed a sterling reputation for upgrading the prison cuisine.

Almost a year after he climbed aboard "The Rock" in San Francisco Bay, he was one of the most popular prisoners—"an old man with a big heart." His first inmate review included the statement: "In spite of his adverse publicity, this man's behavior has always been excellent. He is always polite and respectful and tries hard to get along with everyone. He is a favorite teller of stories."

Though they were now divorced, Spears continued to write to his ex-wife and send little notes to his children. He explained that life was actually good for him, and in many ways, it was the best place at which he was ever incarcerated.

224 / Chapter 27

Then, Robert received a return letter from Frances that dropped him to his knees. On March 11, 1962, his son Kenny had fallen into a coma from juvenile diabetes and was not expected to survive. The news rocked his world, and the normally affable and outgoing man almost immediately began to withdraw and become despondent, no longer caring to live. Prison officials were concerned.

Then came a second blow in rapid succession. News reached him that Donald Loomis' son had been killed at virtually the same time in a horrendous motorcycle accident along a cliff road in Malibu. He began to feel "as if God had it out for me. As if he was meting out some divine punishment for past sins."

Realizing he needed help, Spears turned to prison psychiatrist Dr. Allan Milofsky. The doctor was also eager to peek into the mind of such a serial criminal, so a connection was made. Dr. Spears, who envisioned himself as a bit of a psychiatrist himself, looked forward to the professional interaction, especially at such a dark period in his life.

Dr. Milofsky, however, was less concerned about Robert's mental health and was more interested in developing a criminal profile for a study he was doing with a book in the offing. Put off by the tone of his probing questions that had little, if anything, to do with Spears' immediate situation, the prisoner walked out on him in less than a half-hour.

Offended by the condescending tone of someone he saw as a colleague, Spears bristled at Milofsky's manner and felt insulted at being put under a microscope for purely academic reasons. "I'm not just a bug in a petri dish," he would later comment. He was even more incensed when a guard snuck him a copy of the psychiatrist's report.

> This patient's voluminous record is full of dramatic tidbits and reads a little like a cloak-and-dagger romance, with aliases, mistaken identities, illicit mail, a mysterious plane crash, intrigues, etc. In my short time with the subject, I can only conclude that he is inscrutable and represents a sociopathic personality.

The Rock and the Role / 225

Infuriated by the demeaning report submitted by the analyst, Spears hurried off a letter to Milofsky and copied the warden:

> Dr. Milofsky has submitted a pseudoscientific report which appears to have been completed through a horoscope assessment supplemented by a Ouija board. I would also advise the doctor, as a colleague, to avoid ponderous words such as "inscrutable."
>
> Also, when promulgating or articulating your esoteric, superficial, sentimental or philosophical observations, please shun polysyllabic profundity, superficial sentimentalities, rodomontade, and jejune bafflement. In other words, say what you mean, but please don't use big words.

Dr. Spears may have had the satisfaction of getting in the last word with a "colleague," but it would soon be his health—not his verbal jousting—that would become his primary concern. Five months later, in November 1962, he was transferred out of Alcatraz and reassigned to the Medical Penitentiary in Springfield, Missouri, for prostate surgery. With some complications, it would require a long recovery time—more than eight months. While that was happening, Spears' shortened release date came up.

Thus, in late August 1963, Spears was formally released from prison in Springfield—but only to be handed directly over to Los Angeles County Sheriffs. They would escort him to the Chino Institution for Men in Riverside to begin serving his sentence for performing abortions in California. In a matter of minutes, he was preparing to serve his next five-year sentence.

However, without complaint or anger, he moved on to yet another life in Chino—ready and excited about making new friends, having access to a more well-equipped kitchen, and getting to play bridge and poker with the guards. He loved the weather and the more relaxed environment at Chino. As was always the case at every stop, he was lauded in reviews as a popular and well-behaved inmate.

As Frances and Bob were on the path to becoming comfortable with their new lives, Alice Taylor—far away in Florida—was

226 / Chapter 27

embroiled in a legal nightmare, not of her own making. Since it was necessary for her ex-husband, Al Taylor, to be declared legally dead before any insurance benefits could be awarded, Alice was mired in a mess trying to make that happen.

Courts were slow to take action because no body had ever been recovered, nor any proof given that he was ever on Flight 967. Despite Alice's fervent arguments that Dr. Spears had switched places on the doomed plane with her husband, there was no solid evidence to support her claims. The Tampa police still had him listed as a missing person. Thus, Mutual of Omaha was in no hurry to write a check.

This was further complicated by the fact that there was still a strong contingent within the law enforcement community that Taylor may, in fact, still be alive—faking his own death just as Dr. Spears had attempted to do. The fact that the two men had met earlier with Julian Frank, the New York attorney, not long before Flight 967—and all three ended up connected to an airline crash—just seemed too much of a coincidence for many to ignore.

Al Taylor had been "positively identified" by a co-worker in Nashville around Christmas after the plane went down, and he was still willing to "swear on a stack of Bibles that the man I saw was Al." There had been other alleged sightings as well, but the fire was greatly fueled when Junior—Alice and Al's only child—was summoned to Dallas by the FBI "to have a discussion."

Excited by the possibilities about what that conversation might concern, Junior immediately went on air with radio station KBOX to announce that there may be new developments in the case of his missing father: "I'm on my way to Dallas because the Feds have new information that my father may be alive!"

The news director at the radio station fueled the rumors even more when he related that he had a source who said the FBI in Dallas had found some of Al Taylor's personal belongings. Speculation quickly arose that he was the "other person" William Turska had been first seen with shortly after Spears' arrival in Phoenix, but then was never seen again.

Art Smith of the *Tampa Tribune* merged these rumors and conjecture and began to build a case that Al Taylor was out there

The Rock and the Role / 227

and in hiding somewhere—a mutual plot by both men to disappear and solve their personal issues. All each side needed to do was point to the other as the perpetrator and mastermind and then collect the insurance money for their own dead husband.

Smith wrote: "Before he disappeared, Taylor seemed a tortured, troubled man—not happy in his job or his lonely existence. Dr. Spears was always telling Taylor to look for 'greener pastures.' He played the role of a successful, patronizing elder statesman, passing along his advice and counsel to a poor, mentally depressed friend. It is not unreasonable to assume that Taylor was looking into making himself scarce."

Others agreed, with one stating, "Taylor and Spears were both practiced con men. They'd been pulling schemes for decades together. After all, both had been planning a 'change in their lives.' And perhaps Taylor left the letters where they might be discovered to leave a clue to loved ones—in order to comfort them—that they might both still be alive."

Veteran Tampa police detective John Daniels also did not accept the prevailing view that Al Taylor was an unsuspecting victim of his pal Spears. "Taylor was in debt over his head," he explained. "Both men were together in the confidence rackets before. Taylor's not going to let himself get talked into something as crazy as getting on a plane that's about to blow up. Who knows, but I personally expect that Taylor might show up one day, alive and healthy."

However, it was Willis Flick, attorney for Mutual of Omaha, who really promulgated the theory that Al Taylor was still living. "They are confidence men, for heaven's sake!" he said at one point, slamming a sheet of paper down on the table to serve as evidence. It was a letter written by Dr. Spears to his wife while he was in Tampa on stationery from the Hillsboro Hotel shortly before Flight 967.

In it, he wrote to Frances that Al Taylor was talking about disappearing from Florida for good, citing that he was fed up with his ex-wife and stepson, who always wanted his money but didn't care about him. Frances would later convey the contents of one of the three letters that she received by airmail from her husband on the very day of the plane crash:

228 / Chapter 27

Visited with Al last evening. Al is making—or has already made arrangements—to get away from his domestic situation at home in Tampa for good. Al Jr. is going down the same road as Blaine and between all of them, they have ruined Al's credit and made a wreck out of him. He's absolutely pitiful.

Al says that he is just going to take off somewhere and get away from it all. Doesn't want to ever hear from any of them again. Said he planned on going last week, but was waiting to talk to me first. Guess most everyone has their troubles. We have a couple of "small ones," but those two sure are sweet. So's my wife! All my love, darling!

The letter represented a strong argument that Taylor might still be alive. Although it might have appeared publicly to be an expression of hope and sympathy for the Taylor family, it was actually self-serving. It was in Flick's and Mutual of Omaha's best interests for Taylor not to be declared dead, thus preventing an insurance payment to the beneficiary.

Alice Taylor would not give up, however, in her campaign to place her ex-husband on that fateful flight, and she turned to the most unlikely source imaginable to get that proof. It was a Hail Mary, to be sure, but it was perhaps her last hope to claim the insurance money due to her son.

So—though it left a bitter, acrid taste in her mouth—she picked up the phone and placed another call to her attorney Robert Mann.

Chapter 28

A Book and Movie Deal

The courts notified attorney Robert Mann that the only way William Allen Taylor could be declared legally dead, without waiting the required seven years, would be to obtain a notarized statement from an informed individual. A tall order, to be sure, but Mann had an idea.

In October of that year, Mann was being processed as a visitor with the strict protocols that were in place to prevent anyone from sneaking contraband to inmates at The Rock. It was a bit of a wonder that he had received permission to speak with Dr. Spears—even between a two-inch thick glass wall—because once someone landed at Alcatraz, it was generally their last stop in the prison system, a system that did not give a damn for the personal concerns of its prisoners.

Mann actually benefited from his request because of some unusual timing at Alcatraz. The prison was going through a change of leadership, and the attorney took advantage of it somewhat by manipulating the system.

Paul Madigan was the warden of Alcatraz Federal Penitentiary when Mann's request came through. Having worked his way up from the bottom of the ranks of the enforcement officers to being the head man, Madigan was a virtual one-man institution with a no-nonsense approach. A stout, ruddy-faced, pipe-smoking, devout Irish Catholic, he was a fighter who was single-handedly waging a war with the U.S. Director of Prisons

230 / Chapter 28

in Washington, DC, who wanted to close down the aging, crumbling prison permanently.

Amid this battle, he was replaced by his associate warden Olin Blackwell. If anyone thought that Blackwell would be more compliant, they were wrong. A short and feisty fellow, he picked up the cause and demanded more funds to save the decaying and financially destitute prison.

His own efforts would be ultimately undermined by the fact that he was known as a loose-lipped, fast-living, heavy drinker and smoker, nicknamed "Gypsy" by the guards and known as "Blackie" to his friends. However, in the midst of this transfer of power and confusion, Robert Mann, miraculously, received approval for a face-to-face meeting with Dr. Robert Spears.

Alone in a room, the attorney got straight to the point: "Bob, I need a notarized statement from you attesting to the fact that Al Taylor took your place on Flight 967. It's the only way Junior can get the insurance money that his father wanted for him. It's the right thing to do, Bob, and I hope you see it that way."

Mann reported later that Spears was calm and happy to receive a visitor—he loved to talk, after all—but he could see that the prisoner was worn down and had lost weight. His prostate issues were exacting a toll, as were the harsh conditions of the decrepit facilities. Not hopeful about getting the signed document, Mann was surprised when Spears agreed to cooperate.

Even knowing that Alice Taylor loathed both him and his wife and was calling him out in the press as a mass murderer, Spears wanted to do the right thing for Junior, a good kid whom he always liked and who was now serving his country in the Marines. He also wanted to do the right thing for himself, at least the prudent thing.

The presence of a stenographer and notary gave Dr. Spears the golden opportunity to get his version of the story officially recorded and entered into court records, his own selfish reason in the matter. For some time, he had been itching to get his side of the events out there, and—for the cost of giving his primary accuser her insurance money—he jumped at the chance to "tell all."

A Book and Movie Deal / 231

Robert Mann was also happy to make the trade to get the all-important signature on the statement—though God only knew what Dr. Spears might say when he was given free rein to talk.

And talk he did. In a sworn and notarized statement, Dr. Spears told "the truth and nothing but the truth"—at least as he saw it.

> During the afternoon of November 15, 1959, Mr. Taylor came down to the Hillsboro Hotel in Tampa. I checked out, and we went to his apartment. Previous to that time Mr. Taylor told me he was having trouble with his right arm. He was practically unable to use the arm at all. When we got to his apartment, Mr. Taylor said he wanted to go to Dallas to get his arm taken care of.
>
> Previous to that time, he had had the same trouble, and a doctor in Dallas had been able to straighten him out, and it lasted for almost 10 years. At that time, Taylor asked me to drive his car and let him fly on my ticket. I didn't much want to do it, but he was in such pain that I finally agreed.
>
> Shortly before 12 o'clock, we went to the airport. I checked in, turned my ticket over to the agent, and the agent gave me a boarding pass, or whatever it is that they do for a passenger. I took it back out to the car and gave it to Taylor.
>
> A few minutes later, Taylor got out of the car, took his bag, and went toward the airport terminal. We were both in the front of the terminal at the time. I waited a short while, went across the street to a gas station, picked up a couple of road maps, and eventually took off for Dallas.
>
> Taylor had asked me to drive his car and let him use my ticket on the plane. It's that simple. I never saw him again afterward.

In November 1961, Judge James Bruton officially declared—exactly two years after the airliner crash—that William Allen Taylor was deceased, stating, "No bodies were ever found, and so we don't have firsthand knowledge of it, but there's good circumstantial evidence that Mr. Taylor was aboard the plane.

"Along with Dr. Spears' notarized statement and the testimony of gate attendant, Lloyd Griffin, who confirmed that

232 / Chapter 28

there were thirty-six tickets collected and thirty-six passengers counted on board, from a legal perspective that is sufficient to please the court in this matter."

With that judgment by the court, William Allen Taylor's complete estate was turned over to Alice. Unfortunately, the total of his assets added up to only $400—a rather minuscule amount, in his ex-wife's estimate, for a man who had worked all his life and earned decent salaries. At this point, however, her focus was more on the fact that she was relieved that her son would receive the flight insurance money, along with other funds that came from another Metropolitan Life policy and a settlement from National Airlines.

Alice Taylor was convinced that she could finally rest, having been proven true and vindicated in her exhausting two-year cause. From MetLife and the airlines, in the end, she and Junior would receive well over $200,000 in today's value—a tidy sum with the Mutual of Omaha money still to come.

But would it come?

Willis Flick, attorney for the vending machine insurance company, refused to give in, still maintaining—despite Judge Bruton's ruling and Dr. Spears' statement—that Taylor was alive and he would not authorize the nearly $400,000 (in today's money) payment to Junior. Standing steadfast, he maintained his firm was willing to wait out the seven years before cutting any check. It infuriated Alice, who, once again, found herself in yet another fight.

Just as Alice was forced to turn her attention to a new adversary, so too was Dr. Spears, who was growing increasingly frustrated and irritated by Eddie Barker's constant storytelling and broadcast platforms where, he felt, the newsman was manipulating and brainwashing his wife Frances against him.

Knowing that the self-promoter had finagled his way into the life of his family—often spending the night on their living room couch—he grew progressively incensed and began to focus all of his energy, what there was left at least, on righting the inequities that Barker was putting forth in his wife's name.

A Book and Movie Deal / 233

Even from Alcatraz, Spears was convinced he had plenty of clout, and he intended to use it.

So, he decided to take his adversary head-on by entering the lion's den and extracting a deal with the devil.

"The man thought too highly of himself and needed to be brought down to earth," Spears would later say. "He had been comforting and impressing my wife with his smooth talk and slick ideas, but only I knew the truth . . . and he knew it. I was the big fish he wanted, so I lured him in."

Heaven only knows how he did it, but Dr. Spears—again, always the model prisoner and popular inmate—was able to pull strings and get Eddie Barker a face-to-face interview in prison. Saying he was "an old friend" with news from home, Spears incredibly secured a day-pass for the reporter. The promise of an exclusive with the most nefarious criminal in America was almost overwhelming. Barker took the first plane he could catch to San Francisco, with station KRLD picking up the tab.

Sitting directly across from each other at a metal table in a private room—like two boxers locked in a cage—Spears began to talk, and Barker began to record him on his portable reel-to-reel tape recorder. But this interview was designed to be more than giving Spears yet another chance to tell his story. No, this time there was some serious money behind it.

Barker had been able to send a message in advance to Spears indicating that he had an offer from a publisher of between one and two million dollars (in today's value) for the doctor's "true story," and there was even buzz that MGM was interested in obtaining the film rights. The newsman swore that, aside from that massive payday, he also wanted to work in tandem with Spears to deflect any hint that Frances had been implicit in his crimes by aiding him along the way—an issue that was heating up with the Feds at the time.

"He told me that this was the best way for me to provide for my wife and children," Spears later told FBI agents. "I asked him who would write the book, and he told me he would, saying, 'I'm pretty good on the typewriter, you know, and it won't cost you any commission. All I want is the prestige of breaking the story. It will be good for my career as a journalist.'

234 / Chapter 28

"That sounded pretty good to me. Plus, Barker told me that he was greatly interested in my career as a naturopath and the benefits of alternative medical treatments because it personally fascinated him. He felt that the naturopath story needed to be told, and I'd been interested in doing that for some time."

Thus, the package was simply too good to pass up, and Spears began to talk as the tape wound around the plastic spools.

After nearly six hours, however, Barker felt like he had been given nothing new. It was the same old story: Spears had given his plane ticket to Taylor because of his sore neck and arm and drove his friend's car on up ahead to Dallas with full permission. In this telling, Spears was the consummate and compassionate best friend, and Taylor was simply the hard-luck loser—the sad story of the man's star-crossed life.

At the end of their time together, Eddie Barker stood and blurted out that he felt like he had been played by the serial con man, and if the story didn't have more spice, then the publisher would never be interested—there had to be more to it than that. Calling a guard to unlock the door, Barker told Spears to think it over and see if there was anything else "he could come up with."

In a later letter to Frances, Robert said that Barker became "verbally aggressive" toward him and maintained that such a vanilla story wasn't "saleable." Barker was not willing to give up, however—he was just pitching the wrong person.

Returning to Dallas, Barker almost immediately began to apply pressure on Frances to "have your husband think long and hard about our conversation and the possibilities. He needs to tell me the complete story." She was unclear what this meant, but it would start a thread of letters that would later become significant.

Spears would subsequently tell his wife exactly what Eddie Barker was fishing for, and he would document it as well.

In a letter to Mutual of Omaha insurance investigators, Spears stated: "After Barker got my story on tape, he told me that he wouldn't be able to sell it. He wanted a confession. For hours, he kept telling me that I owed it to my wife and babies to tell the complete story, that it was the only thing that would ensure their future. I said, 'I'm sorry, Eddie, but anything else would have to be a made-up story.'

"Then he said, 'So, let's make one up then!'"

Chapter 29

A Broadcast and a Bestseller

Dr. Robert Spears, who had never been opposed to picking up a quick buck with either a white lie or a detailed deception, turned to his wife to make the call—as recorded in letters between the two. "I finally told him to discuss the matter with you and let me know what you thought of the plan," he wrote. "So you know, Eddie and I decided that he would refer to it as the 'property deal' so we should do that."

Barker was working both sides feverishly, desperate to make this deal work. Hoping to tempt Frances with enough money to live with her children in luxury for the rest of their lives, he also was attempting to squeeze Robert by sending him a news clipping—which he had authored—stating that authorities would soon be bringing in sophisticated military diving equipment to locate the airliner now located at the bottom of the Gulf of Mexico.

Along with the article, he wrote, "Bob, we should consummate the deal as soon as possible. I think you will agree that time is of the essence if the value is to hold up. The story will have little to no value once the plane is found. We must get 'the complete story' on tape as soon as we possibly can, and I give you my word not to divulge anything regarding our conversations unless and until you give me permission. Once we have the recordings, I will keep the tapes in my safety deposit box."

Frances confirmed the offer with her husband and admitted that Barker was talking to her "multiple times a week, both night

235

236 / Chapter 29

and day, in an attempt to set up an extended interview with you. He says that the only way the book deal will go through is if you tell the complete story . . . if you confess."

In a separate letter to insurance investigators, Spears stated:

> My newspaper friend has been in contact with Mrs. Spears two or three times a week for over a year, and he has got her completely sold on the idea that I know what happened to the plane. He said that if I'd tell all about it, then they could forgive me and proceed to help me. That I could be forgiven for my sins.
>
> It is sort of a religious attitude—that one must confess their sins to bring about forgiveness. Trouble is, I don't know what to confess. Frances' words to me are the exact words of Eddie Barker and there is nothing I can say or do that will change her mind.

Without getting any further advice, Bob Spears apparently decided to go along with the hoax and let Barker believe that the need for forgiveness sealed the deal for him, and he was finally ready to tell the all-important "complete story" and deliver the "property."

Thus, from November 17 to November 29, Barker spent dozens of hours taping Spears while incarcerated. "Barker insisted that we put the whole thing on tape so he wouldn't forget any of it."

However, Spears was already beginning to have misgivings. Writing to Frances, he stated, "As the tape rolled, I began to feel that he was only after another scoop and that he cared nothing about a book, or for you and the future of the children, nor what harm he could cause you with his plan. I doubt now whether he ever even intends to write a book."

Continuing, his tone turned melancholy and regretful. "I want to see you more than anything in the world. I'm sorry— sorrier than you'll ever know—and I hope you can visit at least one more time so that I can tell you in person."

During those exhausting days, Eddie Barker did indeed get the scoop of a lifetime. Robert Spears spoke effortlessly and freely and provided details that, until this point, had never

A Broadcast and a Bestseller / 237

been heard. Barker knew he was getting something special, and his enthusiasm for the project was rising by the hour. He just needed to keep Spears talking until he said the magic words, until he gave a full confession of his deeds.

The following was the "complete story" Dr. Robert Vernon Spears told.

> Around October of 1959, I reached out to my friend Al Taylor in Tampa from a pay phone at LA International and told him about the Los Angeles abortion charges. Although it was not the first time I had faced charges, this time, I knew it could be worse. My opportunities in Dallas had dried up because of the legal situation there, and California represented the best option for my wife and kids. If I were to go to prison, at least they would be living in a nice place and probably be close to me.
>
> I considered any number of ways to deal with my upcoming legal situation, including using intimidation of the girl who was the primary witness for the prosecution. I spent some time thinking about how I might take care of her. In an emergency, I decided I would use a bomb. I discussed all of these options with Al because he was an expert with explosives.
>
> At that time, Al said that he could easily obtain explosives from a nearby roadside construction site in Tampa. Then he asked me, "What do you want with them?" I told him that I couldn't discuss the matter over the phone, but I'd try to see him soon, and we could talk about it some more.
>
> In the meantime, I asked Taylor to go ahead and pick up a batch of dynamite, and we agreed to have a conversation about everything in the future. On November 14, I flew into Tampa Airport, and the first thing he asked about was what the dynamite was for. I explained the situation to him, and I told him that there'd be some money in it for him. I told him I could get him $10,000 [$100,000 in current value] if he could get the dynamite to Los Angeles.
>
> To disguise what we were talking about, we called the dynamite plan "The Business." There wasn't really a plan to blow up anything, but we were going to use it to intimidate the girl who was going to testify against me. Taylor constructed a bomb, and we did some test blasting out in the Tampa marshes, way out of the city, and during that time, he set up a

device that could be activated once we were in California. All that was needed was to hook up the timer.

After that, we just had a nice time at the Hillsboro Hotel—it was brand new at the time—before driving to the Tampa Airport. We had already decided that I would drive to Dallas, and Al would use my ticket to fly there. On the way, we stopped at the Morrison's Cafeteria for Al to pick up something for the trip.

We sat for a while in the airport parking lot just shooting the bull, you know, and having a smoke or two. In the backseat was "The Business," so to speak. It was a brown paper-wrapped package that was about twelve inches long and about six inches thick.

After that, I went up to the National Airlines counter, just to the right of the terminal entrance, and checked in. I had no luggage to check because my suitcase was still back in the car with Al. After I had my boarding pass, I went to the airport coffee shop and got the shrimp platter with fries and coleslaw.

When I was done, I went back again to the car and gave Taylor the stamped boarding pass. I said goodbye to Al then and drove out of the lot as he was entering the terminal with my ticket. He only had a briefcase and the wrapped package with him. That was the last time I ever saw Al Taylor.

Of course, we all know now, from the testimony of other witnesses in the airport that night, that Al boarded the plane and then came back out to purchase the flight insurance. There's nothing about that that surprises me. Taylor was sort of a nut on insurance. I can understand him taking out an insurance policy even for that short of a flight. It was only a few quarters, after all.

Even though Al was carrying "The Business" when I last saw him, I'm still of the opinion that the plane—well, that something else happened to it. The fault lies with National Airlines. I'd say mechanical problems, pilot error, or maintenance issues are the most likely cause. If "The Business" did detonate during the flight, well, then it had to be by accident.

Think about it . . . it makes no logical sense for Al to destroy the entire plane—including himself—just for a chance on someone collecting some meager amount of insurance off of him. I am absolutely convinced that Al Taylor did not explode that airliner.

A Broadcast and a Bestseller / 239

Barker was quick to publish his exclusive interview in the *Dallas Times Herald* and aired portions of the actual recordings on his Saturday evening KRLD broadcast. The next day—just in time for the large Sunday editions of every paper in the nation—a syndicated version of the story would land on front pages from coast to coast. The headline in the *Los Angeles Herald Examiner* read: "I Paid to Put a Bomb on the Plane." Others touted: "Robert Spears Tells Grim Bombing Tale" and "Missing Plane Carried Bomb."

In a melodramatic and unnecessary opening statement in the article, Barker wrote, "Spears is the toughest man I ever knew, with cold hard eyes and an evil leer. But these are the grim and truthful facts—gathered over 60 hours of interviews—carefully outlined by the convict himself, who is at the heart of this story."

Barker also began his story with a scene virtually written to be a future movie script. Wanting to kick off his dramatic tale—and perhaps the first chapter of a book—he had Spears describe a harrowing moment at the Bali-Hi during the moment of his arrest.

"I had been tipped off that the agents were arriving soon at the hotel, and so as I sprinted toward the cab's open door, I whipped out a bottle of cyanide, but an agent caught my hand before the bottle could reach my lips. There was enough cyanide in there to kill 300 men, experts told me later, but I was so desperate to avoid the abortion trial that I would have done anything."

Perhaps plant a bomb on an airliner? Eddie Barker's readers and listeners were on the edge of their seats.

The story failed to reveal one important fact, however, which helped explain why a reporter could gain access to an inmate in a maximum security prison with a tape recorder in hand—it turned out that Eddie Barker was working for the FBI. In fact, he had been strategically inserted into the situation to try to get to the bottom of the story, and his tapes were quickly turned over to and analyzed by federal investigators.

An FBI memorandum was later attached to Spears' file that read, "Edward Barker has been permitted to visit Mr. Spears on a number of occasions at the request of the FBI. He has actually

240 / Chapter 29

been cooperating with the FBI in an attempt to get information regarding the plane crash. It was for this reason the tape recordings were made, and not for the publicity purposes that Spears thought."

Two days after the story ran, Barker's name had been crossed off the visitor's list in Alcatraz with a handwritten note that read: *REMOVED*.

Shortly after the recordings, Spears also contacted Richard Ellis, Mutual of Omaha assistant vice president, and gave him this statement: "Barker asked that I make a direct confession. I refused to do this. It was at this point that he became abusive, and I realized that he was not interested in helping my family but was interested in building up a fictional news story for his own benefit.

"So I just went along with it."

This was indeed an interesting twist and one which might help him in a future parole hearing. Spears, in essence, was saying that he was merely trying to please Eddie Barker and make a more "saleable" book when he elaborated on certain story details. This was far from any confession of wrongdoing but rather an amateur scriptwriter wanting to forge his own character's role.

Tempted by a publisher's million-dollar payday and Barker's incessant prodding for the "complete story," he resorted to his finely honed storytelling skills and spun a tale worthy of Hollywood—whose eyes he was trying to attract.

For the general public, who never before had heard Spears' voice, the radio and television broadcasts brought the fascinating con man—who had generated a thousand headlines—into the living rooms of everyday Americans and made him a folk hero of sorts.

With an appealing way with words and an oddly good-natured sense of humor, Spears had somehow managed to reach the pinnacle once again, though for the most unconscionable reasons. Nearly a septuagenarian at this point, he was more grandfatherly than threatening and it was hard for the public not to see him as an affable storyteller in the mold of a Burl Ives than a cunning, heartless killer.

A Broadcast and a Bestseller / 241

During the Barker interviews—60 hours in length—it was hard not to think that Spears was playing the role of his own advance man for a publisher promoting his bestseller. Later, he would say that he was just toying with Barker during those sessions, in part as revenge for manipulating his wife's emotions at such a vulnerable time and turning her affections against him. Then, if a book by Barker did eventually manage to get published, he would see that the joke was on him.

At the moment, however, no one was laughing.

Al Taylor's son immediately reacted to the idea that his father was an expert in explosives and the mastermind of a bomb-building enterprise. "He couldn't even adjust the carburetor of his car," Junior commented derisively. A co-worker at Pioneer Tire agreed, "Taylor couldn't even plug in a television set without doing it wrong. This business about him making a bomb is ridiculous."

Furthermore, Junior dismissed out of hand the thought that his father was committing suicide by taking down an airliner full of innocent passengers.

> My father would not have boarded that plane in Spears' place unless he was drugged or hypnotized. He would never, ever have given his life for Spears.
>
> And that whole thing about him needing to see a doctor about a bad arm and neck is just a bunch of crock. He had a brace once, yes, but it's still out here in the garage. He was healthy. Dad was in a car accident a few years earlier, but there was nothing wrong with him for years.
>
> And I've also wanted to say this for ages. The stories about my father have been one-sided. As far as I'm concerned, he was a fine man. He did many things for me. I didn't appreciate them then, but I appreciate them now.

The reaction to Barker's interview with Bob would also turn out to be Frances Spears' last comment for the press. Exhausted by the years-long ordeal, she had finally accepted that her husband was a fraud and con man and maybe even worse. Tired and defeated, with children to raise and a need to earn a living, she issued her final statement.

242 / Chapter 29

There is nothing I can say at a time like this. I can only say again what I have said so many times before. The Bob Spears I knew, was married to, and who fathered my children was a loving and kind man. The Bob Spears I knew and loved could not have done this thing. Surely, something must have snapped. He is no longer the man I knew.

I have lived for some time with knowledge of this information about the probability of the bomb, dreading the day it would be revealed and searching for a word of comfort for all those who have suffered and been grieved by this terrible thing. I pray God's mercy and forgiveness for Bob.

Chapter 30

Laughing All the Way

After spending time at the federal prison in Chino, California, Dr. Spears—model inmate as always—was eventually transferred to the California Men's Colony in San Luis Obispo, a minimum-security institution. There, he applied for parole on the abortion conviction as soon as he was eligible in 1965. Maintaining that he was a changed man, a doctor, and had never caused any problems while behind bars, he threw himself at the mercy of the panel of reviewers.

Almost before he finished speaking, however, the parole board pronounced that he was "not sufficiently rehabilitated," stamped DENIED on his application, and he was dismissed from the room.

One year later, he was once more eligible and went before the parole board for a hearing. They stamped DENIED on his form once again with little consideration, but this time added, "Mr. Spears, you should be prepared to serve your full sentence and not expect release before August 1968, assuming good behavior."

Spears was discouraged but not defeated. He had another tack that he was willing to try and began working on it as soon as he returned to his cell. *There was always another way.*

This time, he went to work on preparing a legal challenge on his stolen car charge. In a somewhat miraculous turn, he eventually ended up in the court of District Judge William Copple in June 1967. This time around, again acting as his own attorney,

244 / Chapter 30

he was maintaining that he had been coerced into a confession and guilty plea by the FBI. His statement was categorically false.

Standing before the judge, who had a reputation for coming down hard on police corruption, he explained that the FBI agents had told him that they would level the book at both him and his wife—charging her with conspiracy—and make orphans out of his children if he did not agree to the Dyer Act violation. He respectfully described 11 stress-filled days of unrelenting interrogation during which he was consistently denied legal counsel.

Also, if he did not agree to cooperate, they would charge him with interstate narcotics smuggling for transporting abortion treatments that he used in Phoenix, California, and Florida.

As one writer put it, his defense was that "the con man had been conned."

Furthermore, he swore that the FBI told him that they had brokered a deal for him for a maximum three-month sentence and, if convicted in California, those sentences would run concurrently, not consecutively.

The bottom line is that Robert Spears had been intimidated, threatened, tricked, and lied to because the feds were always going to go for the maximum sentence simply because they were frustrated with the fact that they had spent so much time and money trying to prove that he was behind the Flight 967 bombing, and were unable to. It was merely retaliation for their failure and burning humiliation.

After all, a car theft which really wasn't a theft—he steadily maintained that Al Taylor had asked him to drive the car to Dallas—in no way deserved five years in Alcatraz among the nation's hardest and most unrepentant criminals.

His final plea, however, was an emotional one: "More than anything, your Honor, I just want to get out in time to be of some service to my family."

In a September 1967 decision, Judge Copple surprised most legal analysts when he agreed with Spears that he had not been provided legal counsel when he agreed to plead guilty. With the pound of his gavel, the judge dismissed the stolen car conviction.

Laughing All the Way / 245

This vacated sentence, however, instantly introduced another issue.

With Spears having already served his entire five-year sentence on the stolen car charge, there was now hope on his part that—with time already served—his abortion sentence, based on performing just one abortion, would also have been satisfied. After all, Donald Loomis—who had pleaded guilty to performing 500 abortions and was his co-defendant in the case—had only served six months and was now living comfortably in his estate home.

But despite his hope, California didn't seem to be moving in his favor and for months, Spears couldn't get anyone to listen to him, and he was forced to wallow in San Luis Obispo well into the following year. In the eyes of the court system, Spears believed he was serving time for blowing up an airliner, though he had never been charged with the crime.

Then—in what appeared to be a bit of a slap in the face—just 57 days short of serving his full sentence, Robert Vernon Spears was released from the California Men's Colony in San Luis Obispo on July 9, 1968. Walking through the gates, he waited a couple of hours to catch a bus. After a few transfers, he headed for the only place that truly felt like home—Dallas, Texas.

He finally arrived late in the evening and walked several miles until he reached tree-lined Gaston Avenue in the prestigious Lake Highlands suburb. Just as he had done nearly a decade earlier when he was masquerading as his close friend Al Taylor and driving his car with a trunk full of dynamite, he stood across the street from the beautiful brick two-story home marked 6116.

Straining, he thought he saw Frances cross the room as a silhouette. Then, in a flash, his daughter ran to reach her mother. His heart dropped at the sight of it and the memories of the active, full, and privileged life they once shared in that home.

But, of course, he was now divorced and penniless. And there was one other thing.

In 1962, Spears was notified that his son had gone into a diabetic coma. As a result, four-year-old Kenny suffered irreversible

246 / Chapter 30

brain damage and was institutionalized for years. While incarcerated, Spears was told the tragic news—his only son had finally died of respiratory failure. The loss seemed greater than ever as he stood across from the beautiful house with the soft glow of hominess emanating from within.

He hadn't been able to attend his son's funeral to hold his six-year-old daughter's hand. He hadn't been able to convince the parole board to let him go there. The obituary simply listed Kenneth's father as "away in California"—a cold and bitter indictment of the truth of the matter.

Not wanting to be recognized by any neighbors, Spears eventually shuffled along slowly and headed toward the boarding house that would be his home for the next few years. He would never contact Frances again. He would never reach out to Robin, but wherever he went, he hoped to catch a glimpse of either of them. More than once, he tried to anticipate where they might be and waited in the shadows.

He also realized that, at some point, Frances would begin a new life with a new man. He never doubted that she would be a good mother and hoped she would say some kind things to Robin about her father. Perhaps tell her that she was loved by him even if he was never around.

Frances eventually did as Robert expected.

Although she refused ever to be interviewed again on the topic of her ex-husband and the tragedy of Flight 967, she did answer one last question. When asked why she chose not to change her name, she replied, "I must teach my daughter to remember her father with love and that running away solves nothing."

Though he had craved attention and an audience for most of his life, Bob Spears was content to live a most unspectacular life in his 70s. Subsisting on frozen dinners and television, he was merely passing the time. Marking off the days on the calendar.

There were undoubtedly times when the old memories resurfaced to haunt him. Back when he was head of the National Naturopathic Association and leading the fight to bust the monopoly of the American Medical Association. Back when he was rich and admired and sought out as a renowned lecturer.

Back when he and Frances entertained the Dallas' elite in their stunningly decorated home located in the best neighborhood.

He also remembered the years of intense excitement and adventure—always one step ahead of the law and laughing all the way. He missed Al—his forever friend Al Taylor—and no doubt wondered what might have been if. . . .

Still, there was no reason to think too hard about anything. Fate had her hand in everything, after all. Regrets? Sure. Rewards? Too many to count.

In the early morning of May 2, 1969—a gorgeous spring morning in Texas—Robert Spears woke up with some indigestion. His left arm felt numb. Managing to get the operator, he was soon scooped up by paramedics and rushed to the Baylor University Medical Center emergency room. Arriving a few minutes after eight, the 73-year-old man was pronounced dead of a heart attack.

Spears' 10-year-old daughter was named as next of kin, but it was Frances who identified his body. The death certificate, ironically, read: "Retired Physician, MD." Frances would go on to order his headstone—there was no other adult in his life—and she had engraved on it: *Sgt. US Army, World War I*. Perhaps his only legitimate career and semi-noble act of his lifetime. Spears was laid to rest in an honored section of Restland Memorial Park in Dallas named, The Field of Honor.

Three days later, the Reverend William Martin of First Community Church presided over the service while a lengthy obituary ran in the *New York Times*. The generation that may have known of him was now largely gone but his final headline reminds everyone of his place in history: "Robert V. Spears, 73, Is Dead: Figure in Mystery Plane Crash."

Over a span of 39 years, 25 aliases, 28 arrests in 20 cities, and nearly a dozen imprisonments, Robert Spears had lived a life of unparalleled adventure and intrigue. However, his greatest legacy would prove to be the one thing no one would ever know if he did.

When his remaining personal items were packed and stored for auction by the County Coroner's Office, a worker placed a particular book on the top of the pile, undoubtedly not

248 / Chapter 30

understanding its significance. It was a 1940 volume by David W. Maurer entitled *The Big Con, The Story of the Confidence Man.* Inside, one sentence was underlined in red: *"Of all the grifters, the confidence man is the aristocrat."*

OBITUARY
May 3, 1969
St. Petersburg Times
Robert Spears, 1959 Bomb Suspect, Dies in Dallas

Robert Vernon Spears, suspected a decade ago of planting a bomb on a plane that went down in the Gulf of Mexico, died in Baylor Medical Center yesterday. A spokesman for the hospital said Spears was admitted at 8:10 a.m. and died at 8:30 but did not give the cause of death.

Spears was a naturopath. The plane that crashed on Nov. 16, 1959, was a National Airlines transport. Although a bomb was suspected, the cause could never be determined because the water the plane crashed in was too deep.

Spears, for weeks, was assumed to have been one of the passengers. Then, it was discovered that William Taylor of Tampa, a friend, took his place at the last moment.

The change was discovered when Spears was arrested near Phoenix, Ariz., in January, 1969, driving Taylor's car. Spears went to federal prison on a government charge of car theft.

Chapter 31

In the Aftermath

For the reader, in a story as complex as the life of Robert Vernon Spears, there no doubt will be a nagging wonder about what eventually happened to all the characters in this grand drama. It is normal, but it is also a difficult yearning to satisfy for several reasons.

First, and most obvious, is the fact that with a story that begins more than a century ago and hasn't had any noticeable updates in the last 50 years, it is difficult to track the movements of people. Few, if any, are still around.

Second, in a story drenched in heartache and tragedy, those involved—as well as their offspring—are understandably ready to move on from the past. The idea of dredging past pain is never a pleasant prospect, and it takes a hearty soul to willingly reopen the door to sad times.

Finally, a fair amount of the people in this tale were involved in criminal activities and wanted, for all intents and purposes, to disappear. Perhaps not like Robert Spears or Al Taylor, but nevertheless to simply move back into the shadows where there is less exposure. As a result, they leave a scant trail to follow, if any at all. Some, clearly, went to great efforts to cover their tracks.

Donald Loomis, who bore the title of "The Physical Director of Hollywood" and "Flesh Sculptor for the Stars" for MGM Studios, had the highest profile of anyone in this twisted tale. Still, he also had one of the sharpest declines. After having served as a nutritionist, trainer, and exercise partner for scores of movie

250 / Chapter 31

stars such as Jean Harlow, Marlene Dietrich, Ginger Rogers, Joan Crawford, and Kathryn Hepburn for well over a decade, he was dismissed by the studio with no comment.

Observers believed that it was because he knew too much. Or had done too much. According to one report, he performed more than 5,000 abortions during his career, many of which were with starlets, marquee actresses, and mistresses of studio executives. Loomis was a "fixer" in the day—every studio during the Golden Era of Cinema had one or more—and his inside knowledge eventually made him a massive liability.

Hollywood is rife with stories of cinema legends who had "appendicitis attacks" and were rushed to studio-supported clinics for an emergency operation. Later, MGM internal memorandums would reveal that "appendicitis" was a code word for abortion. One anonymous studio source admitted that from the 1930s to the 1950s, "there was an overwhelming epidemic of appendicitis during the era."

When Loomis eventually moved on from MGM into being a full-time medical practitioner—under the large and loose naturopath umbrella—he was watched carefully by industry thugs and undoubtedly lived under certain threats not to open his mouth.

But Loomis thrived in his black market trade, which resulted in him living in a hilltop mansion in Palos Verdes with a view of the Pacific Ocean and featuring an Olympic-size pool, tennis courts, and a putting green. That home is now worth more than $15 million.

Donald Loomis' fall from grace was a steep one, and it all started when he made the unwise decision to partner with Robert Spears. Although Loomis raked in the bulk of the revenue from their short-lived operation, it was Spears' botched abortion that brought down Loomis' lifestyle of wealth and excess.

However, using his extensive network of contacts with the Los Angeles police, the legal community, and the court system, Loomis was able to turn a charge of 500 abortions into a six-month jail sentence—of which he was released early—and a return to the luxury of a Hollywood life.

In the Aftermath / 251

But once again, his brief relationship with Bob Spears came back to haunt him in a big way. In a desperate attempt to shift blame in his own Los Angeles abortion case—though he was only charged with one count—Spears impetuously threw Loomis under the bus by fingering him as the mastermind behind the operation.

This time his vast number of influential contacts and under-the-table payments couldn't save him because Spears—with the hopes of putting his co-conspirator in the spotlight—provided detailed information proving that Loomis had been avoiding taxes for decades. Thus, after completing his short jail sentence, Loomis came home to his Palos Verdes mansion only to find IRS agents waiting for him. After years of delay, he was finally sentenced to a two-year jail-term in 1963 for falsifying his tax return in 1957.

Don Loomis was not happy about that. Not only would he have to go back to jail for even longer—after paying for police protection for years—but his financial empire, Hollywood reputation, and lucrative abortion business were now in shambles.

And so he decided to run.

Quietly and quickly liquidating most of his assets, he headed south, where he was later reported to be living lavishly in an American colony outside of Mexico City. Although it was believed that from time to time, he would sneak back into the States to visit family, he largely disappeared for good.

William Turska—who was also facing abortion charges of his own—also disappeared. Shortly after Spears' arrest in Phoenix, Turska promptly sold his New River compound. However—before the new owners could move in—the building mysteriously burst into flames. It burned to the ground, leaving only the brick patio that he and Bob had built earlier, and a few plumbing pipes sticking out of the ground.

Having remarried yet once again—this time just days after Spears had been arrested—Turska and his new wife Nellie Walker headed to Edmonton, Canada, where he set up a new practice there and continued to evade authorities, now in two countries.

252 / Chapter 31

Eventually, Turska crossed the border once again into Idaho. Although he could easily change countries, he could not change his own stripes as he went on to be named in a series of criminal charges, including assault and battery of his wife in 1971, public drunkenness, unlawful possession of drugs—caught with some 1,500 barbiturate pills—and several drunk driving offenses.

Still supremely confident even with his lengthy record, Bill Turska ran for the office of Idaho County Coroner in 1972 on the Republican ticket. He was soundly defeated in a landslide in a nearly all-red state.

But for the rest of his life, strangely enough, William Turska would enjoy a virtual legendary status within the naturopathic world—though within a decade or so, the number of practitioners dropped from 5,000 to 500. To this day, he is still celebrated as "The Grand Old Maverick." Continuing to practice well into his 80s, he was never shy about embracing controversial and unproven medical methods—even those rejected by his equally unqualified peers.

Frances Spears would later say, "Turska was the one to fear, not Bob." He has since passed and none of his several ex-wives have any desire to talk about him.

Four months after her husband's release from prison in July 1968, Frances married construction worker Jim Baze. The newlyweds settled into a more modest home in a new development on the outskirts of Dallas. There, they raised Bob's daughter together and lived for nearly 30 years until Jim's death. Frances worked most of those years in anonymity as a secretary and would continue to live in the area until she died in 2011 at age 87.

With the official ruling of her ex-husband's death and the resolution of the insurance cases, Alice Steele Taylor drifted out of the limelight. Before she did, however, she managed to utter a final enigmatic statement: "There's a great deal more that I can tell, but before I do, there would need to be a financial contract." She died without revealing anything more. Junior went on to live his own life, leaving the mania and the mystery of Flight 967 far behind.

In an odd and incredibly unexpected twist, Blaine—Alice's son by her earlier marriage—turned out to make headlines of his own. Blaine McKinley Henrie was only 11 years old when Al and Alice married. Despite Al's genuine desire to connect with the boy he inherited, he continually felt like he was falling short.

Most people in the know felt that it was a result of the child being spoiled by his mother, who ensured she had a photographer present at every one of his birthdays for inclusion in the Tampa newspaper society pages. Still, with few friends and limited interests, Blaine was a bit of a loner.

Throughout the saga with his father and Dr. Spears, Blaine seemed to always be in the background, often trying to get one or both of them to help him set up an art business for which he had a singular vision. By his late 20s, though, he had changed his name to *Henrie*—with a French pronunciation of "On-Ree"—and had developed an added touch of European arrogance along with it.

Blaine's entrepreneurial idea was to create wall-sized murals out of song sheets—he saw it as a blockbuster idea—and stepfather Al was too often his "bank," while Spears was his gateway to Hollywood through Don Loomis. It was, by and large, a foolhardy venture, but Al was trying to create a bond with him for Alice's sake, which was the impetus for the road trip to Manhattan.

Blaine—now rebranded once again as Paul Blaine—saw himself as a burgeoning modern artist in his own mind and had managed to place some pieces in a Greenwich Village gallery. Wanting to pitch his work to potential clients, Al agreed to drive him to New York while secretly planning on meeting with Bob Spears and Julian Frank, the doomed lawyer.

Later, Robert Spears would tell authorities, "Blaine was taking advantage of Al's good nature. He had this cockeyed plan to sell large painted murals of sheet music and wanted Al Taylor to finance the whole endeavor. I can tell you, Al Taylor was always borrowing and giving it to Blaine for the project, but the kid never once repaid him. It was just going down a hole. It's one of the reasons Al wanted out of that family."

254 / Chapter 31

After Al's disappearance—or untimely death—Blaine went his own way and ended up in Los Angeles, where he was convinced that he would be embraced by the more eclectic and avant-garde art community there.

Instead, he found a quite unique way of making a living—*forgery*.

Without any knowledge of his stepfather's nefarious past as a serial fraudster, Blaine traveled down a similar path as soon as he began to run short of money while searching for his pot of gold in the art world.

In early 1956—three years before his father disappeared— Blaine was detained for forging signatures on stolen checks to purchase a series of expensive items and then selling them to a fence. It landed him in jail for a stretch of time but, apparently, didn't dull his interest in taking shortcuts to "earn" money.

It amused Taylor that Blaine had no idea that he and Spears had a far more considerable pedigree in forgery and fraud. Blaine was too much of a liability for Taylor and Spears to confide in, but they did begin to take more of an interest in his future potential. That may have been their motivation in offering to help Blaine in his struggling art career.

It was Robert Spears, however, who saw promise in the boy and decided to support him in a fledgling endeavor near his home in Los Angeles. With Taylor putting in a chunk of seed money, Blaine was planning on selling art reproductions to the Hollywood colony where Spears, through Loomis, promised to get him connected for a share of the profits. Ironically, his business launched in November 1959—the same month as the ill-fated Flight 967.

Of course, with all the chaos that soon ensued, neither Spears nor Taylor were available to help out with Blaine's California venture. Surprisingly, however, he did just fine on his own and quickly became a very wealthy young man—though not exactly in the way that his business plan had outlined.

He was indeed beginning a venture of selling art reproductions—but he wasn't talking about poster prints. Rather, Blaine had developed into an expert art forger and could virtually replicate any painting in any style by any artist. Truly gifted in this

In the Aftermath / 255

skill, the wealthy and pretentious in Southern California—who were currently in art collecting fervor—were eager to get their hands on "originals" and paid top dollar and beyond to get newly "obtained" paintings from some of the most noted artists of the time.

Having once again repackaged himself in a way that would no doubt have made Bob Spears proud, Blaine was now "Paul Henrie" and gained national attention for painting large murals while, on the back end, supplying galleries with forgeries. Moving into the exclusive artist enclave of Laguna Beach with his wife and child, he soon had a million-dollar hillside home and several garages full of sports cars.

There, he also painted—in large volume—local seascapes and coastal scenes and sold them to eager tourists, whom he openly mocked while happily exploiting. Henrie was best known for his watercolors and palette-knife oil paintings of California as well as exotic locales he had visited in Tahiti, Mexico, and New Orleans.

Henrie bragged he was the "fastest palette in the west" and could produce several paintings in a day—saying that he only produced the paintings for tourist trap art galleries "when I need a ton of bucks. It may sound crass, but when I hear the bell and see the carrot, I'm off and running."

Despised by the locals and legitimate fine artists as a money-grabber, he clearly couldn't give a damn and boasted of having more than a thousand paintings for sale in galleries across California at any given time. Henrie was criticized for "prostituting his undeniable talent" because he readily admitted to pumping out dozens of paintings at a time simply to underwrite his ostentatious lifestyle.

Still, he was a talented artist of note and eventually became a favorite among the Hollywood crowd, many of whom readily purchased his expensive seascapes for thousands of dollars. With showings at several prestigious galleries, like the Grand Central Art Galleries in New York City, a significant number of celebrities collected his works, including Vincent Price, Frank Sinatra, Princess Margaret, and John Wayne, as well as a silk-screen portrait of the actor entitled, *The Duke.*

256 / Chapter 31

Full of himself, he next moved to Carmel-by-the-Sea and ran on the Republican ticket to be the city's mayor—following Clint Eastwood's term—though unsuccessfully. For all of his high-profile bravado and posturing, however, it would be Paul Blaine Henrie's backroom art forgeries that would make him a fortune.

In one particularly large score, he sold nearly three dozen "original Joan Miró paintings" to a Monterey art gallery for almost $95,000 in current value. Promoting the fact that he had direct access to the Spanish surrealist, Henrie made a killing off his fakes.

Before the era of digital scanning and X-ray examinations, if a painting looked genuine and the seller had a good reputation, then the deal was a good one. Unfortunately for Paul Henrie, however, he had left a palm print in the paint on one of the pieces and before long he was sitting in a courtroom.

Pleading guilty to forgery, Henrie was fined $12,000 and given one year in jail. Thinking that over, he decided to skip the country before he was to report and instead headed for the Mexican border. On the run for some time, Henrie was eventually captured in Santa Fe, New Mexico, where he was working on new art scams and was finally forced to face the music.

Always in and around the Southern California art scene for decades, Paul Blaine McKinley Henrie died in 1999.

However, in a story filled with chaos and mystery, it would fall to Lt. Herman "Bud" Zander—head of the Abortion Squad which ultimately brought down Spears—to be the one who survived the saga in the best shape. At the relatively young age of 46, after 21 years of service beginning in 1942, the homicide detective decided to turn in his retirement papers.

"It was a sudden decision," he stated, noting that, "I will operate a fishing lodge that is now under construction at June Lake near Bishop and while it is being built, my wife Lela and I will take a world cruise on a tramp steamer."

But that would be far from the entire story as it related to Lt. Bud Zander. The FBI investigation into Dr. Robert Spears and the downed airliner also revealed some shocking information. Their report included the following:

In the Aftermath / 257

Dr. Hoppe arranged a meeting between Dr. Spears and Los Angeles attorney Joseph Forno. Forno confirmed what Dr. Hoppe had said—that the key man in the payoff scheme was Lt. Zander of the Homicide Bureau of the Los Angeles Police Department. Also working with Zander were two officers in his department that were identified to me only as Officers Galindo and Hill.

It was stated that everything was all set—that the payoff money had gone to Joseph Forno, who in turn had made the payoff to Zander. Zander then made the payoff to Galindo and Hill.

The perennially "unnamed" cops in the LAPD—who were in on the take with a systematic payoff program for abortionists—were none other than members of the Abortion Squad itself. Those entrusted with tracking down illegal practitioners were, in fact, the ones protecting them through under-the-table payments and Lt. Zander was at the head of it, according to the FBI documents.

Actually, from the very beginning of their investigation, the FBI had everything they needed to close in on Zander and the corrupt LAPD Abortion Squad and shut them down. Robert Spears himself delivered the *coup de grâce* when he provided the following specifics in one of the airmail letters he sent to Frances postmarked the day of the crash.

> You have questioned the payoff deal, but Joe Forno has promised that everything will be ok and that no time will have to be served in the LA case.
>
> It would have been over long ago, if Loomis had played ball. Zander wanted a certain amount for his group—there are four besides himself—and they now have everything that they asked for, according to Joe.
>
> They can't afford not to go through with the deal at this point. Joe has some of his fees already, but I'll have to give him more—but not enough to break us.

The reality was that Zander had been paid by Spears, through Joe Forno, to have his case swept away but—for unknown

258 / Chapter 31

reasons—that never happened. It was something Frances Spears had maintained all along—without naming in the newspapers anyone in particular, though stating she knew exactly who was involved. It appears, from the FBI's perspective, she was correct. Unsurprisingly, it wasn't long after all of this that Lt. Zander resigned quite unexpectedly.

And with his relatively virtual disappearance from the scene, Zander fittingly contributed to the bizarre and head-twisting final chapter of Dr. Robert Spears.

Appendix A

Robert Spears' Alcatraz Case Summary

CONFIDENTIAL
Inmate: Robert Vernon Spears
Case # 1493: Confidence Man
Date: March 17, 1961

This is a rather confused case in which so many stories have been told that it is difficult to know precisely what the truth is. Spears himself has made conflicting statements.

Spears, who was awaiting trial in California for abortion at the time of his arrest on the Federal offense, has a long criminal history dating back to 1917 for forgery, using the mail to defraud, confidence schemes, larceny, and even armed robbery. He is considered a sophisticated and clever, confidence man.

It is impossible to tell how many times he has been arrested, but he has served penitentiary or reformatory sentences in Oklahoma, Ohio, Maryland, Missouri, California, and Canada, and previous sentences in Federal institutions at Milan, Michigan, and Leavenworth, Kansas.

He is a naturopath who has practiced in various places in the South and West and was at one time expelled from the Texas Naturopathic Physicians Association. Although the reason for this action is not stated explicitly, it can reasonably be assumed that it was due to his criminal practices and general lack of ethics.

Spears is presently serving five years for violation of the National Motor Vehicle Theft Act, but this offense is apparently

260 / Appendix A

incidental to an elaborate scheme involving aliases, insurance policies, and an airplane crash in which some suspicion has been attached to Spears.

The inmate was committed to the Federal Correctional Institution at Terminal Island on April 22, 1960, and held there during investigations carried out by the Federal Bureau of Investigation and representatives of the Mutual Benefit Insurance Company. A warrant has been filed against him on the abortion charge by the California authorities.

Bizarre Incidents

On November 15, 1959, Spears flew from Dallas, Texas, to Tampa, Florida, where he met William Allen Taylor, a man he had known while the two of them served sentences in the same institution some years previously. The alleged reason for Spears' trip to Tampa was to sell a formula he had developed to perform abortions.

Spears had taken out an accident insurance policy for $100,000. He stated that he usually made several trips a month between Los Angeles and Dallas and had formerly bought trip insurance but that a girl at the insurance desk had suggested he take out a policy good for a year on any public conveyance. This, he said, was cheaper than trip insurance, and for that reason, he adopted her suggestion.

According to Spears, Taylor planned to drive his car from Tampa to Dallas but, because of severe pain in one of his arms due to an old accident, it was agreed that Spears would drive the car and that Taylor would use Spears' airplane ticket back to Dallas. Accordingly, Spears started out in the automobile on November 16th, and Taylor boarded a National Airlines Plane, Flight 967.

The plane crashed in the Gulf of Mexico, killing all on board.

In the meantime, Spears drove to Phoenix, Arizona, thence to Los Angeles, thence to Yuma, Arizona, where he met an associate, Dr. William Turska, with whom he drove once more to Los

Robert Spears' Alcatraz Case Summary / 261

Angeles, returned to Phoenix, then drove to Ely, Nevada, where he stored the car in a garage.

There, two men registered in motels and hotels under aliases. Spears attempted to obtain a fraudulent Nevada title of registration to the automobile but was unable to do so. He admitted that prior to his trip to Ely, he had purchased 50 pounds of dynamite for the purpose of destroying the car. This dynamite was later found in Dr. Turska's home. On January 17, 1960, he drove the car to New River, Arizona, where FBI agents found it abandoned. All identifying marks had been destroyed.

Spears was arrested in Phoenix, Arizona, on January 20, 1960. He had in his possession an open vial containing potassium cyanide.

During the interval between his departure from Tampa and his arrest, Spears knew of the plane crash but did not reveal that it was Taylor instead of himself who had been killed until, according to his wife, he telephoned her on January 7th.

In the meantime, she had filed claims with three insurance companies in Dallas and another claim under the $100,000 accident insurance policy, being convinced, she said, that her husband had perished in the crash. She denies any action on these claims following January 7th. However, the files of Mutual of Omaha show that a "proof of death" affidavit dated January 9, 1960, was submitted to the company by Mrs. Spears. She herself claims this was signed for her attorneys prior to January 7th.

Spears has consistently denied any implication in the plane crash. However, after his arrest, a wall-type detonating device was found among his photographic equipment and blasting caps were found in his luggage. The mystery has never been solved.

It might never have been known that it was Taylor instead of Spears who perished in the crash had it not been that Taylor himself, before he boarded the plane, purchased $37,500 worth of flight insurance made out to his son. This action on his part spoiled the plot, if it was a plot, by Spears to destroy the plane and have his wife collect his insurance.

The file does not reveal whether or not Mrs. Spears had any knowledge of such a plot, but there is some indication of

262 / Appendix A

estrangement from her husband since his incarceration. According to Spears, this is due to the machinations of a newsman named Ed Barker, who, Spears indicates, may have convinced her that he really was responsible for the plane crash.

Strange Aftermath

In the course of the investigations by representatives of Mutual of Omaha, Spears issued two statements, one of which he told of interviews held with a newspaper man named Ed Barker in November of 1960. He said that Barker obtained from him a recording of the true events leading up to the crash of the National Airlines plane. This tape, he said, was to be used as the basis for a book that Barker estimated would net Spears' family $100,000 or more.

Later, Barker returned to him and said that a story based on the original tape would not be saleable and suggested that they create a more dramatic, fictitious story. They finally decided on one, which was then placed on tape. This story was to the effect that Spears had conspired with Taylor to obtain explosives for the purpose of getting rid of a witness in the abortion case pending in California and that Taylor prepared a device for this purpose which he took onto the plane with him, the implication being that the witness was traveling on the same plane.

Again, Barker returned, saying that there were gaps in the story and that it still was not saleable, and urging Spears to make a "direct confession." This Spears refused to do, as, he said, he didn't "know what to confess." Barker, at this point, became abusive, according to Spears, and the latter realized that Barker was not really interested in helping his family but only in getting a news story for his own benefit.

On January 10, 1961, Mrs. Spears received a telephone call from a person who identified himself as a friend of her husband, intimated that he was a "prison guard" and said that he was forwarding to her an air mail letter from her husband which had been smuggled out of the institution. On January 12, Mrs. Spears received the letter and turned it over to the FBI.

It developed later that Spears had persuaded a new probationary officer to take the letter out for him. Actually, there was nothing in it that would have prevented it from going through regular channels, but since inmates do not have air mail privileges and Spears insisted that haste was the principal consideration, he had persuaded the officer to help him.

He feared that Ed Barker was going to broadcast the tapes he had made, and he wanted his wife to get the information to the FBI as soon as possible—he wanted to stop the broadcast in order to protect his family, he said. Both Spears and the officer insisted that no monetary consideration was involved. Spears forfeited all his statutory good time, and the officer was dismissed.

Spears was transferred to Alcatraz on March 6, 1961.

Inmate Spears is currently 67 years of age. He has been married twice and has two children by his present wife, one three years of age and one two years of age. Records of past incarcerations show that he has usually adjusted well in institutions.

Appendix B

Civil Aeronautics Board Aircraft Accident Report: Case 1-0071

Civil Aeronautics Board
Aircraft Accident Report
File No. 1-0071
Adopted: June 11, 1962
Released: June 14, 1962
National Airlines, Inc, Douglas CD-7B, N 4891C.
Downed in the Gulf of Mexico on November 16, 1959.

Synopsis

National Airlines Flight 967 crashed in the Gulf of Mexico while en route from Tampa, Florida, to New Orleans, Louisiana, on November 16, 1959, about 0055 Central Standard Time. All 42 occupants, 36 passengers and 6 crew members, were killed. There was no radio message of impending trouble.

A radar-observed descent was close to Latitude 29°13′N, Longitude 88°40′W. This position is about 108 miles east-southeast of New Orleans, about 30 miles east of Pilottown, near the mouth of the Mississippi River, and very nearly on the planned course. Intensive sea and air searches resulted in finding nine floating bodies and a small amount of floating debris the following morning. None of this disclosed conclusive evidence as to the genesis of the accident. The main wreckage has not been located despite several well planned searches.

266 / Appendix B

Because of the lack of physical evidence, the probable cause of this accident is unknown.

Investigation

National Airlines Flight 967, on November 15, 1959, was scheduled between Miami, Florida, and New Orleans, Louisiana, with a stop at Tampa, Florida. The aircraft was a DC-7, N 4891C, owned by Delta Air Lines and operated by National under an equipment interchange agreement. The National crew consisted of Captain Frank Eugene Todd, Copilot Dick Sheridan Beebee, Flight Engineer George Henry Clark, Jr., Stewardesses Patricia Ann Hires and Donna Jean Osburn, and additional crew member Jack Atkinson of the Federal Aviation Agency.

The flight departed Miami at 2212 and landed at Tampa at 2300. This segment of the flight was completely routine. At Tampa, some passengers deplaned and others boarded. The passenger manifest for Tampa-New Orleans listed 36 passengers. One of these was not aboard, although a final passenger count showed 36 passengers upon departure from Tampa. This matter will be detailed later in this report.

Otherwise, the loading of the aircraft was normal with the center of gravity located within prescribed limits and the gross weight some 11,000 pounds under maximum permissible for takeoff.

Departure from Tampa, with the same crew, was at 2332. Adequate fuel, with reserve, was carried. The flight release Tampa-New Orleans was in accordance with the Civil Air Regulations and NAL procedures. Current weather reports and forecasts showed both destination and alternates to be and to remain above the approved minimums. No severe weather was forecast, anticipated or reported at flight altitudes over the route. Headwinds of about 15 to 20 knots at the filed flight altitude of 14,000 feet were forecast. The captain and the dispatcher discussed the flight and concurred in the release.

Air Route Traffic Control cleared Flight 967 over the established route across the Gulf from Tampa to New Orleans at

Civil Aeronautics Board Aircraft Accident Report / 267

14,000 feet altitude. The flight was estimated to be at the Crab Intersection, a customary reporting point, at 0004.

At 0005 the flight reported to Tampa company radio as over Crab at 0002 and estimated NL1, also a customary reporting point, at 0031, at 14,000 feet.

At 0014, while between Crab and NL1, the flight received the 0600 New Orleans weather from National Flight 968, which was: "M700 overcast: 2.5 miles visibility; very light drizzle; fog; temperature 54; dewpoint 52; wind northwest 3; altimeter 30.14; ceiling ragged; obstruction lights out of service; see Notice to Air Missions."

The flight's next radio contact was with FAA Pensacola radio at 0031 requesting clearance to New Orleans and reestimating NL1 at 0035. At 0034 the flight reported over NL1 at 0033 at 14,000 feet, estimating New Orleans at 0119, Pensacola replied by delivering a clearance to Flight 967, which stipulated that it had cleared NL1 direct to the MSY (New Orleans) omni via the 116-degree radial, and to descent and maintain 6,000 feet at the pilot's discretion. The flight accepted the clearance and stated it would remain at 14,000 feet a little longer.

At 0044 the flight again contacted FAA Pensacola and advised that it would change over to company frequency and would report to the company when leaving 14,000 feet and 7,000 feet. At this time the flight also contacted New Orleans company radio confirming the ATC clearance and reporting the weather to be CAVU with low solid (undercast) to the WNW.

This is the last known radio contact with Flight 967.

Repeated calls to it, starting at 0106 on company frequency, were not answered. A check by the company at this time showed that FAA, New Orleans Approach Control, and ARTC were also out of contact with Flight 967. Company calls to 967 continued without result for some time.

Two military radar stations had the flight under surveillance. The first, at Dauphin Island, near Mobile, Alabama, reported that Flight 967 continued to flight plan course during the entire time it was under their surveillance. Nothing unusual was observed and no other objects were observed in the vicinity of the flight which indicated to the station that any difficulty was

268 / Appendix B

being encountered. The point of fade from the scope was normal and within correlation limited.

The second radar station at Houma, Louisiana, picked up the flight at 0046, on track and at 14,000 feet altitude. For 3.5 to 4 minutes the flight continued on a normal track of approximately 296 degrees magnetic. It was then observed to turn right approximately 70 degrees and disappear from the scope at 0051 at Lat. 29°13′N, and Long. 88°40′W. The radar observer testified that this disappearance was characteristic of a target going below the scope's limits. Throughout this observation the radar scope indicated no other object.

The aircraft remained unreported. Search and rescue facilities were activated and the Coast Guard had search aircraft and surface craft in the suspect area before daylight. The position of 29°13′N and 88°40′W—at which the aircraft went off the military radar scope—was used as a focal point of search.

At Miami, National Airlines prepared one of its Convair aircraft, which left for the area at 0545 under the command of the company's chief pilot. This aircraft was flown to Tampa then out the NL route toward New Orleans to the position of 29°13′N, 88°40′W, at an altitude of 14,000 feet. This position was determined by VPR bearings taken from 14,000 feet altitude. Low frequency bearings were then taken on Grand Isle, on the New Orleans Range Station, and on the Mobile "H" facility, also from 14,000 feet altitude. (These bearings, could be duplicated at low altitude; the VOR bearings could not be, due to line-of-sight limitations.)

The aircraft was then spiralled over the spot down to an altitude of 500 feet through a stratus deck with a base of approximately 800 feet, and tops of 1,200 to 1,400 feet. While spiralling, radio contact was established with Coast Guard aircraft although no direct contact was possible with Coast Guard surface vessels due to the lack of compatible radio frequencies. Accordingly, communications between Coast Guard surface vessels and the National Airlines Convair were relayed by Coast Guard aircraft. Coast Guard vessels suggested searching an area some distance to the southwest of the position 29°13′N, 88°40′W.

Civil Aeronautics Board Aircraft Accident Report / 269

However, the search party aboard the National Convair had decided that the last known radar position (29°13'N, 88°40'W) would be searched first. Accordingly, the aircraft was flown in a northerly direction for some five to ten miles from the point of spiral-down, whereupon floating debris was seen. This appeared to be bits of upholstery, sound deadening material, and white objects like sponge rubber pillows encased in plastic envelopes. While circling in this general area, several bodies were sighted as well as one life raft that had been broken out of its case but was not inflated and appeared to be about three-fourths submerged.

Two more life rafts were soon seen in a similar condition. An oil slick estimated to be a mile long and possibly 400 yards in width ran in a north-south direction. It appeared that the oil was rising from the northernmost point of this oil slick. All floating debris and bodies were from one-half to two miles east and southeast of this oil slick.

While circling and observing, the National Convair called Coast Guard aircraft with continuous transmission, allowing the latter to hone in on the area. Some twelve to fifteen minutes later a Coast Guard aircraft arrived and dropped smoke markers. Shortly thereafter a Coast Guard helicopter arrived. The National plane was then spiralled in a climbing turn to 7,000 feet in order to obtain VOR bearing for this position.

Once determined, the aircraft were spiralled down to the same site, and the bearings were radioed to the Coast Guard and plotted on their charts as 29°07'N, and 88°33'W. This position is six miles south and about five miles east of the radar-observed descent.

Coast Guard and civil surface craft immediately searched the area exhaustively and retrieved everything sighted. There were nine bodies, a portion of a tenth body, five life rafts, five life vests, and a highly diversified quantity of buoyant debris entirely from within the cabin and baggage compartments directly below it.

This consisted of fragmented bits of upholstery, soundproofing material, cabin linings, seat cushions and backs, metallic

270 / Appendix B

parts of seats attached to and buoyed by these cushions and backs, overhead racks and other light items not essential to the structural integrity of the aircraft.

This material totaled possibly less than one percent of all such material within the fuselage. Some small quantity of clothing and other personal effects and several mail bags were also found. The personal effects consisted of shoes, clothing, parts of leather suitcases and other traveling paraphernalia.

Post-mortem examinations of the nine bodies, all of which were identified by fingerprints, indicated that all had received traumatic injuries. These injuries indicated that all nine persons had been seated at the time the aircraft struck the water. No seat belt abrasions were found. The inertia of the bodies was plainly downward and forward and the forces at impact were severe. None of these nine persons had been subjected to fire or smoke before death, as demonstrated by low carboxyhemoglobin levels in blood and tissue. Some of the bodies showed distinct evidence of burning on portions exposed above their waterlines.

A considerable amount of the floating debris also exhibited signs of burning but only above waterlines. Examination of the life rafts and life vests indicated that they had not been used for their intended purposes or prepared for such use, and all damage had been accidental and random.

Witnesses

A careful search was made for witnesses. Fishermen in the Gulf who were questioned stated that they saw low-flying aircraft, but examination of their testimony indicates that they saw search aircraft shortly after the disaster and not the aircraft involved.

However, at Pilottown, Louisiana, the United States Coast Guard maintains a manned lookout tower for observing surface craft approaching and departing the port of New Orleans. The tower is about 30 miles west of the crash site. The Coast Guardsman on duty saw an unusual light in the sky at an angle which he estimated as about 15 degrees above the horizontal and in the general direction of where N 4891C was lost and at about the time it was lost. He did not log the incident.

His testimony indicates that the light was red or dark red, appearing suddenly, lasting a "couple of seconds," and then producing a vertical, white light which fell with a white trail. He estimates that the white trail took three or four seconds to go "straight down," and that the initial red flash was "almost as big as the sun." He heard no noise.

At the time of these observations the stars were visible, the weather was hazy and there were no surface craft within his range of vision. Subsequent investigation has failed to reveal the use of any marine signal flash or pyrotechnic, which might have had a somewhat similar appearance, at the time and place.

Weather

Investigation disclosed no significant weather conditions in the form of fronts, squally lines, thunderstorms, turbulence or icing affecting the route of flight.

The freezing level along the route was at about 14,000 feet and the winds at that altitude were generally from the northwest at 10–20 knots. Except for the land areas and coastal waters from Mobile westward, skies were virtually clear and visibility excellent.

Low stratus and fog in the area from Mobile to New Orleans and at the New Orleans terminal would have caused the destination to be below limits at the estimated time of arrival. However, there was ample fuel to have proceeded to the flight's planned alternate or to Dallas, the next en route stop.

Water temperatures in the vicinity of the crash were 70 degrees or more. The sea was practically calm with waves about one-half feet high moving from a northerly direction with a period of about five seconds.

Investigation disproved the possibility of collision with another aircraft, either civil or military, and there were no missiles or rockets in flight at the time and place.

272 / Appendix B

Maintenance and Crew Competence

Investigation failed to reveal any item of maintenance of either the aircraft or its powerplants which could be significantly related to the accident. Crew qualifications and experience were amply high in all respects and an investigation disclosed no irregularity in this connection.

No suggestion of unfamiliarity by National crews of Delta interchange aircraft was found during the investigation.

Subsequent Search

The Board obtained search assistance from the United States Navy. The Navy utilized several vessels equipped with advanced apparatus and manned with skilled specialists. Unfortunately, these searches were not successful.

The *U.S.S. Assurance* sailed on November 19, 1959, for position 39°07'~- 88°33'W relieving the Coast Guard Cutter *Nike*, which had been standing by. Searching continued through November 23. The *U.S.S. Penguin* assisted on November 24 and on the following day made sonar contacts at position 29°16.4'N, 88°36.7'W. This position was buoyed and two dives were made in depths of 210 feet.

The search was resumed on November 26, 1959, to the south and west of the previous area based upon drift studies of recovered debris. A strong sharp contact, definitely bottom and metallic, was made at position 29°11.6'N, 88°38.2'W at a depth of 245 feet. Divers established that the contact was a sunken ship.

The United States Fish and Wild Life, *M/V Oregon*, searched for 24 hours on December 14 and 15, 1959, dragging a 35 foot wide net over the bottom at a position centered around Lat. 29°10'N, and Long, 88°39'W. From January 9, 1960, to January 15, 1960, the *U.S.S. Vigor* searched, using Navy sonar. About 72 square miles south of the area originally covered in November was swept and bottom contact approximately 110 feet long was made at Lat. 29°12.3'N, Long. 88°37.3'W. Grapples were

Civil Aeronautics Board Aircraft Accident Report / 273

used and a variety of objects were recovered but none could be related to the aircraft.

From January 27 through 30, 1960, and from February 2 through 5, 1960, the *Vigor* and *Penguin* made four dives on the bottom sonar contact obtained by the *Vigor* on January 10, 1960. During this period an underwater television camera was lowered twice on the contact from the *Vigor* but only marine life was observed.

From March 3 through 13, 1960, the *U.S.S. Assurance* and the *U.S.S. Bittern* obtained four separate bottom contacts at Lat. 29°18.5'N, Long. 88°39'W on March 11, 1960, but the XN3 TV camera revealed it to be marine wreckage. From March 16 through 25, 1960, the *Vital* and the *Bittern* continued searching in other areas and many bottom contacts were obtained but none proved to be aircraft wreckage.

Several months later, on November 7, 1960, a commercial organization was engaged to conduct a one-month search using techniques proven effective in prospecting for underwater oil structures. With the time and funds available it was possible to cover only 29.75 square miles of an area selected after an analysis of wind and current factors and the results of all previous searches. This search was also unsuccessful.

Charts used during the several searches with search areas well-delineated, were coordinated within the various agencies to preclude duplicative and omissive effort. These charts have been preserved for possible future use.

Investigation has disclosed certain details in regard to a last minute boarding of the aircraft at Tampa by a person using another person's ticket. Pertinent details are:

William Allen Taylor, of Tampa, Florida, disappeared November 15, 1959, after telephoning his employer he would be late for work. A few moments before the departure of Flight 967 from Tampa, Taylor purchased a flight insurance policy in the amount of $37,500 from a coin-operated machine at Tampa International Airport making his son the beneficiary and showing his destination as Dallas, Texas. National Airlines records do not show a ticket issued in his name and he was not carried on

274 / Appendix B

their records as a passenger on Flight 967. Taylor's body was not among those recovered.

The Board, with the aid of the Federal Bureau of Investigation, has thoroughly investigated Mr. Spears' activities in order to determine whether they might have had a bearing upon the accident.

Analysis

Analysis of this accident must rest almost entirely on circumstantial evidence for the aircraft's wreckage still lies on the bottom of the Gulf. There is little or no physical evidence upon which to explain this accident.

The aircraft was airworthy at the time of departure, the crew was competent, weather conditions were good, and when disaster struck, the flight was very close to being both on course and on schedule. No operational or maintenance item was found which can reasonably be linked to this accident.

It may safely be concluded that there was no warning of the disaster. This is evident by the lack of any unusual radio messages.

As has been detailed, the fire marks on bodies and on debris were of the type caused exclusively by a flash surface fire, probably both hot and brief, upon impact with the water. Because of the lack of physical evidence, the probable cause of this accident is unknown.

By the Civil Aeronautics Board:
Alan S. Boyd, Chairman
Robert T. Murphy, Vice Chairman
Chan Gurney, Member
G. Joseph Minetti, Member
Whitney Gillilland, Member

Civil Aeronautics Board Aircraft Accident Report / 275

Supplemental Data

Investigation and Hearing

The Board's investigator-in-charge at Miami, Florida, the regional office, was notified immediately when it was established that Flight 967 was missing. An investigation was immediately initiated in accordance with the provisions of Section 720(a)(2) of the Federal Aviation Act of 1958. A public hearing was ordered by the Board and held at the Empress Hotel, Miami Beach, Florida, on January 15 and 16, 1960.

Air Carrier

National Airlines, Inc., is a Florida corporation with its main office at Miami, Florida. The company operates as a scheduled air carrier under a currently effective certificate of public convenience and necessity issued by the Civil Aeronautics Board and an operating certificate issued by the Federal Aviation Agency. These certificates authorize the transportation by air of persons, property and mail between various points in the United States including Miami, Florida; Tampa, Florida; and New Orleans, Louisiana.

Flight Personnel

Captain Frank Eugene Todd, age 43, was employed by National Airlines in 1951. His total piloting tie was 14,700 hours, of which 400 hours had been in DC-7 aircraft. He held all pertinent piloting certification issued by the FAA, was current on his physical examination; had had adequate rest before the subject flight and was also current on his line and instrument checks.

Copilot Dick Sheridan Beebee, age 34, was hired by National in February 1953, and was promoted to captain in January 1957. He had a total piloting time of 8,710 hours, of which 400 had been in DC-7 aircraft. Mr. Beebee held all requisite FAA piloting certification and ratings and was current on his physical examination and his instrument check.

276 / Appendix B

Flight Engineer George Henry Clark, Jr., age 31, was employed by National as an apprentice mechanic in July 1944. In March 1951, he was promoted to mechanic and in December 1952, to flight engineer. His total flying time was 6,585 hours. Mr. Clark held all requisite FAA certifications and additionally held a commercial pilot's certificate.

Mr. Jack Atkinson of the FAA was listed as an additional crew member. His aeronautical qualifications and certifications will not be detailed as they are not germane to the accident.

Both stewardesses, Patricia Ann Hires and Donna Jean Osburn, had been satisfactorily schooled in their duties and in emergency procedures. Both had had adequate rest periods prior to the subject flight.

The Aircraft

The aircraft was a Douglas DC-7Bf owned by Delta Air Lines, Inc., and operated by National under an approved equipment interchange agreement. This aircraft was serial number 45355 and it had a total operational time of 6,578 hours. Records indicate that all maintenance had been satisfactory and was current. The engines were Wright Aeronautical Company's Model R-3350. Their maintenance had been current and all four had had time since overhaul well within the prescribed limit. Propellers were models 34E60-345 with 6921D-3 blades. All hub and blade maintenance had been satisfactory and was current.

Bibliography

A Note About Sourcing

The Robert Spears saga covered more than seven decades starting in 1920. For most of those years, his name—or one of his aliases—could be found in some newspaper, some magazine, some radio program, or some television broadcast.

The breadth of such a project and the persistence needed to accurately assemble all of the pieces of the puzzle required an unprecedented amount of research over years. Along with my head researcher, Julie Estrada, we located, read, reviewed, and cataloged literally thousands of newspaper articles on the topic from hundreds of publications across the nation, many now extinct. In its day, it was a story that pushed nearly everything else off the front pages for months.

To provide veracity and academic validity to this project, we have made every possible effort to provide sourcing information for all pertinent pieces of information on which this true story was constructed. It would have been easy to triple or quadruple the number of references, but we tried to limit the number to only the most essential facts. I apologize if any source was overlooked or went uncredited.

I was especially guided by the most reliable of all sources: two immaculately detailed reports by the Federal Bureau of Investigation based on more than 400 in-person interviews by

278 / Bibliography

special agents from around the country. Amazingly, the two reports comprise a total of 740 pages of single-spaced typewritten sheets and cover every aspect of the case and Spears' life. These were obtained through the Freedom of Information Act and brought to light much critical information that had never surfaced before.

I also want to acknowledge an immense debt to the only two published works on the subject. They are due tremendous respect for their diligence and dedication by unearthing innumerable facts surrounding this virtually absurd and preposterous—but completely accurate—tale.

The first of these is *Self-Styled* by Alan C. Logan. Born in Belfast (Northern Ireland), Logan is an award-winning author, historian, and social commentator who served on the faculty at the Benson-Henry Institute for Mind-Body Medicine at Harvard Medical School. Though he has published extensively in scientific and medical journals, it was his book on Dr. Robert Spears that caught my attention after I was well into my own study of the subject.

His well-researched book served as a roadmap at points for my deep dive into the matter. For those who would like to read more on this twisted true tale, I heartily recommend his book, especially for his insights on the world of naturopathy.

Logan himself drew on a previous work of some 60 years earlier entitled, simply enough, *Flight 967* by Brad Williams. His book was published just shortly after the actual events of this story but well before the end of Dr. Spears' life. His proximity to the story—he was a public relations man for National Airlines—and his access to the families and people provide invaluable perspectives on the emotions and turmoil of those so close to the individuals involved.

Williams' core research was especially valuable many decades after the principals in the event had all passed away—taking with them their recollections and reflections. Virtually no one at the heart of this tale is any longer alive. Thus, as objective researchers, we must rely heavily on and appreciate the journalistic and investigative work of those who labored long before us.

The author would also like to acknowledge the hundreds of other publications including newspapers, magazines, and

Bibliography / 279

periodicals—the majority of which are no longer in print—that provided valuable information throughout the course of our extensive research.

Often, a single fact or bit of data was located in a larger more extensive piece that might be on an unrelated topic. Nevertheless, every scrap of information helped fill out the depth and breadth of this story. If anyone has failed to be credited, it comes with our sincere apologies and our genuine thanks.

This disclaimer is also extended to the photographs included within these pages. Every conceivable effort was made to seek permissions and provide credit for the images used. A large number of the photos came from the author's personal collection—gathered over years—of original photographic prints from the actual dates of the events. Should any credits not be noted, it was not for lack of conscientious searching on our part.

Additionally, there were a number of books, articles, magazines, and reports that were a tremendous resource but were not necessarily confined to any single chapter. These greatly aided in the development of the background and understanding of the times and issues that were in play during the lifetime of Robert Spears.

The people at the United States Bureau of Prisons were especially helpful by working diligently to locate and deliver information which, in many cases, had been buried in files for decades. This is also true of various government agencies that made available their records long since filed away in deep storage. All of these resources are too numerous to list but the author would especially like to acknowledge the following:

"Air Mystery: Cast of Characters," *Newsweek*, February 1, 1960.

Alcatraz Federal Penitentiary Inmate File: Robert Vernon Spears, Case # 1493, March 17, 1961.

Champlin, Charles. "Con Man, Best Man, An Air Crash; A Far Out, Far Up Mystery," *Life*, February 1, 1960.

Collar, Chester. Civil Aeronautics Board Aircraft Accident Report, Case 1-0071, June 14, 1962.

Griffee, Frank P. FBI Case Report: Crash of National Airlines Flight 967, February 29, 1960.

280 / Bibliography

Kirchfeld, Friedhelm and Wade Boyle. *Nature Doctors: Pioneers in Naturopathic Medicine*. Kentfield: Buckeye Press, 1994.

Lader, Lawrence. *Abortion*. Indianapolis: Bobbs-Merrill Co., 1966.

Maurer, David. *The Big Con, The Story of the Confidence Man*. New York: Anchor Books, 2010.

Miller, Joy. "Murder in the Sky," *Santa Barbara News-Press*, February 1, 1960.

Murphy, Emmet J. FBI Case Report: Crash of National Airlines Flight 967, January 28, 1960.

United States Bureau of Prisons, Inmate 1493-AZ (Robert Vernon Spears) File.

"$250,000 Suit Filed in Crash," *Pensacola News Journal*, November 20, 1961.

"$40,000 Alimony Asked by Phila. Woman Now Allowed $3000 a Years," *The Philadelphia Inquirer*, July 23, 1925.

"150 Attend as Naturopaths into Second Day," *Abilene (TX) Reporter-News*, September 16, 1955.

"2nd Air Bombing: L.A. Doctor Linked!," *Los Angeles Mirror*, January 16, 1960.

"3 Anaesthetized in Wild 1,000 Mile Car Ride," *Eau Claire (WI) Leader-Telegram*, November 11, 1941.

"Abandon Search for Ill-Fated Plane," *The Sun Herald (MS)*, November 30, 1959.

"Abortionist Denied California Parole," *Arizona Republic*, January 13, 1966.

Adams, Cedric. "In this Corner: Donald Loomis," *The Minneapolis Star*, April 17, 1936.

"Admits Forging Vouchers to Pay for 'Good Time,'" *St. Louis (MO) Post-Dispatch*, July 26, 1928.

"Adopting Name of War Buddy Exiles a Citizen," *Detroit Free Press*, September 21, 1935.

"Air Crash Mystery Man Seized by FBI in Phoenix," *Arizona Republic*, January 21, 1960.

"Airline Bomb Suspect Admits Auto Theft," *Merced (CA) Sun-Star*, February 1, 1960.

"Airline Crash Cause Is Coming to Light," *Stillwater (OK) News-Press*, January 21, 1960.

"Airliner 'Victim' of Nov. 16 Plunge Is Arrested by FBI," *Poughkeepsie (PA) Journal*, January 21, 1960.

"Air Mystery: Cast of Characters," *Newsweek*, February 1, 1960.

"Alcatraz Lonely, Awesome Island," *The Spokesman-Review (WA)*, July 7, 1961.

Bibliography / 281

"Alcatraz Shutdown Regretted," *Daily Independent Journal (CA)*, May 9, 1963.

Allegato, Rose. "These 42 Traveled on Ill-Fated Flight," *The Miami (FL) Herald*, November 17, 1959.

Allen, Tom. "Air Crash Mysteries," *The New York Daily News*, January 24, 1960.

Ash, Clarke. "It Is For Us, The Living . . . ," *The Miami (FL) News*, November 16, 1959.

Ausubel, Ken. *Hoxsey: Quacks Who Cure Cancer?* Film, 2003.

"Auto Passenger Who Terrorized Three Sentenced," *Blackwell Journal-Tribune (OK)*, March 22, 1942.

Aynesworth, Hugh. *JFK: Breaking the News*. Dallas: International Focus Press, 2003.

Barker, Edmund. "The 'Business': Diagram of Bomb," *Press and Sun-Bulletin (NY)*, February 4, 1962.

———. "Convict Robert Spears Tells Grim Bombing Tale," *The Columbus (OH) Ledger*, February 4, 1962.

———. "Convict Verifies Bomb on Plane That Killed 42," *The Los Angeles Times*, February 4, 1962.

———. "Crime Record Secret to Wife for Eight Years," *Corsicana (TX) Daily Sun*, January 22, 1960.

———. "Good Family Man, Mrs. Spears Insists," *The Austin American*, January 22, 1960.

———. "Missing Plane Carried Bomb," *The Salt Lake Tribune*, February 4, 1962.

———. "Spears Talks: Bomb on Lost NAL Plane," *The Miami Herald*, February 4, 1962.

———. "Spear's Tearful Wife Pictured as Woman Who Craved Love," *The Orange (TX) Leader*, January 22, 1960.

"Believed Headed for Brazil: Dr Spears Just Missed Escape," *The Tampa Times*, January 21, 1960.

Berkman, Leslie. "Peddling the Popular: It Aims to Please and Pay," *The Los Angeles Times*, September 7, 1975.

"Blaine Henrie to Be Given Birthday Party Tomorrow," *The Tampa Tribune*, February 3, 1944.

"Blaine McKinley Henrie Celebrates Second Birthday," *The Tampa Tribune*, May 10, 1934.

"Blast Indicated in Crash of Plane Involving Frank," *Tucson (AZ) Citizen*, January 21, 1960.

Boatman, Kim. "Artist Arrested for Forgery of Paintings," *San Jose Mercury News*, May 27, 1992.

282 / Bibliography

"Body of Millionaire Youth to Be Exhumed by Chicago Officers," *Troy Daily News (OH)*, December 24, 1924.

"Bogus Check Cashed—Katy Depot Robbed," *Mayes County (OK) Democrat*, June 6,1913.

"Bombing Is Denied by Spears," *Arizona Republic*, January 21, 1960.

"Bomb Wiring Said Found in Dallas," *The Tyler (TX) Courier-Times*, January 24, 1960.

"Bomb Witness Gets Tax Evasion Sentence," *The Los Angeles Times*, January 30, 1963.

"Bribe Panel Eyes Possible Payoffs," *The Paris (TX) News*, March 20, 1957.

"Bride of Two Days Says Hubby Jilted Her; Watch Missing," *Muskogee (OK) Times Democrat*, March 29, 1919.

"Bride to Live Here. Mrs. William M. Henrie," *The Tampa Times*, October 10, 1930.

"CAB Ruling Rekindles Suit in Gulf Crash; Was Tampa Man Aboard Ill-fated Flight?," *The Tampa Times*, June 14, 1962.

"The Case of the Violet Paste: 'Doctor' Charles C. Faiman," *Time*, October 18, 1948.

"Cash, Not Brains, Bought Permits," *The Tampa Tribune*, March 17, 1927.

Champlin, Charles. "The Sad Comeuppance of a Devious Doctor," *Life*, February 1, 1960.

"Charge School as Diploma Mill," *The Sedalia (MO) Democrat*, March 17, 1925.

"Chemist's Report Shows McClintock Died of Fever," *Brown County Democrat (ID)*, January 8, 1925.

"Chiropractor Sees Link between Spears and Frank," *Palladium-Item (IN)*, January 19, 1960.

Civil Aeronautics Board Aircraft Accident Report, Case 1-0071, June 14, 1962.

"Claim Filed in Crash," *The Miami Herald*, January 20, 1960.

"Clayton-Spears Wedding," *Miami (FL) Record-Herald*, March 21,1921.

"Clerk Held for Fraud," *The Philadelphia (PA) Inquirer*, July 24, 1934.

Colbert, Haines. "Airliner Crashes in Gulf, 42 Feared Dead on Miami Plane," *The Miami (FL) News*, November 16, 1959.

———. "Storm Scattering Airline Wreckage," *The Miami News*, November 18, 1959.

"Crash Suspect Dies," *Fort Worth Star-Telegram*, May 3, 1969.

"Crash 'Victim' Arrested by FBI in Plane Probe," *Deseret News (UT)*, January 21, 1960.

Bibliography / 283

"Crash 'Victim' Found Alive in Arizona," *The Vernon (TX) Daily Record*, January 21, 1960.

"Crash Victim Left Tangled Web of Shady Transactions," *The Edwardsville (IL) Intelligencer*, January 16, 1960.

"Dallas Resident Linked to Ill-Fated Gulf-Flight," *Fort Worth Star-Telegram*, January 17, 1960.

"'Dead Man' Returns," *Longview (WA) Daily News*, January 21, 1960.

"'Dead' Plane Passenger Sentenced." *The Great Falls (MT) Leader*, September 9, 1960.

"Degrees Cost $10, But Sold Up to $1000," *The Tampa Tribune*, March 17, 1927.

Delano, Ruth. "Her Real-Life Experience Worse Than a Dime-Novel Thriller," *The San Francisco Examiner*, February 13, 1927.

Dempsey, John Mark. *Eddie Barker's Notebook*. Houston: John M. Hardy Publishing, 2006.

Department of Corrections: Inmate Robert Vernon Spears, Case # 1493, March 17, 1961.

"Distributor of Naturopath Funds to Face Bribe Probers from House," *Corsicana (TX) Daily Sun*, March 20, 1957.

"Divorces Granted; Turska, Annette D. vs. William A.," *Arizona Republic*, March 11, 1959.

Dobbs, Ricky. *Yellow Dogs and Republicans: Allan Shivers and Texas Politics*. Texas A&M University Publishing, 2005.

"Doctor's Wife Remains Mum about Hubby," *Deadwood (SD) Pioneer-Times*, January 21, 1960.

"Dorothy Eastwood Hayes Engagement," *The San Francisco Examiner*, December 7, 1920.

Doubleday, Douglas. "Plane Plummets into Foggy Gulf," *Tampa Bay (FL) Times*, November 17, 1959.

"Driver Gets Four Years," *The McAlester (OK) News-Capital*, March 21, 1942.

"Dr. Spears' Hideout," *Arizona Republic*. January 22, 1960.

"Dr. Spears, Reported Lost in Gulf with Airliner, Located in Phoenix," *Morning Democrat (IA)*, January 21, 1960.

"Dr. William Albert Turska (42) and Dorothy Annette Sowa (39) to Wed. Portland, Oregon," *The Des Moines (IA) Register*, August 14, 1952.

"Dr. William Turska Accused of Assault and Battery on Wife," *Idaho Free Press*, September 15, 1971.

Dugger, Ronnie. "What Corrupted Texas?," *Harper's Magazine*, March 1957.

284 / Bibliography

"Each of Wives Says Mate Killer," *The Galveston (TN) Daily News*, January 18, 1960.

"Echo of '59 Air Crash: Robert V. Spears, 73, Dies in Dallas Hospital Emergency Room," *The Kansas City Times*, May 3, 1969.

"Empty Wallet Called Frank's One Mistake," *Tampa Bay (FL) Times*, January 20, 1960.

"Engagement: Dorothy Eastwood Hayes, Robert Vernon Spears," *Oakland (CA) Tribune*, December 26, 1920.

"Ex-Convict Linked to Gulf Crash," *Arizona Republic*, January 17, 1960.

"Experts Grope for Plane Crash Cause," *The Daily News-Texan*, November 17, 1959.

"Explosives Found: Secrecy Surrounds Spears Case," *Johnson City (TN) Press*, January 22, 1960.

"Explosives in Luggage of Bomb Suspect," *Tucson (AZ) Citizen*, January 21, 1960.

"Explosives Said Found in Dr. Spears' Luggage," *The Tampa Times*, January 21, 1960.

"Ex-Wife Denies Taylor Needed Medical Aid," *Tampa Bay Times*, January 23, 1960.

"Faiman Tells of Shepherd's Bribe Offer; Typhoid Germs Sold for Offer of $100,000," *Messenger-Inquirer (KY)*, March 17, 1925.

"FBI Agents Continue to Grill Spears," *Valley Morning Star (TX)*, January 27, 1960.

"FBI Agents Search Dr. Spears' Home," *Arizona Republic*, January 22, 1960.

"The FBI and Mrs. Spears," *The Paris (TX) News*, January 25, 1960.

"Find 9 Bodies of Gulf Plane Crash Victims; Fear 42 Dead," *Chicago Tribune*, November 17, 1959.

"Find Ex-Convict Alive, Not Killed in Air Crash," *The Journal Times (WI)*, January 21, 1960.

"Findings against Reddick, Board to Be Circulated," *The Daily Times (MD)*, August 23, 1956.

"Five Arrested in Alleged Abortion Mill in LA," *The San Bernardino (CA) County Sun*, May 27, 1954.

Flashy Clothes Lead to Arrest on Check Charge. *The St. Louis (MO) Star and Times*, July 26, 1928.

"Flight Insurance Kiosks and the Jet Age," https://www.jetageart.com/new-blog/2019/4/8/flight-insurance-kiosks-and-the-jet-age.

"Flight Insurance Vending Machines," https://airandspace.si.edu/multimedia-gallery/14310hjpg.

Bibliography / 285

Foley, Jack. "Artist Admits Forging Work, Claiming It Was by Surrealist Miro," *San Jose Mercury News*, October 16, 1992.

"Forger to Be Freed: Reddick Issued License for Medicine to Auto Mechanic," *New York Times*, April 2, 1961.

"Former Church Worker Sent to Prison," *Minneapolis Daily Times*, March 21, 1942.

"Four Arrested in Swindling; Men Trapped Because Telegram Sent Instead of Letter," *The Billings (MT) Gazette*, August 23, 1934.

"Four in Illegal Surgery Mill Go to Prison," *Long Beach (CA) Independent*, October 12, 1956.

"Frank Was Attorney for Missing Doctor; Plane Crash Mysteries Linked," *The San Francisco Examiner*, January 19, 1960.

"Freedom Asked by Osteopath," *The Kilgore News Herald*, June 12, 1967.

"Friend Links Suspects in Two Air Crashes," *Oakland (CA) Tribune*, January 19, 1960.

"Friend of Spears Seeks Out Probers," *The Birmingham (AL) News*, January 24, 1960.

"Funeral Notice: Spears, Robert V.," *Dallas Morning News*, May 5, 1969.

Greene, Juanita. "Hush of Tragedy Fills the Homes of Plane Officers," *The Miami (FL) Herald*, November 17, 1959.

"Gulf Air Crash Mystery Man Found Alive in Phoenix Motel," *The Los Angeles Times*, January 21, 1960.

"Gulf Crash Victim Arrested in Motel," *Daily World (WA)*, January 21, 1960.

"Gulf Plane Crash Suspect Got Medical License Here," *The Baltimore Sun*, January 19, 1960.

"'Happy' Best Describes Paul Henrie's Paintings," *Arizona Republic*, March 22, 1964.

Hardeman, D. Bernard. "Shivers of Texas: A Tragedy in Three Acts," *Harper's Magazine*, November 1956.

Hendershot, Heather. "What's Fair on the Air," *University of Chicago Press*, 2011.

"'He's Dead,' Says Wife of Spears," *Richmond (VA) Times-Dispatch*, January 18, 1960.

Hillsborough County, Probate Case # 47699: William Allen Taylor, 1961.

"His Salary Is Less, But He Bosses the Movie Stars," *The Des Moines (IA) Register*, June 21, 1936.

"Homeopaths' Licenses Dispute to be Reviewed," *The Baltimore Sun*, April 29, 1957.

286 / Bibliography

"House Bribe Group 'Shifts, Suspends,'" *San Angelo (TX) Evening Standard*, April 3, 1957.

"House of Love," *Tampa Bay Times*, January 16, 1960.

"House Panel Delays Bribery Investigation Till Next Week," *Longview (TX) News-Journal*, March 21, 1957.

Hoxsey, Harry M. ND. *You Don't Have to Die: The Hoxsey Cancer Treatment*. Oregon: Milestone Books, 1956.

"Husband Keeps Bail Money, Wife Charges. Hayes-Spears Divorce," *Oakland (CA) Tribune*, July 25, 1923.

"Hypnotized Man, Not Doctor, Killed on Plane, Ex-Wife Says," *The Morning News (TX)*, January 18, 1960.

"'I Don't Feel Anything, Don't Know Anything,' Woman Says on Learning Husband Is Alive," *The Santa Fe New Mexican*, January 21, 1960.

"Impersonation of Bald New Mexican Leads to Arrest of Robert V. Spears," *The St. Louis (MO) Star and Times*, August 17, 1926.

Inglis, Tom. "Confidant Doubts Taylor Dead. Says Wasn't on Plane," *The Tampa Times*, January 22, 1960.

———. "Flight Insurance: Suit Asks $64,625 for Crash Damages," *The Tampa Times*, September 7, 1962.

———. "Mystery Plane Crash Back in Public Eye," *The Tampa Times*, January 27, 1964.

———. "Photo Shows Spears, Taylor with Mystery Woman," *The Tampa Times*, January 25, 1960.

"Insurance Co. Balks at Paying Frank's Widow," *Hartford (CT) Courant*, June 25, 1960.

"Insurance Plot Hinted in Gulf Air Crash," *Oakland (CA) Tribune*, January 16, 1960.

"Insurance Plot Theory Linked to Dallas Man," *The Daily Oklahoman*, January 17, 1960.

"Interstate Statute Broken by Spears," *The Montreal (Canada) Star*, February 2, 1960.

"Investigation Revives Bizarre Story," *The Weatherford (OK) News*, January 21, 1960.

Johnson, C. W. "The Big Plane Crash Mystery," *The Tampa Times*, January 22, 1960.

Joint Naturopathic Convention, Journal of the American Association of Naturopathic Physicians, September 1956.

Juhnke, Eric S. *Quacks and Crusaders: The Fabulous Careers of John Brinkley, Norman Baker, and Harry Hoxsey*. Lawrence: University Press of Kansas, 2002.

Bibliography / 287

"Knew Husband Was Alive? Wife's Silent!," *Deseret News (UT)*, January 21, 1960.

"Lad Frees One Who Robbed Him; Confession Is Made," *The Daily Oklahoman*, December 31, 1917.

Lake, Clancy. "Why Did Plane Fall with No SOS Call?," *The Miami (FL) Herald*, November 17, 1959.

"Let Chips Fall Where They May," *Evansville (IN) Press*, January 22, 1960.

"Lethal Links Checked in Air Crashes," *Chillicothe (OH) Gazette*, January 19, 1960.

Lewis, Roger. "Bombing Is Denied by Spears," *Arizona Republic*, January 21, 1960.

———. "Seized by FBI in Phoenix," *Arizona Republic*, January 21, 1960.

"Listed among Dead, Ex-Con Alive," *Star-Phoenix*, January 21, 1960.

"Looking for Clyde Porter," *The Tulsa (OK) Daily World*, May 2, 1917.

"Loomis, Associate of Spears, Sent to Jail," *The Los Angeles Times*, February 17, 1960.

"Loomis Says Spears Feared Prison Term. Had $10,000 Policy," *The Daily Advocate (OH)*, January 23, 1960.

"Loyal to 'Dead' Husband," *The Times (IN)*, January 24, 1960.

Madison, Arnold. *Great Unsolved Cases*. New York: Franklin Watts Publishing, 1979.

Mahoney, Ralph. "Mum, Glum, Spears Gets Five Years," *Arizona Republic*, February 16, 1960.

"Man Accused in LA Case Linked to Air Tragedy," *The Los Angeles Times*, January 17, 1960.

"Man in Brown Traced by CAB," *Pensacola (FL) News Journal*, January 16, 1960.

"Man Listed as Dead Captured by FBI in Phoenix," *Oakland (CA) Tribune*, January 21, 1960.

"Man Reported Killed in Gulf Air Crash Found Alive, Well in Phoenix," *The Tampa Tribune*, January 21, 1960.

"Man Ruled Legally Dead in Air Crash," *The Tampa Tribune*, November 18, 1961.

"Man Seeks Annulment on Grounds Wife of One Hour Tricked Him to Obtain $1,000," *Denver Post*, April 27, 1925.

"Man Suspected as Being Faiman Held as Forger," *The Miami (FL) News*, July 4, 1926.

"Many Friends Witness Hayes-Spears Wedding," *Oakland (CA) Enquirer*, June 16, 1921.

288 / Bibliography

"Many Go by Spears Residence," *Dallas Morning News,* January 25, 1960.

Marriage License Applications: Spears-Foster. Minneapolis, MN, November 5, 1941.

"Marriage of Donald Loomis and Elsie Fjerstad," *Star Tribune (MN),* March 8, 1931.

Maurer, David W. *The Big Con: The Story of the Confidence Man.* Indianapolis: Bobbs-Merrill Company, 1940.

"May Be Tie-In of Two Plane Crashes," *The Childress (TX) Index,* January 21, 1960.

Mayes County Court, Docket Book No. 1. Pryor, Oklahoma, Case of Clyde Stringer, September 11, 1913.

"Methods of Averting Sabotage Are Sought," *Greensboro (NC) News and Record,* January 31, 1960.

McConnell, Virginia. *Fatal Fortune: The Death of Chicago's Millionaire Orphan.* Westport: Praeger Press, 2005.

McCormick, Harry. "Spears Quiz Continues at Rapid Pace," *Dallas Morning News,* January 24, 1960.

———. "Spears' Wife Admits He Came Back to Dallas on January 7th for 4-Day Visit," *Dallas Morning News,* January 22, 1960.

———. "Woman Hints 'Proxy' Hypnotized by Spears," *Dallas (TX) Morning News,* January 18, 1960.

"Medicine: Homeopathic Hassle," *Time,* August 20, 1956.

"Minneapolis Youth Writes Story on Night of Terror," *Weatherford (OK) News,* November 13, 1941.

"Minnesotan Gets 4 Years for Terrorizing Three," *Fremont (NE) Tribune,* March 21, 1942.

"Missing Airline Passenger Found by FBI," *The Oneonta (NY) Star,* January 21, 1960.

"Missing Man Reported Seen in Nashville," *The Leaf-Chronicle (TN),* January 7, 1960.

"Missing Man's Insurance Asked," *The Tampa Times,* January 19, 1960.

"Missing Plane 'Victim' Nabbed Leaving Resort," *Herald-Times-Reporter (WI),* January 21, 1960.

"More Prison for 'Crash Victim,'" *The Messenger (KY),* September 10, 1960.

"Morning Wedding in St. Paul's," *Oakland (CA) Tribune,* June 25, 1921.

"Mrs. Alice Henrie and W. Allen Taylor Marry," *The Tampa (FL) Tribune,* April 29, 1942.

"Mrs. Alice Mae Steele and WM Henrie Married," *The Tampa (FL) Tribune,* October 5, 1930.

Bibliography / 289

"Mrs. Julian Frank Has Miscarriage," *The Tyler (TX) Courier-Times*, January 24, 1960.

"Mrs. Spears Back at Office of FBI," *Fort Worth Star-Telegram*, January 24, 1960.

"Mrs. Spears Bares 'Racket,'" *Wichita (KS) Falls Times*, February 21,1960.

"Mrs. Spears Breaks Down at News: Wife of Mystery Man in Dallas," *The Palm Beach (FL) Post*, January 22, 1960.

"Mrs. Spears Says She Feels Numb," *Tyler (TX) Morning Telegraph*, January 21, 1960.

"Mrs. Spears Sends Wire to Husband Today," *Woodward Daily Press (OK)*, January 21, 1960.

"Mrs. Spears Upset," *The Daily Advance (VA)*, January 21, 1960.

"Mrs. Taylor Waiting for Spears to Tell Her 'What Happened' to Ex-Husband," *The Tampa Tribune*, January 21, 1960.

Murphy, Emmet J. Federal Bureau of Investigation File #149-42, February 28, 1960.

"Mystery Deepens in Gulf Airline Crash," *The Times (IN)*, January 18, 1960.

"Mystery Man Gets 5 Years," *The Vancouver (Canada) Sun*, September 10, 1960.

"Mystery Package Linked to Spears?," *The Daily Oklahoman*, January 31, 1960.

National Archives and Records Administration, San Bruno. Robert Vernon Spears, Alcatraz Files: Location 3140E.

"The Naturopath," *Time*, February 1, 1960.

"Naturopath Has 'Chit-Chat' with FBI," *El Paso Times*, January 24, 1960.

"Naturopathic Medicine," Entry in the Gale Encyclopedia of Alternative Medicine, 2001.

"Naturopathic Meeting Starts Here Today; Dr Robert Spears, President," *Abilene (TX) Reporter-News*, October 14, 1954.

"Naturopaths Appear in Bribe Case," *The Mexia (TX) Daily News*, April 19, 1957.

"Naturopath's Parole Bid Turned Down," *Corpus Christi Caller-Times*, January 13, 1966.

"Navy Minesweeper Hunts Wreckage," *The Shreveport (LA) Journal*, November 20, 1959.

"Navy Scouring Gulf's Bottom for Lost National Airliner," *Fort Lauderdale News*, February 2, 1960.

"New Mystery Added to Spears Case," *The Winston-Salem (NC) Sentinel*, January 30, 1960.

290 / Bibliography

"New Piece Added to Puzzle Surrounding Robert Spears," *The Newport (VT) Express*, January 30, 1960.

"News of Religion," *The Greenville (SC) News*, May 1, 1960.

"Nine Ways to Gain Beauty and Relaxation with MGM's Donald Loomis," *Chicago (IL)Tribune*, May 23, 1967.

"No. 1 Cancer Quack Will Speak Here; Harry M. Hoxsey, Dallas Naturopath," *Cleveland Plain Dealer*, April 18, 1957.

"Officer Says He Believes Tampan Was on Plane," *The Shreveport (LA) Journal*, November 20, 1959.

Ohio State Penitentiary Records: Robert V. Spears (#63006, aka Robert Lane) and William Allen Taylor (#63015, aka Albert Oliver Thompson).

"One Youth in Serious Condition," *The Minneapolis Star*, November 10, 1941.

"Parole Denied Abortionist Robert Spears," *The Los Angeles Times*, January 13, 1966.

"Passenger Goes Berserk Shoots Two, Self," *Fort Worth Star-Telegram*, November 11, 1941.

"Passengers, Crewman on Doomed Plane," *The Los Angeles Times*, November 17, 1959.

"Payoffs to LA Cops Charged by Mrs. Spears," *Oakland Tribune*, February 21, 1960.

"'Perfect Figure' Exercises with a Partner," *The Fresno (CA) Bee*, October 17, 1937.

"Pioneer Tire Company," Tampa-Hillsborough County Public Library Archives.

Piser, Bob. "Small Stucco House in Desert Hid Plane Crash Mystery Man," *Arizona Republic*, January 22, 1960.

Pizzorno, Joseph and Michael Murray. *Textbook of Natural Medicine*. London: Churchill Livingstone, 2020.

"Plane Crash Hoaxer Given Term for Illegal Operation," *The Ogden (UT) Standard-Examiner*, September 11, 1960.

"Plane Crash 'Victim' Found Alive," *The Albuquerque (NM) Tribune*, January 21, 1960.

"Plane Falls in Gulf," *Waco (TX) Times Herald*, November 16, 1959.

"Plot to Pass Bad Checks in Hotels Fails," *Bradford (PA) Evening Star and The Bradford Daily Record*, August 23, 1934.

"Police Arrest Peninsula Pair," *San Pedro News-Pilot*, August 1, 1959.

"Police Expert on Homicides Retires at 46; Lt. Herman Zander," *Los Angeles Times*, August 3, 1962.

Bibliography / 291

"Police Jail Terror Driver," *The Amarillo (TX) Globe-Times*, November 12, 1941.

"Police Kept Eyes on 'Abortion House,'" *Long Beach (CA) Independent*, August 16, 1956.

"Police Seek Swindler of Convention Guests," *St. Louis (MO) Post-Dispatch*, August 17, 1926.

Porterfield, Bill. "H. L. Hunt's Long Goodbye," *Texas Monthly*, March 1975.

"The Press: Dallas News Beat," *Time*, February 1, 1960.

"Prison Sentence Assessed against Robert V. Spears," *The Mexia (TX) Daily News*, February 15, 1960.

"Racketeer's Friend on Crashed Plane," *The Monroe (LA) News-Star*, November 19, 1959.

"Reddick Fined on Charge of Beating Wife," *The Evening Sun (MD)*, June 25, 1957.

"Reynolds Was Ancestor," *Oakland (CA) Tribune*, November 29, 1911.

"Rich Man's Wife Charges Plot to Ruin Good Name," *Courier-Post (NJ)*, December 23, 1926.

"Robbery Charge Is Drawn at Clinton," *The Enid (OK) Morning News*, November 12, 1941.

"Robbery Charge to be Filed in Weatherford Case," *Anadarko (OK) Daily News*, November 11, 1941.

"Robbery Trial Near End; Yokely Johnson and James Weiss," *The Los Angeles (CA) Times*, May, 4 1932.

"Robert Spears, 1959 Bomb Suspect, Dies in Dallas," *Tampa Bay Times*, May 3, 1969.

"Robert Spears, 71, Has Term Extended," *Wichita Falls Times*, January 13, 1966.

"Robert Spears Gets Sentence for Abortion," *Marshfield (WI) News-Herald*, September 10, 1960.

"Robert Spears Guilty of Stolen Car Charge," *The Daily Telegraph (London)*, February 2, 1960.

"Robert Spears Nabbed by FBI," *Corvallis (OR) Gazette-Times*, January 21, 1960.

Sanford, Vern. "Highlights and Sidelights from Your State Capitol," *The Canyon (CA) News*, April 3, 1957.

Sannella, Roy. *My Nine Lives*. Bloomington: iUniverse Publishing, 2005.

Schertzer, Leo. "President of Miller High School," *The Minneapolis Star*, November 23, 1937.

Schiappa, Tony. "Does Crashed Plane Hold Answer to Tampa Mystery?," *The Tampa (FL) Times*, December 10, 1959.

292 / Bibliography

———. "Evidence Shows Tampan Was on Gulf Plane, Insurance Taken Out Here," *The Tampa (FL) Times*, December 11, 1959.

———. "Insurance Policy Taken Out Here. Evidence Shows Tampan Was on Gulf Plane," *The Tampa (FL) Times*, December 11, 1959.

———. "Tampan Not Sure He Saw Missing Man," *The Tampa Times*, January 20, 1960.

———. "Wife Says Missing Tampan 'A Man Obsessed by Fear'; Periods of Moody Silence," *The Tampa (FL) Times*, January 18, 1960.

Schnier, Sanford. "It's a Tough Job . . . Breaking the News," *The Miami (FL) News*, November 16, 1959.

"Searchers Find 10 Bodies in Shark Waters," *The Orlando Sentinel*, November 17, 1959.

"Search Goes on for Air Victims," *The Orlando Sentinel*. November 18, 1959.

"Senders Get Gulf Crash Letters Back," *The Miami Herald*, November 30, 1959.

"Sentenced to 4 Years," *The Arapaho Bee (OK)*, March 20, 1942.

"Sentence Set Aside after Being Served," *Arizona Republic*, September 27, 1967.

"Sentencing Delayed for Informant," *Los Angeles Mirror*, January 19, 1960.

"The Sign of the Unholy Three: Polio Serum," Keep America Committee Pamphlet, 1955.

"Sister of Long Beach Man on Tragic Flight," *Biloxi (MS) Sun Herald*, November 17, 1959.

Smith, Art. "Diner Workers Say Missing Tampan Told Them about Plans for a Trip to Dallas," *The Tampa Tribune*, January 19, 1960.

———. "Skeptical Detective Says Taylor May Yet Show Up," *The Tampa Tribune*, January 27, 1960.

———. "Spears Missed Lecture Date at 'House of Love,'" *The Tampa Tribune*, January 23, 1960.

———. "Vanished Tampan Seen in Nashville, Police Told Here," *The Tampa Tribune*, January 7, 1960.

"Son of Dead Man Denies Dad Took Bomb on Plane," *San Angelo (TX) Standard-Times*, February 5, 1962.

"Spears Admits He Stole Car, Crash Still Mystery," *The Morning News (DE)*, February 2, 1960.

"Spears Admits to Auto Charge," *Chattanooga (TN) Daily Times*, February 2, 1960.

"Spears Arrest Nets Caps, Too," *The Austin American*, January 23, 1960.

"Spears Awaits Sentence," *Fort Lauderdale News*, February 2, 1960.

Bibliography / 293

"Spears Could 'Clear Up' Crash," *Arizona Daily Star*, March 4, 1960.

"Spears Gets Full Sentence," *Denton Record-Chronicle*, January 13, 1966.

"Spears Given 5-Year Term," *The San Bernardino (CA) County Sun*, February 16, 1960.

"Spears Going to Jail," *The York (PA) Dispatch*, February 16, 1960.

"Spears Grilled Nine Hours in Crash of Gulf Airliner," *The Gaffney (SC) Ledger*, January 28, 1960.

"Spears Had Explosives," *Austin (TX) American-Statesman*, January 21, 1960.

"Spears Held on Federal Charge," *Kansas City Post*, August 18, 1926.

"Spears Hypnotized Taylor, Son Says," *Long Beach Independent*, February 5, 1962.

"Spears 'Model Husband' Says 36-Year-Old Wife," *The Times of Shreveport (LA)*, January 23, 1960.

"Spears Pal Given Year," *Tulsa (OK) World*, February 17, 1960.

"Spears' Pal Talks with FBI Agents," *The Lexington Herald (KY)*, January 25, 1960.

"Spears Pleads Guilty to Transporting Taylor's Car," *The Tampa Tribune*, February 2, 1960.

"Spears Serving Term on Coast," *Arizona Daily Star*, April 26, 1960.

"Spears Shown as Kindly Advisor of Missing Man," *The Tampa Tribune*, January 22, 1960.

"Spears, Taylor Served Missouri Prison Terms," *St. Louis Post-Dispatch*, January 22, 1960.

"Spears' Wife Says Pay Given to California Cops, Cites Police Racket in Abortions," *Ft. Worth (TX) Star-Telegram*, February 21, 1960.

"Spears' Wife Says Taylor on Airliner," *The Tampa Times*, January 22, 1960.

"Spears Wife Seeks Divorce: 'Cruel, Excessive and Abusive Treatment,'" *Dallas Morning News*, April 10, 1961.

"Spears' Wife Sends Telegram: 'The Babies and I Are Well,'" *The Waco (TX) Times-Herald*, January 21, 1960.

St. Louis Police Department. Robert V. Spears, alias Oscar Delano. File No. W17-207. 1926.

"St. Paul Man Sent to Oklahoma Prison on Robbery Charge," *The Oshkosh Northwestern (WI)*, March 21, 1942.

Stafford, Charles. "Story of Spears Resented: 'He was Hypnotized or Drugged' Son Says," *The Greenville (SC) News*, February 5, 1962.

Sturm, Virginia. "Hour of Exercise Worth 10 Pounds Lost by Diet; MGM Physical Culture Expert," *Dayton (OH) Daily News*, August 22, 1937.

294 / Bibliography

"Suburban Retreat Near New River School for Sale," *Arizona Republic,* September 30, 1959.

"Suit Filed against Fred L. Bonney," *The San Francisco Examiner,* June 25, 1936.

Superior Court, County of Maricopa: Turska, Annette D. vs. Turska, William A., Decree of Divorce #53057, March 6, 1959.

"Suspect in Crash of Airliner Appeals Car Theft Conviction," *Arizona Republic,* June 10, 1967.

"Suspect's Wife Goes to Hospital," *The Austin (TX) American,* January 23, 1960.

"'Switched Identity' Eyed in Gulf Airliner Crash," *The Vernon Daily Record (TX),* January 28, 1960.

"Tale of Bomb on Airliner at Sea," *Oakland (CA) Tribune,* February 4, 1962.

"Taylor Jailed with Spears Here in 1933," *Evening Star (Washington DC),* January 28, 1960.

"Taylor's Widow Sues Two Airlines," *The Miami Herald,* November 19, 1961.

Tereba, Tere. *Mickey Cohen: The Life and Crimes of LA's Notorious Mobster.* Toronto: ECW Press, 2012.

"Term as Terrorist for Former Local Man," *The Minneapolis Star,* March 21, 1942.

"Texan Linked to Another Plane Blast," *The Lawton (OK) Constitution and Morning Press,* January 17, 1960.

"They Lived 6 Minutes of Horror," *The Miami (FL) News,* February 14, 1960.

Thompson, Larry. "42 People Had Nothing in Common . . . Before They Began Their Last Flight," *The Miami (FL) Herald,* November 17, 1959.

"Three Former Tar Heels among Plane Passengers," *The Raleigh (NC) News and Observer,* November 17, 1959.

"Tip from Pal Nabbed Dr Spears," *The Tampa Tribune,* January 22, 1960.

"Trip to Pacific Coast Winds Up in Mystery Robbery Case," *Sapulpa (OK) Herald,* November 10, 1941.

Tucker William. "Suspects Were Pals. Spears Called Frank for Aid." *The Miami (FL) News,* January 18, 1960.

"Tulsa Arrest in 1917 Initial Entry in Spears' Lengthy Criminal Record," *Tulsa (OK) World,* January 21, 1960.

"Turska Clinic. Ano-Rectal Disorders; Female Organs," *Arizona Republic,* April 26, 1955.

"Turska Requests FBI Interview," *Leader-Telegram (WI),* January 24, 1960.

Tuttle, Rick. "An Hour Meant Life or Death," *The Miami (FL) Herald,* November 17, 1959.

"Two Air Crash Suspects Served Time in Maryland," *The Evening Sun (MD)*, January 21, 1960.

"Two-Day Hubby Arrested for Deserting Wife; Spears and Watch Disappeared at Same Time, Wife Says," *Muskogee (OK) Times-Democrat,* April 22, 1919.

"Two Forgers Get Five Years in Pen," *The Baltimore (MD) Sun,* March 9, 1937.

"Two Men Are Missing; Which One Boarded Ill-Fated Plane?," *The Telegram-Tribune (CA)*, January 18, 1960.

"Unanswered Questions Pile Up about Spears, Taylor, Frank," *Arizona Republic*, January 21, 1960.

United States Bureau of Prisons, Robert V. Spears, Inmate File 1493-AZ.

United States District Court records, Judge Dave Ling, State of Arizona, February 11, 1960.

The United States vs. Lionel Byam. Case #22784 of 1934, held at the National Archives, Chicago, IL.

"Universal Temple of Love," *Tampa Bay Times*, March 21, 1959.

"Used Ether in Robbery," *The San Luis Obispo (CA) Tribune*, November 1941.

"Van Nuys Physician and Wife Aboard Plane," *The Los Angeles (CA) Times*, November 17, 1959.

Varhola, Michael. *Texas Confidential: Sex, Scandal, Murder, and Mayhem in the Lone Star State.* Kentucky: Clerisy Press, 2011.

"Victim Is 'Bagged,'" *Pittsburgh Sun-Telegraph*, January 21, 1960.

"Was Hypnotized Man Aboard NAL Plane?," *The Miami (FL) Herald*, June 24, 1960.

"'Widow' May Fly to Aid of Spears," *The Town Talk (LA)*, January 21, 1960.

"Wife Calls Spears 'Model Husband,'" *Tyler (TX) Morning Telegraph*, January 23, 2960.

"Wife of Air Crash 'Victim' Will Fly to Comfort Him," *El Paso (TX) Herald-Post*, January 21, 1960.

"Wife of Spears Gets News, Sobs," *The Greenville (SC) News*, January 21, 1960.

"Wives of Missing Men Differ on Plane Substitute," *Victoria (TX) Advocate*, January 18, 1960.

296 / Bibliography

"Woman Ends Visit to Jailed Husband," *Arizona Daily Star*, March 4, 1960.

"Yeazel Funeral Monday," *The Miami Herald*, November 21, 1959.

"Your Figure, Madam!" *Lansing (MI) State Journal*, May 24, 1937.

"Youth with Bullet Through His Chest Stops Assailant with Flying Tackle," *The Weatherford (OK) News*, November 13, 1941.

Index

abortion industry, 61–62, 167
abortionists, 60, 119–20
"abortion paste," 125
abortions: "appendicitis attacks" as code for, 250; botched, 65; clinic at Turska, W., residence, 144; 'deafness clinic' as code for, 200, 206; Euro-Clear Creme, 66, 67, 68; "gook" and, 167–71; "Go-OK" ointment, 207; Loomis and, 60, 62–63, 245, 250; Metro-Vac, 65–66, 125–26; "Mobile Motel Service" for, 66; naturopathy and, 63, 188; price for, 81; "Rectal Exams" as code for, 63; self-aborting products, 206–7; shipping network for, 206–7; UCLA student, 80–81, 83
"Abortion Spa," 73
abortion squad, LAPD, 217, 257–58, *P9*
abuse, 218
accomplice testimony, 91
Aircraft Accident Report, CAB, 265–76

Albert Oliver Thompson (Taylor, W., alias), 42–47, 96
Alcatraz Federal Penitentiary, 222–23, 229, 233; Spears, R., case summary from, 259–63; Spears, R., file from, *P14*
aliases: Albert Oliver Thompson (Taylor, W.), 42–47, 96; Charles Howard (Spears, R.), 110, 111; Clyde Porter (Spears, R.), 110; Clyde Stringer (Spears, R.), 108–10; George Rhodes (Spears, R.), 74–75, 76–77, 155; Henry G. Tremmel (Spears, R.), 43–44; Oscar Delano (Spears, R.), 113–16; Robert Howard (May), 46–47; of Spears, R., 7, 119; of Taylor, W., 48
alternative medical industry, 127
AMA. *See* American Medical Association
American abortion mills, 61
American Association of Naturopathic Physicians, 127
American Fidelity and Casualty Company, 85

297

298 / Index

American Football League, 53
American Medical Association
  (AMA), 52, 63, 127
American Medical Monopoly,
  246
American Naturopathic
  Association, 18, 63–64
anonymous tips, 204
apartment, of Taylor, W., 33
"appendicitis attacks," code for
  abortions, 250
Apple Creek State Mental
  Hospital, 54–55
appliance store sales, 105–6
Arizona, 29, 70, *P5*
Arizona State Board of
  Naturopathic Examiners, 188
arrests: of Faiman, 124; of
  Loomis, 82; of Spears, R., 45,
  111, 152, 155, 175; of Taylor,
  W., 42
asphyxiation, 6
assassination, JFK, 53
attempted murder, 134
automobile accident, Taylor, W.,
  94

bail bond, 154
bail money, squandering, 105
Bali-Hi Motel, 144–46, 184
Baltimore, cons in, 45–46
Barbee, Napoleon Bonaparte, 66
Barker, Eddie, 96, 97–99, *P13*;
  complete story, by Spears, R.,
  237–39, 240–41; FBI working
  with, 239–40; interviewing
  Spears, F., 158–62, 215–16,
  219; interviewing Spears, R.,
  233–34, 235–36, 241; as press
  agent, 193–95; "property deal,"
  235–37

Baze, Jim, 252
Bilderback, John, 171
"Black Box" recorders, 24
Blackwell, Olin G., 230, *P13*
Blodgett, Julian, 216–17
Board of Naturopathic
  Examiners, Texas, 54
"Bogus Check Cashed—Katy
  Depot Robbed" article, 109
bombs, 32, 85, 239; on planes,
  86
Bonnie Bantz. *See* Foster, Bonita
book story, 240
bootlegger smuggling operation,
  103–4
bribery scandal, 65
"Bride of Two Days Says Her
  Husband Jilted Her. Watch
  Missing" article, 107
"Broker's Fee Scam," 115–16
Brown, Charles, Jr., 19
Brown, Madeleine Duncan, 53
"B-Slim Reducing Pills.," 56
Bulova watch, 9
"The Business" plan, 237–38

CAB. *See* Civil Aeronautics Board
California, Spears family moving
  to, 67
California Men's Colony in San
  Luis Obispo, 243
Capone, Al, 152–53
car, of Taylor, W., 35
car crash, 4–5
Carlson, Dolores, 155–56, 157
car theft, 244
"The Case of the Violet Paste"
  article, 124–25
case summary, for Spears, R.,
  from Alcatraz, 259–63
Cave Creek, 137

Charles Howard (Spears, R., alias), 110, 111
Chatwood, Levi, 187
chemist, 168
Chevy coupe, 1
Chicago murders, 122–23
children, of Spears, R., 29
Chino Institution for Men in Riverside, 225, 243
Christie, Robert, 32
cinema, "Golden Era" of, 250
Civil Aeronautics Board (CAB), 23, 24–25, 136; Aircraft Accident Report, 265–76; on Flight 967, 90–91, 92
Classified listings, 114–15
Clayton, Ora, 107–8
Clyde Porter (Spears, R., alias), 110
Clyde Stringer (Spears, R., alias), 108–10
Cohen, Mickey, 17–18
complete story, by Spears, R., 237–39, 240–41
"Conference Grift" scam, 44–46
confession, looking for, 236–37
"Confidant Doubts Taylor Dead. Says Wasn't on Plane" article, 130
Connecticut, 113
cons, 43–44; in Baltimore, 45–46; mail-order diploma mill, 120–21; in Miami, 45–46; roadblocks to, 45. *See also* scams
conspiracy theories, JFK, 53
conventions, midwest scam, 113–14
cooking "gook," 169–70
Cool Jazz, 10
Copple, William, 243–44

cops, corrupt, 84, 216. *See also* police
cornbread, baking, 185
Coronado Hotel, 42
court hearing, 211–13
Cox, James, 64–65
crash. *See* Flight 967 crash
crash site, Flight 967, 23, 24–25
criminal history sheet, *P14*
criminal profile, for study, 224–25
Cunningham, Charles Fredrick, 46–47

Dallas, Texas, 127; death in, 248; Gaston Avenue home in, 193; meeting in, 170, 238–39; Spears, R., life in, 18–19, 57–58; Vice Squad, 66
Daniels, John, 35–36
dark arts, 174
Darnell, Albert, 134
DC-7 plane, *P4*
""Dead" Dr. Spears Arises From Out of the Sea!" article, 158
'deafness clinic,' abortion code, 200, 206
deal, "property," 235–37
death: of Spears, K., 246; of Spears, R., 247–48
death certificate, 225–26, 229, 232
death insurance plot, 158
defrauding scam, 114
Delano, Oscar L., 113, 117–18
Delano, Ruth, 117–18
Del Rio Motel, 11–12
DeLuxe Motel, 70
divorce, 37, 106
doctors, naturopathic, 52
"Doctor's Wife Shocked, Sedated Over Story" article, 177
domestic conflict, 36

domestic violence, 252
"Dr. Spears' Wife Shuns Mrs.
  Taylor" article, 200
Dyer Act of 1919, 152–53, 154,
  244
dynamite, 137, 171, 183–85, 237

Eastern Mystic Kigab Gypterm
  (Guru Gypterm), 116
Eisenberg, Moxie, 117–18
electromagnetic radiation (EMR),
  56
"Electro-Psychrometer," 56
electroshock therapy, 55
Ellis, Richard, 240
Ely, Nevada, 72, 137, 189
embezzlement, 39
EMR. *See* electromagnetic
  radiation
Erickson, Herbert, 2
escaping FBI, 143–45
Estep, Joseph, 189
ether poisoning, 4, 133–34
Euro-Clear Creme, 66, 67, 68
evading FBI, 146
Evans, Bill, 5–6
event, at Universal Temple of
  Love, 207–8
evidence, 126, 198; incriminating,
  212; lack of, 25, 212, 217
"Ex-Convict Linked to Gulf
  Crash" article, 138
explosions: of Flight 967, 25; of
  Flight 2511, 86; Spears, R., as
  expert on, 87–88
explosives, 77, 171, 237–38

Faiman, Charles, 65–66, 120–21,
  122–26
FDA. *See* Food & Drug
  Administration

Federal Bureau of Investigation
  (FBI), 20, 32, 136, 146, 203;
  Barker working with, 240;
  catching Spears, R., 148,
  149–50; escaping, 143–45,
  147; finding Spears, R., 143;
  on Flight 967 crash, 256–57;
  Gene Rembert pseudonym,
  221; interrogations of Spears,
  R., 154–55; Spears, F., and,
  57, 75, 195; Spears family
  home searched by, 179–80;
  suspicious of Spears, R.,
  79; Taylor, A., and, 201;
  Turska, W., working with,
  183–84. *See* Federal Bureau of
  Investigation
"the fellow" mystery, 164–65, 167
first-degree robbery, 134
"Flamenco Sketches" (song), 10
Flick, Willis, 227, 228
Flight 967 crash: Aircraft
  Accident Report, CAB, 265–76;
  CAB on, 90–91, 92; complete
  story by Spears, R., 237–39;
  crash site, 23, 24–25; FBI
  report on, 256–57; Frank, J.,
  connected to, 91; maintenance
  and crew of, 272; national
  broadcast of, 13; passengers
  of, *P4*; on radio, 10; report on,
  25; search for, 272–74; Spears,
  F., recounting, 19–20; Spears,
  R., as victim of, 11, 36; Spears,
  R., responsible for, 85–86;
  supplemental date about,
  275–76; synopsis of, 265;
  Taylor, W., on, 35–36, 153, 163,
  194, 231; theories on, 17, 185;
  victims of, 12, 15–16; weather
  during, 271; witnesses to,

270–71. *See also* investigation, Flight 967

Flight 2511 crash, 86–87; Frank, J., and, 90; Spears, R., connection to, 89

flight insurance, 34, 173–74, 238, *P5*

"Flim Flam" men, 43

Florida, 9

Florida State Penitentiary, 47

Flower Children, 205

Food & Drug Administration (FDA), 125–26

Ford, Mary, 70

forgery, 108–9; art, 254–56

forgiveness, 236

Forno, Joseph, 20, 83–84, 257

fortune-telling scam, 116

Foster, Bonita (Bonnie Bantz), 131–32, 204, 209–10

Frank, Janet, 86, 87, *P8*

Frank, Julian Andrew, 86–87, 204; Flight 967 crash connected to, 91; meeting Spears, R., and Taylor, W., 90

fraud, 60, 178, 254; insurance, 85; mail, 42; wire, 117

Frost, Robert, 28

Gable, Clark, 62

Gaston Avenue home, 193

Gastro-Majic, 54

Gene Rembert, FBI pseudonym, 221

George Rhodes (Spears, R., alias), 74–75, 76–77, 144, 155

Gibbons, Joel M., 16

Gilbert, Cecil, 111

glycerin, 170, 171

going on the run, 71

"Golden Era of Cinema," 250

good bad guys, 45

"good person" persona, Turska, W., 189–90

"gook," 167–71

"Go-OK" ointment, 207

Griffin, Eli (Mahdah Love), 203–5, 207–9

Griffin, Lloyd, 232

grifts. *See* scams

guilty plea, 212–13

Gulf of Mexico, 13, 24

gunfight, in Oklahoma, 134

gunshot wounds, 5

Guru Gypterm. *See* Eastern Mystic Kigab Gypterm

Hale, Emmet, 109

hand-tailored suits, 43

harboring, a fugitive, 159

Harmon, Howard, 64

Hawaii, 78

Hayes, Dorothy Eastwood, 99–107

Hedrick, Jack, 108

Henrie, Blaine, 37–38, 129, 194, 201; art forgery and, 253–56

Henrie, William, 37

Henry G. Tremmel (Spears, R., alias), 43–44

Hillsboro Hotel meeting, 172

Hires, Patricia Ann, 16–17

Holcomb, Florence, 173

Hollywood, 58–59, 250

Hoover, J. Edgar, 53, 80, 143, 149

Hotel Desert Sun, 145

House of Love. *See* Universal Temple of Love

Hoxsey, Harry M., 52–53

Hubbard, Vivian, 62

Hunt, H. L., 53–54

Hunt, Lamar, 53

302 / Index

"Husband and Watch Both Disappear Says Wife" article, 107

"Husband Keeps Bail Money, Drops Wife" article, 106

Huxley, Aldous, 208

hypnosis, 95, 186, 191; Mahdah Love and, 208; of Spears, F., 174–75; of Taylor, W., 241

"Hypnotized Man, Not Doctor, Killed on Plane, Ex-Wife Says" article, 95

incarceration, as teen, 108–9

incriminating evidence, 211

insurance: death plot, 158; flight, 34, 173–74, *P5*; fraud, 85, 99; life, 69, 85, 86, 151; mortgage, 85

insurance payout, 228, 230

insurance plot, 99–100

"Insurance Plot Hinted in Gulf Air Crash" article, 99

intake form, prison, 222–23

Internal Revenue Service (IRS), 82

interrogations, of Spears, R., 154–55

interview: with Spears, F., 98, 128, 178–79, 194, 215–16; with Turska, W., 185–87, 191

investigation, Flight 967, 23–24, 35–36, 266–70; Spears, R., suspicions, 79–80; suicide-by-proxy theory, 90–91

IRS. *See* Internal Revenue Service

jail, Spears, R., in, 104

JFK. *See* Kennedy, John F.

JFK conspiracy theories, 53

Johnson, Lyndon, 53

journalism, 131–32

judges, corrupt, 84

Kansas City, 3, 116

Kansas City Chiefs, 53

Kennedy, John F. (JFK), 53, 97

kidnapping, of Delano wife, 117

Kilbreth, Floy, 187

Kinney, Aaron, 145

KY Jelly, 170

"Lad Frees the One Who Robbed Him" article, 111

Lakewood Hotel, 74–75

LAPD. *See* Los Angeles police

Leavenworth Federal Penitentiary, 42

Lee, John, *P3*

letters: from prison, 223–24; from Spears, R., 20–21, 228; Taylor, W., and Spears, R., 33–34, 168, 197–200

library, prison, 223

life insurance, 86, 151; fraud, 85, 99; payout, 69; purchasing, 85

Life magazine interview, Taylor, A., 164–65

Lilly soft soap, 169–70

Ling, David W., 211

Loomis, Donald, 58, 67, *P7*; abortions and, 60, 62–63, 68, 245, 250; arrest of, 82; downfall of, 250–51; extortion by Spears R., 79–80, 82–83; getting revenge on Spears, R., 87–88; pleading guilty, 222

Loomis-Spears case, 80–81, 83–84

loophole, naturopathy, 54

Los Angeles police (LAPD), 68; abortion squad, 217, 257–58, *P9*; as corrupt, 216–17;

informant for, 84; Spears, R., paying off, 83
Love, Robert, 204
Lust, Benedict, 52
Lynnhurst community, 2

Madigan, Paul, 229–30
Mafia, 17
Mahdah Love. *See* Griffin, Eli
mail fraud, 42
mail-order diploma mill, 120–21
Mandel, Ellis "Itchy," 17
Manhattan Project, 54
Mann, Robert, 36–37, 38, 92, 96, 128; death certificate and, 229; meeting with Spears, R., 230
Marco, Pedro, 16
marijuana, 60
marijuana operations, 188
marriage, of Taylor, W., and Taylor A., 38
Martinez, Juana, 84
Maryland State Penitentiary, 47
Matheson, Joseph, 56–57
May, Joey, 46–47
McClintock, Billy, 121–22
McClintock, Emma, 121
McElreath, R. M., 20
McGavern, C. L., 15
medical equipment, retrieving, 77
medical licenses, fake, 55
Medical Penitentiary, 225
Memphis, 38
mental health, 224
mental health practices, 55
mercury poisoning, 123
Metro-Vac, 65–66, 125–26
Mexico, planning escape to, 152
Meyers, Laura, 112–13
Miami, 45–46

midwest conventions scam, 113–14
Miles Davis' Sextet, 10
military, Spears, R., in, 100–101
"Milk Routes," 55–56
mills, American abortion, 61
Milofsky, Allan, 224–25
Minneapolis, Minnesota, 131
Minneapolis Wesley Methodist Church, 131
miscarriage, 66; Frank, J., suffering, 87
Missing Persons Bureau, 36
Mississippi, 10
Missouri State Prison, 42
"Mobile Motel Service" for abortions, 66
modern medicine, 186
Morrison's Cafeteria, 173
mortgage insurance policy, 85
motel rooms, as abortion clinics, 81
mugshot, Spears, R., *P1*
Murchison, Clint, 53
murder: attempted, 134; typhoid germs, 121–22
"Muriel," Taylor, W., friend, 128–30
Murphy, Emmet, 217
Mutual Benefit Health and Accident Association, 85

narcissism, 135
narcotics smuggling, 244
National Convention of Naturopathic Physicians, St. Louis, 58
National University of Sciences, 120
naturopathy, 51–52, 54–55, 185; abortions and, 63, 188;

304 / Index

American Naturopathic Association, 18, 63–64, 127; Loomis and, 59
Naturopathy Medical Centers, 51
Ness, Eliot, 103–4
"Neuro-Calometer," 56
Nevada, 72
New Age Movement, 205
New Mexico, 78
New Orleans, 24
New River compound, 73, 136–37, 140–41, *P5*
newspaper articles, 135
nitroglycerin, 171
Nixon, Richard, 53
nolo contendere plea, 212
North Carolina, 86
Novack, Adam, 2, 3–6, 133

Oakland, California, 101, 105–6
obituary, of Spears, R., 248
Oklahoma, 1, 107, 110; gunfight in, 134
Oklahoma State Penitentiary, 48, 134
Osburn, Donna, 24
Oscar Delano (Spears, R., alias), 113–16
outlaw era, 44–45

painting, 255–56
paranoia, 146
Parker, William H., 216
Parole Board hearing, 243–44
passengers, of Flight 967, *P4*
"Passenger Swap Eyed in Plane Crash and 'Dead Man' May Be Alive" article, 80
Pentkowski, James, 146, 147
Phoenix, 138, 139–40, 144
Phoenix city jail, 154

Phoenix International Airport, 147
"Physical Culture" trend, 58
"Physicians' Prescription Products," 125
Pioneer Tire and Appliance, 48
Pioneer Tire Company, 13
Pitts, Eloise, 16
plane crash, as suicide, 86
plane ticket, trading, 151
plea: guilty, 212–13; nolo contendere, 212
Plymouth sedan, Taylor, W., 9, 71, 72, 78, 136–37, 152; Dyer Act and, 174
poem, by Frost, R., 28
poisoning, 121–23; ether, 4, 133–34
police: corrupt, 84, 216; paying off, 84–85; St. Louis, 115–16; Tampa, 35. *See also* LAPD
polio epidemic, 54
Pope, Isabelle, 121
Porham, Pete, 109–10
Powers, Melvin, 174
pregnancies, unwanted, 61
press: Barker as agent of, 193–95; Spears, F., in, 160–61, 177–78, 193–95; Taylor, A., in, 162–64, 175, 177, 196–97
Price, Bessie, 172, 174–75
Prince, Richard, 24
prison: Feiman in, 125; intake form for, 222–23; letters from, 223–24; Spears, R., in, 42–43, 47, 48, 217–18, 223; Spears, R., released from, 245–46. *See also specific prisons*
prisoners, 229
prison library, 223
Program for Progress, 65

Index / 305

"property deal," 235–37
prostate surgery, 225
pseudoscience, 56

racism, 53
radio, news of Flight 967 crash, 10
"Radionics Machine," 56
"Rectal Exams," as code for abortions, 63
Reddick, Robert H., 54–55, 120, 124
Reed, George, 46
rehabilitation, 243
reporters, 149, 157, 197, 201
roadblocks, to cons, 45
robbery, first-degree, 134
Robert Howard (May alias), 46–47
Roosevelt, Franklin, 37
"rubber cheques," 43

Saatz, Ella, 131
St. Louis: National Convention of Naturopathic Physicians, 58; Taylor, W., life in, 41–42
St. Louis police, 115–16
Salk vaccine, 54
San Pedro, 221
scams: "Broker's Fee," 115–16; "Conference Grift," 44; fortune-telling, 116; looking for, 51; midwest conventions, 113–14
Schertzer, Leo, 1, 2–5, 132, 134
Schertzer, Mollie, 1, 2, 5
Schiappa, Tony, 177
science fiction, 175
search and rescue mission, 23
Seattle, 103–5

"2ND AIR BOMBING: L.A. DOCTOR LINKED!" article, 85
self-aborting products, 206–7
self-representation, in court, 211–13
sexual desires, 106
Shepherd, William and Julia, 121–23
Shietal, Neil, 206
shipping network, for abortion products, 206–7
Shivers, Robert Allan, 58, 65
Shutts, John, 15
Simpson, Tom, 5
Smith, Art, 177, 226–27
smuggling: bootlegger operation, 103–4; narcotics, 244
soft soap, 170–71
SOS signal, 24
spa, abortion, 73
Spears, Frances, 19, 27–28, 29, 48–49, 73–74, *P9*, *P10*, *P12*; as accessory to crime, 159–60, 177–78; Barker interviewing, 158–62, 215–16, 219; defending Spears, R., 92, 95, 158, 168–69, 215; family life of, 178; FBI and, 57, 75, 195; helping Spears, R., on the run, 77–78, 179; hypnosis of, 174–75; interview with, 98, 128, 178–81, 194; learning of abortion charges, 67; marrying Baze, 252; meeting Spears, R., 57–58; in the press, 160–61, 177–78, 193–95; as "psychiatrist," 57; public campaign by, 97–98; seeing Spears, R., alive, 75–76; Taylor, A., and, 95, 157–58, 181; visiting Spears, R., in prison, 217–18

306 / Index

Spears, Kenneth "Kenny," 224, 246

Spears, Robert (Bob) Vernon, 2–6, *P1*, *P2*, *P3*, *P7*, *P8*, *P11*, *P12*, *P13*, *P14*; abortion charges and, 18, 67, 68, 80, 189–90; Albert Oliver Thompson and, 42–47; Alcatraz file for, *P14*; appliance store job, 105–6; arrest of, 45, 111, 152, 155, 175; Barker interviewing, 233–34, 235–36, 241; bootlegger smuggling operation, 103–4; bribery scandal, 65; Charles Howard alias, 110, 111; children of, 29; Clayton married to, 107–8; Clyde Porter alias, 110; Clyde Stringer alias, 108–10; complete story by, 237–39, 240–41; criminal history sheet, *P14*; Dallas life, 18–19, 57–58; death of, 247–48; defrauded by wife, 112; early life of, 108–9; FBI catching, 148, 149–50; Foster marrying, 131–32; George Rhodes alias, 74–75, 76–77, 144, 155; Hayes married to, 100–101, 103–5; Henry G., Tremmel alias, 43–44; hypnosis of Taylor, W., 95; hypnosis practiced by, 174–75; interrogations of, 154–55; as journalist, 131–32; letters from, 20–21, 228; letters to Taylor, W., 33–34, 168, 197–200; Loomis and, 59–60, 78–80; Loomis extorted by, 79–80, 82–83; Loomis-Spears case, 80–81; Los Angeles police paid off by, 83; Meyers marrying, 112–13;

in military, 100–101; "Milk Routes," 55–56; "Mobile Motel Service," 66; naturopathy and, 63–64, 124–25; "new beginning," 151; obituary of, 248; official statement from, 231; Oscar Delano alias, 113–16; as a physician, 49, 51, 54–56, 124, 126; in prison, 42–43, 47, 48, 217–18, 223; prison release of, 245–46; self-representation in court, 211–13; Spears, F., and, 57–58, 73–74; suspected alive, 79–80; Taylor, A., suspicious of, 36–37, 93–95; Taylor, W., and, 12, 35, 48–49, 93–95, 130–31; as Taylor, W., 28–29; Turska, W., and, 60, 69–70, 71–73; as victim of Flight 967 crash, 11, 36. *See also* aliases

Spears-Taylor criminal partnership, 48

state lines, crossing, 154

stolen car charge, 245

stress interrogation, 155

suicide, plane crash as, 86

suicide-by-proxy theory, 90–91

suits, hand-tailored, 43

Super Bowl, 53

surgery, prostate, 225

Surplus Underwriters company, 85

survivors, search for, 25

Tampa, 48, 93, 95

Tampa International Airport, 10, 34, 150, 238, *P4*

Tampa Police, 35

Tampa Police Department, 32

Tampa reporters, 201

Index / 307

tax evasion, 153
Taylor, Alice, 12–13, 20, 31, *P6*;
defending Taylor, W., 92; early
life of, 37–38; end of life of,
252; FBI and, 201; hypnosis
claims by, 95; legal battle, 225–
26; Life magazine interview
with, 164–65; looking for
Taylor, W., 32–35; meeting
Taylor, W., 37–38; in the press,
162–64, 175, 177, 196–99;
Spears, F., and, 95, 157–58, 181;
suspicious of Spears, R., 36–37,
93–95, 163
Taylor, Allen Junior, 31–32, 75,
172–73, 226; insurance payout
and, 230
Taylor, Charles Newton, 38
Taylor, Ruth, 39, 42
Taylor, William Allen, 12, 25, 150,
180–81, *P2*; as Albert Oliver
Thompson alias, 42–47, 96;
apartment of, 33; arrest of,
42; automobile accident, 94;
car of, 35; death certificate
for, 225–26, 232; death of, 70;
early life of, 38; on Flight 967,
35–36, 153, 163, 194, 231; flight
insurance for, 76, 238; hearing
of flight 967 crash, 9–11;
hypnosis of, 95, 241; legally
dead, 229; letters to Spears,
R., 33–34, 168, 197–200; life
in St. Louis, 41–42; meeting
Taylor, A., 37–38; missing,
31–32; "Muriel" and, 128–29;
neck injury, 197; new scheme
by, 90; Plymouth sedan, 9, 71,
72, 78; police pulling over,
26; possibly alive, 226–28; in
prison, 42; professional life,
38–39; sales career, 48; Spears,
R., and, 12, 35, 48–49, 93–94,
130–31; Spears, R., pretending
to be, 28–29; in Tennessee,
91–92; traveling to New York,
89–90; true story of, 93–94;
visiting Spears home, 27–28
teargas, 6
Tennessee, Taylor, W., in, 91–92
Terminal Island Federal Prison,
221
Tessmer, Charles, 98, 159–61, *P10*
Texas, 54
Texas Naturopathic Association,
56, 127
theft, car, 244
therapy, electroshock, 55
314th Aero Squadron, U.S. Army,
100, 112
"Too Much Hair Traps Man In
Wire Frauds" article, 45
Trailways, Continental, 206
trial, for abortion charges, 18, 69
trial, for Spears, R., 154
Turska, Annette, 139–40
Turska, William, 29, 58, 59–60,
69, 74, *P6*; abortion charges
against, 187–88; as accessory
to crime, 189; convictions, 73;
disappearance of, 251–52; FBI
finding, 144; "good person"
persona, 189–90; helping
Spears, R., 71–73, 77–78, 135–
41; interview with, 185–87,
191; working with FBI, 183–84
typhoid germs murder, 121–22

UCLA Medical Center, 68
UCLA student abortion, 80–81,
83
Umman, Harry, 61

308 / Index

Universal Temple of Love
(House of Love), 203, 205–6
The Untouchables officers, 104
unwanted pregnancies, 61
U.S. Army, 100

vaccine, Salk, 54
vending machine, flight
insurance, 34, 173–74, *P5*
Vice Squad, Dallas, 66
victims, of Flight 967 crash, 12,
15–16

"war of the widows," 96
Weatherford, Oklahoma, 4–5
weight loss treatments, 55
Weiler, C. P., 114
Weiss, James, 62

Welch, Wenton, 67
Westlake Construction Company,
46
White, Leonard, 5–6
wife abandonment, 108
Williams, Doyle, 19, 64
Willis, C. C., 45–46
Wilson, Carey, 154
wire fraud charges, 117
"Wives of Missing Men Differ on
Plane Substitute" article, 96
Wolff, Oscar, 122

Yuma, Arizona, 71–72

Zander, Herman "Bud," 17–18,
256–58, *P9*; discovering
abortion services, 81–83

About the Author

For nearly forty years, **Jerry Jamison** has been an award-winning advertising copywriter with more than fifty national writing commendations during his career. As the principal in a California-based advertising agency, he helped create and guide successful and memorable campaigns for a wide range of clients throughout the country.

Following his years as a copywriter, Jamison turned to a career as a novelist, generating more than thirty books in a wide range of genres. He currently focuses on stories based on true events in history that are largely undiscovered. These include in-depth projects that require hundreds of hours of meticulous research through tens of thousands of contemporary news articles. With a detective-like nose for the truth, he utilizes

310 / About the Author

newspapers, magazines, and other credible sources from the actual times of the events and constructs accurate re-creations of some of America's most horrific crimes and most unique criminals not previously covered.

Jamison has been the recipient of numerous national awards during his career including a national commendation, alongside Senator Edward Kennedy, for his service to underserved communities.

Jamison graduated from Westmont College with a degree in sociology and currently lives with his wife in Chula Vista, California.